CAPITAL MARKETS IN THE DEVELOPMENT PROCESS

PITT LATIN AMERICAN SERIES
Cole Blasier, Editor

Selected titles

THE STATE AND CAPITAL ACCUMULATION IN LATIN
AMERICA (2 vols.)
Christian Anglade and Carlos Fortin, *Editors*

THE MANIPULATION OF CONSENT: The State and Working-
Class Consciousness in Brazil
Youssef Cohen

EXTERNAL CONSTRAINTS ON ECONOMIC POLICY IN
BRAZIL,1889–1930
Winston Fritsch

THE POLITICS OF SOCIAL SECURITY IN BRAZIL
James M. Malloy

POLITICS WITHIN THE STATE: Elite Bureaucrats and Industrial
Policy in Authoritarian Brazil
Ben Ross Schneider

UNEQUAL GIANTS: Diplomatic Relations Between the United
States and Brazil, 1889–1930
Joseph Smith

Capital Markets in the Development Process

The Case of Brazil

John H. Welch
Economist, Federal Reserve Bank of Dallas

University of Pittsburgh Press

Published in the U.S.A. by the University of Pittsburgh Press

Published in Great Britain by The Macmillan Press Ltd

Copyright © 1993 by John H. Welch

Printed in Hong Kong

Library of Congress Cataloging-in-Publication Data
Welch, John H., 1959–
    Capital markets in the development process : the case of Brazil /
John H. Welch.
        p.   cm. —(Pitt Latin American series)
    Includes bibliographical references and index.
    ISBN 0–8229–1163–9
    1. Capital market—Brazil.   2. Finance—Brazil.   I. Title.
II. Series.
HG5332.W45   1993
332'.0414'0981—dc20   91–8338
                                                          CIP

To the memory of Howard A. Welch, Jr.

Contents

Preface		xi
Introduction		1

1 Financial Growth and Economic Development — **16**

1.1	Introduction	16
1.2	The Relationship between Financial Development and Economic Growth	16
1.3	The Neo-liberal Solution	22
1.4	The Neo-structuralist Approach	35
1.5	Trouble in the Southern Cone	37
1.6	A Reconsideration of the Theory of the Financial Aspects of Economic Development	40
1.7	Summary and Conclusions	43

2 Development with Inflationary Finance: 1945–63 — **45**

2.1	Introduction	45
2.2	The 'Duplicata' Discount and the Bills of Exchange Market	53
2.3	The Structure of the Brazilian Monetary Authorities: 1945–64	62
2.4	Summary and Conclusions	65

3 The Reforms of 1964–5 — **67**

3.1	Introduction	67
3.2	The Financial Market Reforms	68
3.3	The Housing Finance System and the National Housing Bank	69
3.4	Short-term Credit Institutions	71
3.5	Medium- and Long-term Credit Institutions	72
3.6	Institutional Investors	73
3.7	Equities Markets	73
3.8	A Summary of Special Programmes and Funds	76
3.9	Structural Changes in Brazilian Financial Markets, 1964–85	77
3.10	The Structure of Brazilian Monetary Authorities	84

vii

3.11 Summary and Conclusions   88

4 The Development of Equities Markets: 1964–85   91

4.1 Introduction   91
4.2 Historical Experience: 1964–85   92
4.3 An Interpretation   99
4.4 The Tax Structure of Financial Instruments   107
4.5 The Performance of Decree Law 157 Funds   110
4.6 Mutual Funds and Venture Capital Companies   113
4.7 The Role of the BNDE   115
4.8 Summary and Conclusions   121

5 The Indexation of Financial Assets   124

5.1 Introduction   124
5.2 The Desirability of Indexed Bonds   126
5.3 Government Indexed Bonds and the
     Inflation Tax   128
5.4 The Brazilian Experience with Financial
     Indexation   136
5.5 The Inflation Rate, Inflation Variance, and
     Uncertainty   149
5.6 Summary and Conclusions   150

**6 Commercial Banks, Investment Banks, Conglomeration,
    and the Financial Structure of Firms   152**

6.1 Introduction   152
6.2 The Structure of Commercial Banks, 1964–85   153
6.3 The Structure of Investment Banks   158
6.4 Conglomeration   160
6.5 International Evidence on the Efficiency of
     Brazilian Financial Intermediaries   169
6.6 Firm Financial Structure After 1964   172
6.7 Summary and Conclusions   178

**7 Summary and Concluding Remarks: Towards a New
    Financial Reform in Brazil   181**

Notes   185

Bibliography   212

Index   223

Preface

The importance of financial and capital markets has become a focal point of recent research in economic development. Views on the benefits from vigorous financial and capital markets range from efficiently allocating scarce capital resources to increasing domestic saving and investment to enhancing macroeconomic stability. The trick, however, is to create working financial and capital markets where none exist. Recent policy prescriptions have emphasized liberalizing financial markets, allowing the free play of market forces to establish the incentives for the creation of financial institutions and instruments that heretofore had not existed. The financial reforms whose only instrument was liberalization, however, have been failures on the whole, e.g. the Southern Cone countries of Latin America of Argentina, Chile, and Uruguay.

The distinguishing characteristic of the Brazilian experience is that not only were reformers successful in creating robust financial and capital markets: they also combined the liberalizing technique of increasing real interest rates to borrowers and lenders with an institution-building approach. Brazilian reformers created a Central Bank, a National Housing System with the centrepiece the National Housing Bank (BNH), expanded the powers of the National Development Bank (BNDES), created tax incentives for the issuance of common stock, and, most importantly, created inflation indexation of financial assets. The reforms and institutions did encounter problems and failures but the financial system grew throughout the economically turbulent 1970s and 1980s.

An understanding of the motivations of the reforms, the resulting financial structure, and the performance and problems of the resulting financial system should provide some insight into the Brazilian success story and indicate where improvements are needed. This study is meant to systematically analyze developments in Brazilian financial and capital markets to this end.

This book is the culmination of six years of research. I hope it will prove an important step in understanding the role of financial markets in Brazil and in Latin America and developing countries in general. This work would not have been possible if not for the help of many people. I would like to thank Werner Baer, who as adviser and friend guided my research and writing from start to finish. Further, I would like to thank the Fulbright-Hayes Foundation, the University of Illinois, Oakland University School of Business Administration, and the University of North Texas for funding my research in Brazil. I would like to thank all the faculty and students at the University of São Paulo who provided an intellectual home away from home, especially Roberto B. M. Macedo, Celso L. Martone, Carlos Alberto Primo Braga, and Paulo de Tarso Afonso de André. I would like to thank Sergio Sister and Airton Ribeiro of *Análise Financeira* for their help in data collection and for sharing their understanding of the behavior of Brazilian financial intermediaries. Thanks also go to Eliza Willis of Tulane University, Leslie Armijo of Northeastern University, Luigi Manzetti of Southern Methodist University, Robert McComb of the Texas Tech University, and Sylvia Maxfield of Yale University for helpful comments on earlier versions of the manuscript. I would like to thank the members of my dissertation committee, Donald Coes, Paul Newbold, and Case Sprenkle, whose comments and work improved the quality of the study immensely. Finally, I would not have been able to persevere without the love and help of my wife, Debbie, and son, Cory.

JOHN H. WELCH

Acknowledgements

The author and publishers are grateful to the following for permission to reproduce copyright material: The Ohio State University Press for a diagram from 'Money and Capital or Financial Deepening in Economic Development?' by Maxwell L. Fry, *Journal of Money, Credit and Banking*, Vol. 10, No. 4 (November 1978) © by the Ohio State University Press; The American Economic Association for diagrams from 'Credit Rationing in Markets with Imperfect Information', by Joseph E. Stiglitz and Andrew Weiss in *American Economic Review*, June 1981.

Introduction

Brazil has actively pursued and achieved significant financial development since 1964. Tables I.1–I.3 confirm this proposition in a general
way, showing that the ratio of financial institution assets to GNP rose
from 0.53 in 1956 to 1.11 in 1976. Further, total non-monetary assets
as a proportion of GDP increased from 0.2% in 1961 to 25% in 1984.
Not only has the quantity of financial assets grown but so has the
quality, as should become evident in this study.

The financial environment before 1964 can be adequately described as one of 'financial repression'. Table I.1 reveals that the size
of the financial sector was small compared with other countries, both
developed and less developed. In the subsequent process of financial
deepening, Brazil encountered many difficulties (the theoretical
possibility of which is described in Chapter 1) such as stagflation
during the initial liberalisation phase, the loss of a numeraire (because of indexation) for the economy in later stages of the process,
and destabilising capital flows. The resolution of one or a subset of
these problems, unfortunately, has often meant a deterioration in the
state of another. Consequently, there emerged two main issues that
pervaded policy debate in the period following the 1964–5 reforms:
(1) whether interest rates should be controlled or left to be determined by the market, and (2) whether the development of a strong
financial structure compromised other policy objectives such as price
stability and the equitable distribution of income.

This study analyses the Brazilian attempt at financial market development. It will look at the reformers' original objectives, the reforms
themselves, and identify the successes and failures of these reforms.
The distinguishing characteristic of Brazilian financial policy as compared with other Southern Cone financial liberalisation attempts was
that it concentrated not only on interest rate policy but also on
creating and fortifying financial institutions that either did not exist or
played a marginal role in financing development.[1] These institutions,
as we shall see, were able to prevent some market failures but also
created new ones.

This study is organised as follows. Chapter 1 surveys recent theoretical and empirical work concerning financial market development
and its role in economic development and stabilisation policy. I
then turn to an analysis of Brazil's development of its financial

1

2   *Capital Markets in the Development Process*

Table I.1   Ratio of Financial Institution Assets to GNP—1963

Country	Ratio	Country	Ratio
France	2.72	Egypt	1.11
Japan	2.22	Spain	1.08
Holland	1.79	South Africa	0.92
Italy	1.74	Greece	0.83
Rhodesia	1.69	Philippines	0.67
U.S.A.	1.67	Venezuela	0.66
Denmark	1.66	Argentina	0.56
United Kingdom	1.63	Brazil	0.55
Belgium	1.61	Mexico	0.55
Sweden	1.48	India	0.53
Norway	1.48	Jamaica	0.50
Canada	1.40	Thailand	0.47
Israel	1.38	Pakistan	0.39
New Zealand	1.30	Nigeria	0.20
Australia	1.29		

Sources: Raymond W. Goldsmith (1969): *Financial Structure and Development* (New Haven: Yale University Press), pp. 502–54; Walter L. Ness, Jr (1977): *A Influência da Correção Monetária no Sistema Financeiro* (Rio de Janeiro: IBMEC), p. 35.

Table I.2   Brazil: Ratio of Total Financial Institution Assets to GNP[a]

Year	Ratio	Year	Ratio
1952	0.63	1965	0.50
1953	0.63	1966	0.40
1954	0.57	1967	0.46
1955	0.54	1968	0.50
1956	0.53	1969	0.55
1957	0.56	1970	0.60
1958	0.58	1971	0.70
1959	0.56	1972	0.83
1960	0.58	1973	0.91
1961	0.56	1974	0.96
1962	0.56	1975	1.07
1963	0.50	1976	1.11
1964	0.44		

[a] As the National Accounts were revised in 1959 and 1965–76, it is impossible to make an exact comparison between these years and the periods 1952–8 and 1960–4.
Sources: Walter J. Ness (1977), op. cit., p. 36; Banco Central do Brasil, *Boletim*; *Conjuntura Economica*.

Table I.3   Brazil: Financial-Assets-to-GDP Ratios, 1950–4

Year	(1)M_1/GDP*	(2)M_2/GDP†	(3)NM/GDP‡	(4) 2+3
1950	0.23	0.29		
1961	0.20	0.22	0.002	0.22
1964	0.17	0.17	0.008	0.18
1970	0.15	0.16	0.100	0.26
1975	0.14	0.20	0.210	0.41
1979	0.10	0.16	0.210	0.36
1984	0.04	0.10	0.250	0.35

* M_1 is defined as currency in circulation plus demand deposits.
† M_2 is M_1 plus time deposits.
‡ NM signifies non-monetary assets which include letras de cambio, ORTNs and LTNs (after 1965), and savings accounts.
Sources: Banco Central do Brasil, *Boletim*; Claudio R. Contador (1974): *Mercado de Ativos Financeiros no Brasil* (Rio de Janeiro: IBMEC); Carlos M. Pelaez and Wilson Suzigan (1981): *História Monetária do Brasil* (Brasília: Editora Universidade de Brasília); and *Conjuntura Economica*.

markets. Chapter 2 analyses the pre-reform financial market. Chapter 3 looks at the structure of Brazilian financial markets resulting from the 1964–5 reforms and their experience over the period 1964–85. Chapter 4 examines the failed attempt to develop the Brazilian stock market. Chapter 5 is devoted to examining Brazil's experiment with financial indexation. Chapter 6 examines the roles of commercial banks, investment banks, and conglomeration in Brazilian financial markets. Finally, Chapter 7 offers some conclusions from this study.

The remainder of this chapter will establish a chronology of stylised events that directly and indirectly affected financial market growth. It is meant to serve as a backdrop for the analysis of Brazil's financial experience in the succeeding chapters of this study.

DIVIDING THE PERIOD 1945–85

Although the study concentrates on the post-reform era 1964–85, a clear understanding of the financial system that existed before the reforms is necessary in evaluating Brazil's transition from 'financially repressed' to 'financially deepened'. Chapter 2 is therefore devoted to an analysis of the structure of Brazilian financial markets from

1945 to 1964. The period was characterised by severe interest rate controls embodied in the usury law of 1933, which put a 12% nominal ceiling on all interest rates.

In order to better develop the macroeconomic backdrop of the Brazilian post-reform experience, I will first divide the whole period into subperiods according to certain stylised facts. Firstly, the post-reform era (1964–86) can be divided into two large halves. The dividing line is the first oil shock of 1973. The performance of the Brazilian economy was distinctly different in these two periods. From 1964 to 1973, a relatively successful stabilisation policy was carried out with increased internationalisation of both goods and financial markets. Inflation subsided and a strong recovery was experienced between 1967 and 1973 after an initial recession from 1964 to 1967. Foreign debt grew, but not at worrisome rates. After the 1973 oil embargo, however, inflation returned and the current account of the balance of payments deteriorated. Brazil's growth rate was not at first severely affected by these events, as balance of payments adjustment was postponed by borrowing in foreign capital markets. The second oil price shock in 1979 put further pressure on Brazil's current account. As international funds channelled to Brazil dried up, especially after the Mexican moratorium of 1982, adjustment measures could no longer be put off. A massive foreign debt deflation was attempted, pushing the Brazilian economy into a depression in 1982 and 1983. Inflation accelerated throughout the period. Recovery began in 1984 led by exports and continued in 1985 and 1986 owing to an increase in the real wage bill.

These two large periods can then be divided into sub-periods determined by the interest rate regime in effect. The divisions correspond to whether or not interest rates were controlled in the portion of the financial market referred to by many as the 'free market'. The periods are as follows: 1964–7, in which interest rates were relatively unrestricted; 1968–73, in which they were controlled during an expansion; 1974–6, in which they were gradually adjusted upward; 1977–9, in which they were again allowed to move freely; 1980, in which controls were again imposed; and finally 1981–5, in which policy flip-flopped between controls and free interest rates.[2]

AN OVERVIEW OF THE PERIOD

This section briefly reviews some of the main stylised facts concerning the Brazilian economy and financial markets during each of these

Table I.4   Brazil: Real Rates of Growth and Inflation, 1964–85

	Real growth[a]			Inflation[b]		
	Total	Industry	Agriculture	General price index	Wholesale prices	Consumer prices
1964	2.6	5.6	−1.3	91.9		
1965	2.1	−2.6	20.1	34.5		
1966	5.4	9.9	−14.6	38.2		
1967	4.7	3.1	9.2	25.0		
1968	11.0	13.3	4.5	25.5	24.2	24.5
1969	10.2	12.2	3.8	21.4	21.6	24.2
1970	8.3	10.5	1.5	19.8	19.4	20.9
1971	12.0	11.8	11.3	18.7	20.0	18.1
1972	11.1	12.7	4.1	16.8	17.7	14.0
1973	14.0	16.0	3.6	16.2	16.7	13.0
1974	9.5	9.1	8.2	33.8	34.1	33.8
1975	5.6	5.6	5.2	30.1	30.6	31.2
1976	9.7	12.5	2.9	48.2	48.1	44.8
1977	5.4	3.9	11.8	38.6	35.3	43.1
1978	4.8	7.4	−2.6	40.5	42.3	38.7
1979	6.8	6.6	5.0	76.8	79.5	76.0
1980	7.9	7.9	6.3	110.2	100.8	86.3
1981[c]	−1.6	−5.5	6.4	95.2	112.8	100.6
1982	0.9	0.6	−2.5	99.7	97.6	101.8
1983	−3.2	−6.8	2.2	211.0	234.0	177.9
1984	4.5	6.0	3.2	223.8	230.3	208.7
1985	8.3	9.0	8.8	235.1	225.7	248.5

[a] Source: Ralph M. Zerkowski and Maria A. G. Veloso (1982): 'Seis Décadas de Economia Brasileira Através do PIB,' in *Revista Brasileira de Economia*, Vol. 36, No. 3, July–Sept.
[b] Source: *Conjuntura Economica*.
[c] The growth series after 1980 comes from *Conjuntura Economica*. It is not perfectly comparable with the other series owing to the use of different sectoral weights.

periods. Table I.4 presents some growth and inflation indicators which will be referred to throughout the balance of this introduction.

1945–64

This period was characterised by import substitution industrialisation financed by money creation (i.e. inflation). Inflation interacting with the usury law (1933), which restricted nominal interest rates below 12%, severely crippled financial and stock market growth.[3] This fact was accentuated by the large amount of disintermediation that occurred when inflation accelerated at the end of this period, reaching nearly a 100% annual rate at the beginning of 1964.

Money creation was not governed by a single central bank with executive power during this period. The National Treasury, the Superintendency of Money and Credit (SUMOC), and the Bank of Brazil all had (and used) the power to create base money independently of one another. Any severe liquidity crisis or government deficit was translated into money creation because foreign borrowing was not significantly utilised and the demand for government bonds had vanished owing to the usury law and inflation.

The inflationary bias of the Brazilian economy with no effective control mechanism culminated in the reforms of 1964–5 and a rigorous stabilisation policy. These reforms were introduced by a military government which had taken power in March 1964, and whose ascendancy was, in part, precipitated by the inflationary chaos of 1963–4.

1964–7

The Castello Branco administration attempted simultaneously to resolve the shortcomings of the financial system and stabilise prices through widespread financial and stock market reforms, a fiscal reform, a restrictive monetary policy, and the suppression of wages. Another goal was to integrate product and financial markets into the international market through export promotion and the regulation of direct foreign borrowing.

The capital market reform after 1964 proceeded mainly through the introduction of three laws. The Housing Financial System (SFH), whose central institution was the National Housing Bank (BNH), was created by Law 4380 of 1964. Later, a forced-saving fund called the Job Tenure Guarantee Fund (FGTS) was created and deposited at the BNH. The FGTS was funded by social-security-type taxes and indexed to the inflation rate. The 'Bank Reform Act' (Law 4595 of 1964) created the Central Bank which replaced SUMOC, redefined the Bank of Brazil's role as a monetary authority, expanded the functions of the National Economic (and Social) Development Bank (BNDE), and created the National Monetary Council (CMN), which was to coordinate the actions of these sectoral financial institutions. The 'Capital Markets Law' (Law 4728 of 1965) created 'open-capital companies' and provided firms with fiscal (tax) incentives to issue common stock. Finally, the government created *ex post* indexed government bonds (ORTNs) to bypass the usury law and give asset holders a way to hedge inflation risk, which had eliminated the demand for government bonds in the prior period. This allowed the government to finance deficits by direct internal borrowing, as opposed to resorting to printing money. This also paved the way for the use of indexed private obligations, which was intended as a way to reduce real interest rates by reducing the inflation risk premium.

The initial steps for financial opening to international capital flows were taken before the 1964–5 reforms.[4] Law 4131 of 1962 allowed firms and individuals to contract foreign debt in order to finance fixed and working capital investment. The salient feature of this law was that it gave the Central Bank control over the terms and interest rates of these loans. Complementary legislation in 1970 gave the Central Bank control over amortisation schedules as well.[5] Instruction 289 of the now extinct SUMOC in 1965 allowed firms to contract short-term working capital loans of six to twelve months' maturity in which the borrower incurred the foreign exchange risk while the Central Bank provided foreign exchange cover for interest and amortisation payments. Instruction 289 was revoked in 1972.[6] Finally, perhaps the most important legislation in this regard was Resolution 63 of 1967, which allowed commercial and investment banks to contract foreign loans to be re-lent within Brazil for fixed and working capital investment.

With the *de facto* liberalisation of interest rates and the restrictive monetary and fiscal policy imposed after 1964, the Brazilian economy moved into a recession.[7] Interest rates stayed at high real levels as inflation declined. Attempts were made to persuade the private sector to index its debt obligations. This would have decreased the implicit inflation premium and, with it, interest rates.[8] The private sector resisted, however. This resulted in the strange situation, where private sector debt carried 'pre-fixed' indexation (the rate of indexation was set *a priori* by the government), while government debt carried 'post-fixed' indexation.[9]

It is curious that indexed bonds were also not widely accepted on the demand side. Individuals preferred to invest in the legal and illegal bills of exchange markets, despite the fact that the credit crunch of this period forced an increasing number of shaky firms into this market. Only after a default by a large concern in 1966 did individuals move into indexed assets in a significant way.[10]

The same open market crisis precipitated more drastic stock market legislation, as firms resisted issuing common stock despite the fiscal incentives created by the 'capital markets law'. At the end of the Castello Branco administration, a forced-savings fund was created, the so-called '157 funds' named after Decree Law 157. Individuals were allowed to purchase securities in lieu of paying a portion of income taxes. The emergence of 157 funds marked the beginning of a stock market boom, fanned by the easy credit conditions of the following period which culminated in the stock market crash of 1972. These funds, however, did little in and of themselves to ease the working capital crisis of 1966. Even though they were created for this purpose, there is no theoretical reason why one should have expected this result.[11]

The persistence of high real interest and high inflation rates, coupled with a large degree of excess capacity, led many economists to believe that inflation was no longer demand-determined as it had been in 1964. They saw it as being fed on the supply side by high interest costs. The policy prescription consistent with this evaluation was to bring interest rates down and expand the economy by an easing of credit. The incoming Costa e Silva administration, with Minister of Finance Antonio Delfim-Netto, was sympathetic to this viewpoint.[12]

1967–73

The order of the day at the beginning of this period was to decrease interest rates and expand credit, using the newly installed financial apparatus. Interest rate controls were re-introduced. Firstly, financial incentives were given to banks which lowered interest rates, starting in 1968 and 1969, by allowing them to hold a larger proportion of compulsory reserves in the form of indexed government bonds. By 1970, full-fledged interest controls had been re-established.[13] These controls, however, allowed positive real interest rates as long as inflation did not accelerate.

This policy contributed to a vigorous economic recovery, starting with consumer durables and then spreading to capital goods and more basic industry.[14] Inflation also declined gradually throughout the remainder of this period. A good portion of this expansion was financed through the contraction of foreign debt, facilitated by the introduction of a 'minidevaluation' or crawling-peg exchange rate adjustment system in 1968. This proved to be an important catalyst to foreign capital inflows, as it decreased exchange rate uncertainty and lagged behind the inflation rate to a small degree. The effective interest rates on these loans (mainly through Resolution 63) were lower than internal interest rates. The main source of these loans was the growing Eurodollar loan market, especially in the early 1970s.

Prior to 1970, the Brazilian monetary authorities had no instrument for short-term monetary control. In 1970, National Treasury Bills (LTNs) were created with which to perform open market operations. For the most part, the Central Bank was able to sterilise the formidable foreign capital inflows using open market operations, except in 1973, when they were larger than expected.

Finally, two more forced-savings funds were created in this period. The Programme for Social Integration (PIS) and the Public Employees Financial Reserve Fund (PASEP) were to be managed by the BNDE to finance long-term loans to business.[15]

The large economic expansion stimulated import demand as new investments took place, financed by significant increases in foreign debt. Brazil's balance of payments situation was not too precarious on the eve of the first oil shock but it seems that the expansion could not continue as Brazil's economy reached full capacity in 1973. External adjustment, in retrospect, was imminent in the medium term if external debt was to grow at a sustainable rate. The oil price shock of 1973, along with price increases of agricultural goods and other raw materials, rendered future adjustment a current policy issue. As we shall see, Brazilian policy makers chose to postpone adjustment by further increases in foreign debt.

1974–6

The balance of payments problems and the acceleration of inflation in this period underscores two contradictions in the development strategy of the prior period. Firstly, growth at such high rates was incompatible with stable prices and reasonable deficits in the current account of the balance of payments as the economy reached full employment in 1973. The incoming Geisel administration, however, was committed to political opening and saw recession as a threat to this process. This perception emanated from the fact that the military regime's sole claim to legitimacy was that it could in some way ensure high economic growth compared with alternative regimes.[16] Secondly, financial markets and institutions had grown but intermediation remained costly. This is exemplified by the fact that when interest rates were liberated once again in 1976, they surged to and remained at high real levels. It was felt that the high overhead costs inherited from the pre-reform era were the main culprits. In order to exploit possible economies of scale in intermediation, Brazilian authorities embarked on a policy of promoting conglomeration of financial firms.[17]

A policy conflict between expansionary fiscal policy, supported by the Minister of Planning, and restrictive monetary policy, supported by the Minister of Finance, came to the fore at this time. The expansionary fiscal stance was embodied in the economy-wide investment programme, the Second National Development Plan (PND-II). Restrictive monetary policy was seen as necessary owing to balance of payments problems and accelerating inflation. Political forces favouring the expansionary policies dominated, as mentioned above, in lieu of the political decompression being pursued. This program was ultimately financed by foreign loans. In order to stimulate such capital inflows, interest rates had to be increased in real terms, especially after the inflation rate surpassed the nominal interest rate ceilings.

Another source of pressure on interest rates came from the portfolio shifts that occurred during this period. As inflation rates pushed against interest rate ceilings on 'pre-fixed' indexed assets, a movement into 'post-fixed' indexed assets ensued. Before long, financial institutions which had 'pre-fixed' indexed liabilities became extremely illiquid, while financial institutions that had 'post-fixed' indexed liabilities saw an unsustainable buildup in their liabilities.[18] Since there was no market mechanism by which one set of financial institutions could lend to the other, government financial institutions set up schemes of 're-lending' ('repasses'), in addition to Central Bank 'compulsory financing' to aid in the adjustment.[19]

Interest rates were adjusted upward in discrete steps while interest rate ceilings were maintained. The movement towards austerity in 1976 precipitated the full liberalisation of interest rates.

1976–9

In 1976, Minister of Finance Mario Simonsen coordinated a broad-based stabilisation policy, replacing the expansionary stance of the prior period. Domestic credit expansion was curtailed with the liberalisation of interest rates and by attempts at controlling government spending. Although domestic absorption was diminished, the higher domestic interest rates nourished a large expansion of foreign debt, mainly in the Eurodollar market, larger than that compatible with the level of investment prevailing at the time.[20]

In order to spread out the use of these resources, the Central Bank created dollar-denominated accounts in 1977, better known as '432 accounts' after Central Bank resolution 432.[21] Firms which had contracted foreign loans could deposit the full value in 432 accounts. The Central Bank guaranteed interest and the dollar value of these deposits. Unfortunately, a side effect of the existence of these deposits was that it created an interest arbitrage mechanism, the result of which was the linking of domestic interest rates (and money supply) to foreign interest rates, in the manner of textbook interest parity arrangements. This *de facto* interest parity effect occurred in spite of the fact that Brazilians were prohibited from holding foreign bonds or deposits.

The arbitrage mechanism worked in the following way. If domestic interest rates were higher than the interest rates on foreign debt plus expected exchange depreciation, firms would liquidate domestic liabilities by drawing down 432 accounts. Domestic interest rates fell as credit demand eased and the money supply rose. If domestic interest rates were lower than interest rates on foreign debt plus expected exchange depreciation, firms contracted domestic loans while depositing funds in 432 accounts. Domestic interest rates rose with the increase in credit demand as the money supply contracted. Hence, 432 accounts provided (another) source of endogeneity of the money supply and made interest rates on foreign debt serve as a floor to domestic interest rates.[22]

The inflow of foreign resources did not subside to sustainable levels. The government imposed a series of quantitative restrictions in an attempt to slow the inflow of capital. At the end of 1977 and beginning of 1978, compulsory deposits were created on all new foreign loans (resolutions 449 and 479). In April 1979, 50% of new foreign loans were frozen in compulsory deposits for a year without interest or exchange correction (resolution 532).[23]

In early 1979, as Minister of Finance Simonsen became Planning Minister of the incoming Figueiredo administration, suspicions about the sustainability of these capital inflows became manifest. The second oil price shock in mid-1979 with the outbreak of the Iran–Iraq war made these suspicions a reality.

1980

The year 1980 witnessed Brazil's brief experiment with inflation expectations manipulation similar to that in Argentina under Martinez de Hoz.[24] Unfortunately, this policy proved disastrous and it was quickly abandoned.

In August 1979, Mario Simonsen resigned as Planning Minister as inflation accelerated owing to the second oil shock and poor agricultural harvests. Antonio Delfim-Netto was named the new Planning Minister and was determined to reduce inflation through growth, as he had done between 1968 and 1972.[25] Two additional sources of cost-push inflation occurred in late 1979. The first was the change from annual to semi-annual adjustments for inflation in wage contracts in November. It can be shown, under fairly general assumptions, that the shrinking of the period of adjustment provides a significant cost impetus to higher inflation.[26] The second was the 'maxidevaluation' of the cruzeiro of 30% relative to the dollar in December.

Indexation (of government bonds, wages, exchange rates, and term contracts) was prefixed at 45% at the beginning of 1980 for that year in an attempt to dampen inflation expectations in conjunction with restrictive monetary and credit targets. In order to offset the poor agricultural performance, the government pursued a 'super-harvest' through high minimum-price guarantees and the expansion of subsidised credit to agriculture. Much as the objective of the 'tablitas' was pursued in Southern Cone countries, the rate of mini-devaluation of the cruzeiro was slowed after the maxidevaluation in the hope that the rate of inflation would eventually converge to the rate of exchange depreciation.[27] Unfortunately, this did not occur.

The prefixing of the indexation rate was combined with nominal interest rate ceilings. Interest rate control cannot be implemented with credit and monetary controls, as was soon obvious in the Brazilian case. By mid-1980, inflation had already reached the cumulative rate of 45% and it ended the year at around 100%. Real interest rates turned sharply negative and disintermediation set in once again. National domestic savings declined dramatically and remained at low levels through 1985. The decline in the saving rate was due first to the negative interest rates and later to the recession that followed the liberalisation of interest rates.

The decline in savings rates and its mirror image in excess demand for goods led to a quick decline in Brazil's international reserves,

side is less direct, however. Indexing of government liabilities (bonds and private sector loans to public enterprise) tends to make monetary accommodation more likely. If a good portion of government contracts are linked to the inflation rate and tax receipts are not completely elastic to inflation rate changes, fiscal austerity becomes extremely difficult. Monetary restraint through the floating of government bonds lacked credibility because new government bond issues were financed mainly by commercial banks in the overnight market. Because government finance during the adjustment period fell heavily on commercial banks, they acquired an even greater political power than previously. When faced with any liquidity problems (owing many times to a tightening of monetary stance), commercial banks could eventually force the Central Bank to monetise government bonds by simply refusing to buy any new issues of government bonds in the so-called 'go-round' auctions.

The recovery of 1984 strengthened in 1985 owing mainly to rising real wages. A new acceleration of inflation in late 1985 and early 1986 fuelled by an expansionary monetary stance starting in August 1985 along with poor agricultural harvests precipitated a new 'heterodox' attempt at stabilisation. This program, named the Cruzado Plan after the new currency, consisted mainly of price and wage controls coupled with a monetary reform with the objective of completely de-indexing the economy. Unfortunately, as in the experiment with partial de-indexation in 1980, excess demand completely undid the recent attempt at inflation stabilisation at the cost of external balance.[32]

The sudden, although temporary, evaporation of the inflation tax revealed overnight the extent of the inefficiencies in Brazil's financial markets. The ability of commercial banks to capture a significant portion of the 'inflation tax' through the creation of demand deposits led to a large expansion of agencies much as had occurred prior to 1964. The short-term adjustment taken by commercial banks was to fire a large portion of their labour force. With the renewed acceleration of inflation and the very high profit rates earned in the financial sector of the Brazilian economy calls for a new financial reform (along with the more radical calls for interest rate ceilings) returned. Extensive proposals by public and private sector institutions for financial reform are now being discussed as a central theme of Brazil's long-term economic agendas.

1 Financial Growth and Economic Development

1.1 INTRODUCTION

An increased separation between saving and investment decisions, i.e. large increases in financial assets relative to tangible assets, is seen by many economists[1] to be a necessary if not sufficient condition for the self-sustained growth of an economy. Over the last three decades extensive theoretical and empirical research has focused on the relationship of financial development and economic development.

The main policy proposed to generate robust financial markets that could be a leading sector in the process of economic development and growth has been the complete liberalisation of all prices directly or indirectly affecting the valuation of all assets (e.g. interest rates, exchange rates, etc.). The distinguishing characteristic of the Brazilian case is that policy makers combined partial liberalisation through the indexation of financial assets and the exchange rate to the inflation rate with institution building. The result was a financial market which is the most robust and dynamic in Latin America, although perhaps not as efficient as some. Further, the Brazilian financial system did not suffer the same degree of instability as its Southern Cone counterparts.

This chapter surveys many of the arguments for and against such liberalisation policies. Theory leaves many questions unanswered. Many conclusions depend upon specific aspects of economic structure. This fact accentuates the value of case studies. The lack of clear theoretical conclusions concerning financial market liberalisation and other policies is one of the main motivations for this case study of the Brazilian experience.

1.2 THE RELATIONSHIP BETWEEN FINANCIAL DEVELOPMENT AND ECONOMIC GROWTH

Much of the early literature concerned itself with defining the exact role financial markets play in an economy. Microeconomics, as well as a good part of macroeconomics, dealt mainly with the real side of the economy, *in vacuo*. Those theoretical works that did include financial assets usually included only money, eliminating the bond market by Walras's law. Gurley and Shaw (1955) attempted to dispel this taste for aggregation of financial markets into only two assets.[2]

Financial markets have two main functions: (1) to transfer resources from surplus agents to deficit agents (the primary market) and (2) to provide liquidity to debt instruments, allowing agents to sell off positions in financial assets when necessary (the secondary market). In order to evaluate how well financial markets accomplish these goals necessitates (a) a disaggregated view of the economy, especially in reference to finance, based upon sectoral flows of funds statements and balance sheets, and (b) some type of measure in order to gauge the degree to which these goals are realised (for example, velocities or turnover rates might indicate the degree of liquidity different financial instruments possess).

Gurley and Shaw (1955) first sketch a design of a set of social accounts.[3] Agents are divided into those who incur deficits, surpluses, and balanced budgets. Agents (or sectors) with deficits are those that spend more than their income, generating a demand for loanable funds, issuing financial assets or debt. Their financial assets fall relative to their liabilities and equity. Agents with surplus budgets are those that have an excess of income over expenditures (for a defined period), which increases the amount they either save or invest. If they save, their financial assets increase relative to their liabilities. Surplus agents that invest fall into the balanced budget class, whose expenditure keeps in line with their income. Hence, agents with balanced budgets experience no change in financial assets relative to liabilities and equity. Equilibrium may be described as an *ex ante* equality between desired spending and income in the goods market, which implies *ex ante* equality between supply and demand for loanable funds.

The same authors then identify the determinants of the ratios of debt to income and of debt to wealth. The first relationship may be described as follows:

$$D/Y = \phi\beta \qquad\qquad (1.1)$$

where D is the stock of debt outstanding, Y is income, ϕ is the ratio of borrowing to deficits, and β is the ratio of deficits to income. The second relationship is:

$$D/W = v\phi\beta \tag{1.2}$$

where W is total (tangible) wealth and v is the income to wealth ratio. If the income–wealth ratio, v, remains constant over the long term, the debt–income ratio and the debt–wealth ratio (and the changes in them) are determined by the same variables, ϕ, β, and growth in Y.[4] It should be noted that both ϕ and β contain a government policy component: how government deficits are financed and the size of the deficit relative to national income.

Clearly, the behavioural determinants of ϕ, β, and v in addition to Y are what is interesting in the financial process.[5] The ratio of borrowing to deficits depends upon, as we will see, whether deficits are financed by direct finance or indirect finance; it depends upon the degree of layering of the financial system. The ratio of deficits to income depends upon all those institutional, historical and policy factors that determine the degree of division between investment and saving decisions. It also depends upon the propensity to consume out of income and the degree to which consumption is financed externally. The wealth–income ratio depends upon the extent to which spending is transformed into capital formation, technological advances, and effective demand.[6]

Each of these different agents must finance their expenditure. Agents with balanced budgets self-finance their expenditure. Agents with budget deficits must finance a portion of their expenditure externally. External finance may be divided into two categories: (1) direct finance and (2) indirect finance. Direct finance is effectuated by the selling of debt directly to agents with budget surpluses. Indirect finance is furnished by intermediaries who finance these loans by issuing debt of their own to surplus agents.[7] Clearly, the degree of financial layering, and thus the debt–income and debt–wealth ratios, increases with the number of the size of financial intermediaries. According to Gurley and Shaw (1955), the increased division of labour between investment and saving decisions through increases in indirect finance enhances the possibilities of economic growth:

> Economic development is retarded if only self-finance and direct finance are accessible . . . The rise of intermediaries—of institutional savers and investors—does not affect at all the basic equalities in a complete social accounting system between budgetary deficits and surpluses, purchases and sales of loanable funds, or accumulation of financial assets and debts. But total debt, in-

cluding direct debt that intermediaries buy and the indirect debt of their own that they issue, rises at a faster pace relative to income and wealth than when finance is either direct or arranged internally. Institutionalisation of saving and investment quickens the growth rate of debt relative to the growth rates of income and wealth.[8]

Gurley and Shaw (1955) thus provide us with two important theoretical hypotheses: (1) as mentioned above, that the neglect of most monetary theory in the macroeconomics of financial structure is a hindrance to the understanding of economic growth and stabilisation, and (2) that financial growth or deepening is a *sine qua non* for economic development (growth).

These authors defend the first hypothesis in the context of the methodology outlined above in the following way. They first identify commercial banks as the first type of intermediary to appear which enhances financial layering. When one considers a world where the only financial intermediaries are commercial banks, one dwells in a world in which financial structure can be reduced to the money market (the liabilities of the commercial banks or the banking system) by eliminating the bond market (the market for direct debt outside the banking system). If the stock of money and bonds is held constant, money is held to the extent to which banks hold bonds. If there is excess demand for bonds, bond prices rise, and banks sell off positions in bonds (that portion of their assets which is negotiable) as individuals move out of money into bonds. Excess demand for money occurs if commercial banks hold no bonds (or too few of them), bond prices are low, and interest rates are high.[9] In a more sophisticated financial environment, if one ignores the other financial institutions that have developed over the years in different countries, one makes a grave mistake of exclusion.[10]

How non-monetary financial intermediaries fit into a complete set of social accounts is clear. In the process of economic change and development, spending units with surpluses accumulate financial assets, direct and indirect, with the indirect assets taking more variegated form. Spending units with deficits accumulate indebtedness, with the debt outstanding to more diversified bodies of creditors. Aggregate debt rises at a faster pace relative to wealth if deficits and surpluses rise relative to income, if income rises relative to wealth, and if an increasing proportion of direct debt moves into the portfolios of financial intermediaries.[11]

Hence, one should not net out any financial layering as double counting of debt because it would eliminate information pertaining to important determinants of aggregate expenditure and thus economic growth and stability.[12] Further, Gurley and Shaw take exception to the view that banks stand apart in their ability to create loanable funds out of hand, while other intermediaries are busy with the modest brokerage function of transmitting loanable funds that are somehow generated elsewhere.[13] They argue that neither type of financial intermediaries creates loanable funds, which are actually created by surplus agents. Financial intermediaries create different forms of financial assets that surplus agents purchase, i.e. intermediaries tailor their assets and liabilities to the tastes of deficit and surplus agents, respectively. The shares of certain assets in the financial system are determined by the tastes (or preferences) of spending units.

These authors' view of economic growth depends very much on this argument.[14] They first reformulate liquidity preference theory. The first modification they make is to allow for growth in the stocks of bonds and money which might influence the division of labour between saving and investment activities.[15] They argue that if direct debt increases with income, then a diversification demand for money may arise. Further increases in the supply of bonds may be absorbed with a rise in interest rate only if the money supply is held constant. The higher levels of interest rates may decrease spending (especially investment spending) by deficit sectors, truncating economic growth. A proper increase in the money supply should ease this deflationary tendency.[16] Extending this diversification demand to financial assets other than money and bonds leads Gurley and Shaw to conclude that any impediments to financial market growth hinder economic growth as well.[17]

Gurley and Shaw's view of economic growth is thus inherently deflationary, especially if financial market expansion does not validate such growth. For many, however, growth (at least accelerated growth) is an inherently inflationary process. Consider an economy where all direct debt is absorbed by the banking system and most of the assets of commercial banks are not negotiable in the short run. Suppose there exists only a small bond market outside the banking system owing possibly to chronic inflation, poorly enforced bankruptcy laws or low nominal interest rate ceilings. Expenditure (and thus economic growth) is financed by retained earnings (self-finance) and by bank loans (money creation). Economic growth generates a diversification demand for bonds pushing bond prices up (in real terms) and interest rates down (once risk premiums are discounted). Banks cannot sell off their assets. Expenditure increases and inflation may increase. The government could stem this pressure by fortifying the bond market (perhaps by lifting the ceilings on bond rates, both bond and deposit rates) and selling safe government bonds. In contrast to Gurley and Shaw's analysis, a certain proportion of direct debt sold directly to households may be necessary for price stability.

Nevertheless, the conclusion of Gurley and Shaw's analysis remains: financial growth is essential for sustained economic growth. The business of monetary policy becomes more complicated, however. The optimal rate of growth of the money supply depends on the degree of financial market sophistication. In this context, monetary policy rules which follow $x\%$ growth rates seem inappropriate. Further, restrictive monetary policy may be undone by financial market innovation, which tends to increase velocity as higher interest rates spur competition by non-bank intermediaries.[18] Regulatory problems result:

> The lag of regulatory techniques behind the institutional development of intermediaries can be overcome when it is appreciated that financial control should supplant monetary control. Monetary control limits the supply of one financial asset, money. With a sophisticated financial structure providing assets, other than money and bonds, in increasing proportion to both, control over money alone is a decreasingly efficient means of regulating flows of loanable funds and spending on goods and services. Financial control, as the successor to monetary control, would regulate creation of financial assets in all forms that are competitive with direct securities in spending unit's portfolios. 'Tight finance' and 'cheap finance' are the sequels to 'tight money' and 'cheap money'.[19]

Raymond Goldsmith (1969) provides some rough international evidence for some of the propositions in Gurley and Shaw (1955). The most important findings for this analysis are: (1) Debt-to-income ratios increase in general during economic growth; (2) less-developed countries (LDCs) have lower debt-to-income ratios than do economically developed nations; (3) the share of financial institutions in the financial system increases with economic growth, although he warns against interpreting this phenomenon in a theory of the 'stages of growth' type; (4) growth has been concentrated in debt rather than equity; (5) the share of money first increases then decreases during growth; (6) the share of the banking system in the financial system has decreased; and (7) within countries, financial development roughly accompanies economic growth rates.[20]

Given that financial development should be pursued in the course of economic development,[21] the question now is how to achieve this goal.

1.3   THE NEO-LIBERAL SOLUTION

The foundations of the so-called neo-liberal approach to financial growth can be found in the pathbreaking studies of Ronald McKinnon (1973) and Edward S. Shaw (1972). McKinnon (1973) and Shaw (1972) initiate the development of their respective financial theories of economic growth by attacking the existing monetary growth theory.[22] They find unacceptable the conclusion that growth in the financial system (as measured by growth in money) would lead to a lower rate of capital accumulation (and a lower steady-state capital–labour ratio).[23] The respective alternative theories they propose, however, differ in a fundamental way: Shaw's argument, the 'debt-intermediation' view, stresses the importance of outside money as in Gurley and Shaw (1955 and 1960), while McKinnon's analysis uses an inside money model. Consequently, their models are different; the policy conclusions they make, however, are strikingly similar. Financial growth is beneficial to economic growth and any impediments to financial deepening, specifically nominal interest rate ceilings, exchange rate controls, and strict import tariff and quota restrictions, should be eliminated.

As mentioned above, Shaw's debt-intermediation model is an outside-money model where money is not viewed as wealth,[24] nor does it enter the production function directly.[25] Factors of production used in the monetary sector and the monetary technology affect the production of non-monetary goods by increasing the set of production techniques (technology) available to that sector. A larger monetary sector also increases accessibility to markets and economises on capital and labour used for transactions in a barter economy (or better, a less monetised economy). Monetary services are thus seen as intermediate inputs to production in all non-monetary sectors, including households. Growth in real money balances affects income in two opposite directions: (1) in a positive way by increasing the average and marginal products of factors of production, and (2) in a negative way by drawing factors of production from other activities to produce monetary services.[26]

It should prove instructive to reproduce the set of social accounts that Shaw (1973) develops, as extensive use will be made of them throughout this chapter (and this book). Shaw (1973) divides the economy into four sectors[27]: (1) a deficit sector; (2) a surplus sector; (3) the monetary sector; and (4) the non-monetary intermediary sector. The sectoral balance sheets appear in Table 1.1.

Notice that in the consolidated balance sheet for the entire economy, money is eliminated. Money is not real wealth and is seen only as a means of payment. Notice also that no reserves are held by the monetary sector. Inside money could be introduced into the analysis by introducing bank reserves and by separating the central bank from the consolidated balance sheet of the monetary sector. Such caveats will be used later in this chapter to evaluate policy measures.

Money demand for Shaw (1973), like wealth for Keynes, increases with real income (y), the real return to money ($i^d - \pi^e$), where i^d is the nominal deposit rate and π^e is the expected inflation rate, and decreases with (a vector of) opportunity costs to holding money (z):[28]

$$\frac{M^D}{P} = L(y, i^d - \pi^e, Z), \qquad L_1, L_2 > 0, \qquad L_3 < 0 \qquad (1.3)$$

Money supply depends positively on the real loan rate ($i - \pi^e$) and negatively on the real deposit rate ($i^d - \pi^e$) and a vector of other costs to intermediation (ω):

$$\frac{M^S}{P} = m(i - \pi^e, i^d - \pi^e, \omega), \qquad m_1 \gtrless 0; \qquad m_2, m_3 \lessgtr 0 \qquad (1.4$$

Increases in the real stock of money may occur because of an increase in the real deposit rate. The net effect upon income depends upon which effect dominates: either (1) the substitution effect between capital and money or (2) the technological advantage of using money as an intermediate input to production. Further, if saving is increased owing to the higher return on money, there may be a positive flow of funds from unproductive activities and/or consumption to productive activities. Hence, an increase in the deposit rate, which increases money or financial deepening, may increase growth rates because of two different reasons: (1) the quality of investment

Table 1.1 Sectoral balance sheets[29]

Deficit sectors (d)		Surplus sectors (s)	
Assets	Liabilities	Assets	Liabilities
K^d	$\dfrac{B}{iP}$	M^s	NW^s
M^d	NW^d	$\dfrac{M^s}{P}$	

Monetary sector (m)		Non-monetary intermediary sector (NM)	
Assets	Liabilities	Assets	Liabilities
K^m	$\dfrac{M}{P}$	K^{NM}	$\dfrac{NM}{P}$
$\dfrac{B^m}{iP}$		$\dfrac{B^{NM}}{iP}$	
		$\dfrac{M^{NM}}{P}$	

K	= capital stock.	P	= price level.
$\dfrac{B}{iP}$	= real stock of bonds.	$\dfrac{M}{P}$	= real money stock.
$1/i$	= price of a bond.	$\dfrac{NM}{P}$	= the real stock of non-monet-
i	= the nominal interest rate		ary financial assets.

will be improved and (2) an increase in saving will allow investment to increase. Whether this actually occurs is an empirical question crucial to the analysis and will be looked at in more detail later in this chapter.

McKinnon (1973) takes exception to the view that (inside) money and capital are substitutes in LDCs, a view that may be appropriate for developed and highly monetised economies but not for developing nations that have fragmented markets and primitive modes of production. He assumes that most investment activity is self-financed and that there exist economies of scale in production that are not being exploited. Since investment is 'lumpy', individuals must save over time in order to accumulate enough resources to make the desired investment. If deposit rates are kept (individually) low, desired money balances will be low and only small amounts will be invested in primitive (low-return) technologies. If deposit rates are raised, desired real money balances will increase, allowing for a larger accumulation of saving for larger investments in more advanced technologies. The agent does not mind paying higher interest rates (in an opportunity cost sense), because the increase in the return on his investment more than compensates the increase in interest rates.[30]

This complementarity between money and capital may be reflected in the demand for money in the following way. Demand for real money balances depends positively on real income (y), the real (average) return on capital (ρ), and the real deposit rate ($i^d - \pi^e$):[31]

$$\frac{M^D}{P} = L(y, \rho, i^d - \pi^e), \qquad L_1, L_2, L_3 > 0 \tag{1.5}$$

Conversely, the McKinnon hypothesis may also be reflected in the investment function:[32]

$$I^D = I(\rho, i^d - \pi^e), \qquad I_1, I_2, > 0 \tag{1.6}$$

For McKinnon (1973), raising the deposit rate is beneficial to economic growth, which is equivalent to Shaw's (1973) conclusion. The quality of the capital stock improves and, since saving increases, investment demand increases. Furthermore, if external finance exists, even higher growth rates may be possible. It should be noted that Fry (1978) presents empirical evidence that supports Shaw's (1973) view as opposed to McKinnon's (1973). Most of the models we will consider throughout the balance of this chapter fall generally under the 'debt-intermediation' view.

McKinnon (1973) and Shaw (1973) then apply their models to a stylised condition found in many LDCs, which they refer to as financial repression. They both assume that there exist good investment opportunities which are not being exploited in typical LDCs. The credit market is usually highly segmented, a condition whose distinguishing characteristic is chronic excess demand for loanable funds at prevailing interest rates. They briefly mention some natural causes of financial repression but these are played down. The main culprits in this story are usury laws, which hold nominal (and real) interest rates below their equilibrium rates, and state intervention of an even more direct nature via the extension of subsidised credit to priority sectors, which are usually accompanied by high import duties used in import-substitution industrialisation strategies.[33] Financial differentiation in monopolistically competitive financial markets by artificial means, i.e. a low nominal interest rate ceiling, which creates markets for other assets in the development of institutions for captive groups of savers, does not represent financial deepening because the allocation of saving is not improved.[34] These types of policies generate incentives for black or 'curb' lending markets, which lead to further financially repressive policies. Additionally, these interest rate ceilings (both deposit and lending) substantially decrease the opportunity costs of consumption, creating excess demand for goods and inflation. Hence, financial repression through interest rate ceilings causes growth to be hindered and also price instability, the opposite of what occurs with financial deepening. The allocation of saving is suboptimal, with funds flowing to low-return projects and the level of saving is low, resulting in slow growth in the capital stock. This condition is accompanied by chronic inflation.

Clearly, according to this line of reasoning, liberating loan and deposit rates would be the appropriate policy. We can illustrate this in the following way.[35] If we use Figure 1.1, saving ($S(y)$) is seen as an increasing function of real deposit rates and investment (I) as a decreasing function of real loan rates. Let ($i_0^d - \pi^e$) be the legally imposed real deposit rate and ($i_0 - \pi^e$) be the legally imposed loan rate.

If the deposit rate and loan rate ceiling are equal (ignoring other variable costs and reserve requirements), bank profits will then be zero. If the banks are able to charge i_0, then their profits are equal to the area *abcd*. More than likely, they can increase the effective interest rate on their loans to i_1 by requiring compensating balances, increasing bank profits to *abfe*. In either case, investment is restricted to I_0, a low level. Further, to the extent that loan rate restrictions are effective, these loans will tend to be directed towards safe projects, rationing riskier ones with higher returns.

If deposit and loan rates are lifted both will experience an initial jump to point g with investment increasing to I_1. If loan rate restrictions are effective, the effective loan and deposit rates will initially increase. If we are at f, however, the effective loan rate will decrease as the deposit rate increases. Higher investment at I_1 will increase saving from $S(y_0)$ to $S(y_1)$. A higher investment rate I_2 and lower real deposit and loan rates will obtain. This process continues until an equilibrium interest rate is reached that is lower than the interest rates experienced during the transition period. Investment, and therefore growth in output, increases to a higher rate.

The above outcome for a closed economy depends very much upon the sensitivity of saving to real deposit rates. Fry (1978 and 1980) presents empirical evidence showing that national saving in LDCs is

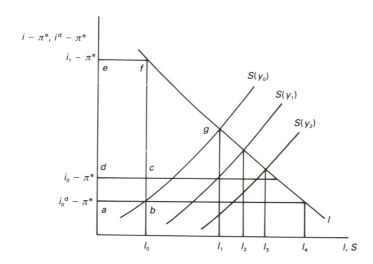

Figure 1.1

sensitive to changes in real deposit rates. Giovannini (1985), however, shows that this probably is not the case. Fry (1978 and 1980)
uses data that do not separate government saving from net national
saving, including in his study countries that underwent simultaneous
financial and fiscal reforms. Fry's conclusion that saving is sensitive to
real interest rates may have been due to increased government
receipts during the period of interest rate liberalisation. Giovannini
(1985) re-estimates the savings function excluding those countries
that fall into this category, finding no evidence that savings is
interest-rate-sensitive. Further, he finds that in only 5 of 18 countries
is intertemporal substitution of consumption sensitive to real interest
rate changes.[36]

The analysis changes if one explicitly accounts for risk. Stiglitz and
Weiss (1981) have shown that in capital markets where projects must
be evaluated with a high amount of risk, i.e. a wide dispersion of
(perceived) possible rates of return from projects, a competitive
equilibrium entails credit rationing. This situation coincides with the
one described by McKinnon (1973) and Shaw (1973) as being appropriate for analysing LDCs: fragmented markets with a large dispersion of possible returns to a heterogeneous capital stock. The
reasoning is that the expected returns to banks from loans decreases
as a larger share of loans is extended to riskier projects. Higher
interest rates ration safe, low-return project applicants out of the

credit market while only risky, high-return project applicants remain. Increases in interest rates past a certain point decrease bank returns.[37] Hence, if one observes (non-price) rationing of credit in an economy, the conclusion that financial repression is due to government policy does not necessarily follow.

McKinnon (1973) and Shaw (1973) maintain that interest rate ceilings intensify risk aversion. This, however, is not necessarily the case.[38] If we consider the Stiglitz and Weiss (1981) model (as described in note 37), the comparative statics of Figure 1.1 must be modified. Suppose deposit rates are held below their competitive equilibrium rate ρ^*_0 at ρ^*_1 (Figure 1.2). Competition for deposits forces the average real return to loans, ρ^*_1, to equal the real deposit rate, ρ_1.

Notice that at ρ^*_1 there are two possible loan rates, r^*_1 and $r^{*'}_1$, with a supply of funds L_0^s. Both situations A and B exhibit credit rationing, with excess demand greater at A than at B. We may look at B as the case where loan interest rate ceilings are not effective, either because they are not legally limited or because there is circumvention of usury laws by the use of compensating balances.

Consider the comparative statics of full interest rate liberalisation. If we are at A when interest rates are liberated, loan rates will rise from r^*_1 to r^*_0 and the amount loaned will rise from L_1 to L_0. The bank's portfolio of loans will become riskier and the expected return will increase. If we are at B, however, loan rates will fall from r^*_1 to r^*_0 and loans will increase from L_1^s to L_0^s, but the degree of credit rationing may increase while the riskiness of the banking system's loan portfolio decreases. In situation A, since the riskiness of the banking system's portfolio increases, growth may be increased as the return on investment increases, shifting the supply of funds from L_0^s to L_1^s. There is no reason to believe that the increase in the loanable fund schedule, however, will eliminate excess demand for funds. Further, the decrease in riskiness of the banking system's loan portfolio in situation B results in a perverse income effect. This would exacerbate credit rationing.

Situation A represents a modified version of the McKinnon–Shaw hypothesis while B is a counter-argument. One might argue, however, that banks, especially in LDCs, are risk-averse and that situation A is more likely to obtain. In countries which have large curb markets or have a portion of the organised financial sector operating as a so-called 'free market', however, there seems to be a high degree of risk taking.[39] Also, the incidence of compensating balances reveals that actual loan rates usually fall above loan rate ceilings. Other types

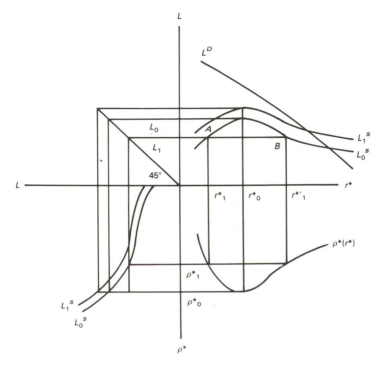

Figure 1.2

of collateral requirements may allow banks to charge a higher rate. These observations are empirical questions, idiosyncratic to each economy, and will not be taken up here. The main conclusion, however, is that there are reasonable arguments to the effect that the outcome of interest rate liberalisation predicted by McKinnon and Shaw may not obtain. Other conditions under which adverse growth and price stability effects result from interest rate liberalisation will be discussed later in the chapter.

Still working within the framework of a closed economy, McKinnon (1973) proposes an alternative anti-inflationary monetary policy to orthodox monetary restriction. He proposes increasing the demand for money by increasing the real return on money (i.e. increasing the real deposit rate). Orthodox deflation usually entails an inordinate contraction in the production of goods and services.

In contrast to the Keynesian view, complementary between the real stock of money and the stock of capital holds during short-run deflations as well as over longer periods of growth. In the process of deflation over the short-run, the key component of investment that is influenced the most is working capital, as is demonstrated by Samuel Morley's analysis of the Brazilian deflation[40] . . . With plant capacity essentially fixed during the time period over which one hopes the deflation will occur, an incidental concentration in M/P in the course of trying to control M may well force severe disintermediation on the banking system. This in turn forces firms dependent on bank finance to reduce working capital: inventories of goods in process, trade credit, and advances to workers prior to actual sales.

The result is unemployed labour and underutilised plant capacity.[41]

McKinnon feels that increasing the demand for money by increasing the real deposit rate will stabilise prices without the adverse output effects of orthodox policy. People will consume less and hold more real money balances.

The desired deflationary impact on the aggregate demand for commodities will be achieved, thereby reducing the rate of increase in the price level, even as the competitiveness and real size of the banking system increases. Real credit—albeit at much higher nominal rates of interest—can then expand rather than contract, and the typical squeeze on working capital can be avoided all together.[42]

Again, this argument depends upon the sensitivity of (private) saving to real interest rates. If saving is inelastic in relation to interest rates, real credit may not expand. Further, if the shift into money comes from productive financial assets with a lower degree of intermediation than the banking system and not from unproductive assets, as we will see, real credit supply may contract.[43] Also, if working capital financial costs are important (in magnitude), output may contract and prices may rise.

The balance of the discussion of McKinnon (1973) and Shaw's (1973) arguments will deal with liberalisation in the context of an open economy. Trade liberalisation and fiscal budget balance are seen by both as essential to successful financial reform, but a discussion of how these should be achieved will be suppressed. Suffice it to say that trade liberalisation should be just that, it is argued, and not merely export promotion, which leaves the fiscal structure acquired during the import-substitution period intact.[44] Fiscal balance must be achieved by increases in explicit taxes and decreases in credit subsidies because interest rate liberalisation may be subverted by unnecessary expansion of the money supply owing to fiscal deficits.[45]

Exchange rate policy, in effect a well-managed devaluation, is a crucial part of interest rate liberalisation.[46] Suppose government policy is to undertake full liberalisation of the economy in order to decrease inflation and increase growth. The government raises taxes and prices of publicly produced goods and services and liberates loan and deposit rates. According to McKinnon (1973), this will decrease inflation and increase output growth. An even reduction in import restrictions should be undertaken. The sharp rise in interest rates coupled with import liberalisation, however, may cause a large inflow of foreign capital, not easily absorbed in the short run except by an increase in imports. Devaluation is hindered, hurting exports. Such capital inflows could undermine the inflation stabilisation policy by causing a large expansion of the money base. Long-run growth prospects may be hurt by the suppression of exports and because of future foreign debt service problems. A reversal of policy may take place with consequent increases in import restrictions, capital flow restrictions, and the reinstating of interest rate ceilings.

In order to avoid such adverse and destabilising capital flows, one should keep the return to capital in the domestic country in line with the rest of the world by devaluation.[47] Devaluation suppresses the increased return to capital in the LDC from the viewpoint of foreigners. The timing of different policy measures, as we will see later, is very important to this line of argument.

To help maintain external balance, however, there is a case for also having the foreign exchange rate depreciate slowly in a predictable way after the initial surprise devaluation. Instead of devaluing fully to 'the' equilibrium exchange rate associated with free trade, suppose the authorities undertake a somewhat smaller discrete devaluation. Initially trade restrictions are evenly relaxed, although not removed entirely. Then the exchange rate begins to depreciate smoothly at an annual percentage rate that reflects the difference between foreign and domestic nominal rates of interest—with a suitable risk premium subtracted from the latter. A large inflow of foreign short-term capital is avoided because users and lenders of foreign short-term capital (trade credit) take the continuing considerations into account.[48]

The above argument could play on nationalistic sentiments; stabilisation and growth (development) can be achieved without unnecessary increases in foreign debt. The foreign exchange constraint may be relaxed if policies are pursued that increase internal saving without allowing foreign saving to crowd out domestic thrift. The viability of such a scheme depends upon assumptions, pointed out earlier in the chapter, that may or may not hold.

A considerable amount of effort has gone into formalising many of the propositions put forth in McKinnon (1973) and Shaw (1973).[49] The first formalisation of the McKinnon–Shaw model was formulated by Kapur (1976).[50] His objective is to show that increases in deposit rates are a viable alternative to orthodox stabilisation policies and to develop the dynamics of such adjustment. Kapur's (1976) model shows the dynamics of the McKinnon (1973) hypothesis in spite of the fact that he assumes that money is not neutral. Considering the non-neutrality of money, it seems that this model is designed to show just this conclusion. Non-neutrality of money does not seem like a bad assumption, because both McKinnon (1973) and Shaw (1973) consider money as non-neutral, at least in the context of financial repression. The manner in which money is made non-neutral, however, is suspect in Kapur's (1976) model and subverts its usefulness to a certain degree.[51]

Mathieson (1980) develops a model that improves upon Kapur (1976) by allowing money to be neutral in competitive equilibrium but not in the context of financial repression.[52] He does this by allowing a fixed proportion of all investment (including fixed capital, net working capital and replacement working capital) to be financed by bank loans. He also incorporates a savings function. The distinguishing feature of Mathieson's (1980) analysis is not, however, the neutrality of money in competitive equilibrium, but the fact that financial institutions might fail with sudden increases in the cost of their funding. If deposit and loan rates are liberated completely at a discrete point in time then the cost of the banks' liabilities will exceed the earnings on their assets because there will be a stock of loans outstanding that still earns the pre-reform interest rate.[53] Interest rate liberalisation could lead to bankruptcies of financial institutions, which would threaten the health of the financial system or cause the government to abort stabilisation policies by injecting resources into the financial sector. The problem then becomes to administer a financial reform while avoiding large losses to the financial sector.

Mathieson (1980) uses optimal control methods to determine the optimal stabilisation and interest rate liberalisation scheme under assumptions of both adaptive and rational expectations. In general, the solution under both adaptive and rational (perfect foresight) expectations entails two phases to the program: an initial stage where a 'shock' treatment is adopted in which policy variables take discrete jumps, and a subsequent 'gradualist' treatment where variables smoothly adjust to their state values. This dichotomy stems from the fact that the solution is saddle-point stable in money growth and loan interest rates, the deposit interest rate being adjusted in line with π^e in order to maintain continual money market equilibrium.[54] In other words, even in the case where (private) individuals are assumed to have adaptive expectations, the government is assumed to have rational expectations, being able to calculate the exact jumps in the policy variables that put the system on its unique (and shifting) convergent path.

Mathieson's (1980) model retains the conclusions of Kapur (1976): price stabilisation can be achieved with higher economic growth by using interest rate liberalisation policy. Timing in the use of policy variables becomes important when one considers the portfolio structure of the financial system. The avoidance of conflicts between growth and inflation is due to the assumptions of a positive saving effect, simple household asset portfolios, and ignoring the cost of working capital.

Further work extends these formalisations to the context of an open economy. Basically, the models developed looked at the proposition that a well-executed devaluation will avoid any incipient excess capital flows due to interest rate liberalisation. Further, the arguments maintain that growth will still increase and inflation decrease.

Kapur (1983) extends his original model to the open economy by introducing an imported input to production and a balance of payments relationship. Growth is inhibited by rising costs of imported inputs. This allows for the possibility of a stagflationary devaluation where the trade deficit worsens as output contracts. He uses optimal control methods to derive an optimal policy. As in Mathieson (1979 and 1980), the solution entails discrete jumps in policy variables. The government shoots for trade balance, lower inflation, and higher growth. At the time of the liberalisation of interest rates, a discrete depreciation is undertaken which undershoots the long-run value of the exchange rate and then depreciates to it. Because of the imported input, a depreciation which is too large could cause excessive capital inflows, i.e. the current account could worsen as expected exchange depreciation worsens. The effect on growth is ambiguous, because a depreciation could decrease growth owing to higher working capital costs, but also allows for a higher deposit rate, which increases the demand for money. The net effect depends upon whether the negative effect of increasing working capital costs dominates the positive supply of credit effects, which in turn depend upon the assumptions about saving behaviour described earlier.

Mathieson (1979) modifies his (1980) model by explicitly accounting for portfolio balance in addition to the balance of payments, foreign reserves in the monetary base, and an expectations-augmented Phillips curve. Again, the objective is to perform a financial liberalisation while simultaneously keeping bank profits at normal levels and avoiding excessive capital inflows. As before, Mathieson (1979) uses optimal control methods to solve for the optimal policy paths. The policy variables are the exchange rate, the deposit rate, the loan rate, and the stock of domestic credit as the total money supply is determined endogenously.

The solution is again saddle-point stable in the deposit rate and the exchange rate. This calls, therefore, for initial jumps in the policy variables, followed by smooth adjustment to the steady state. Further, the optimal mix of policy generated by what he calls a 'patient, anti-inflationary programme' will always be stable. An 'impatient, growth-oriented programme' may yield an unstable adjustment.

Unlike in Kapur (1983), the optimal solution in Mathieson (1979) entails an overdepreciation of the exchange rate as well as jumps in deposit and loan rates which overshoot their long-run values. This stems from the fact that there is no imported input in production. The exchange rate must overshoot its target value in order to avoid large capital inflows[55] as deposit rates overshoot their target values. Because of the increased availability of credit and an improvement in the balance of trade, growth initially overshoots its steady-state value. The inflation rate does not jump but begins immediately a continuous decline. The second phase of the programme has policy variables smoothly moving, as before, to their long-run values.

Mathieson (1979 and 1980) concentrates on the timing and coordination of optimal policies. This timing element results not only from the necessity of keeping the banking system solvent, as before, but also from the necessity of external balance. Exchange rate policy must be carefully coordinated in order to avoid excessive capital inflows. It should be noted that the typical explanation of failures of interest rate liberalisation policies (specifically in Latin America) which follow the above argument usually focus on incorrect timing rather than on the viability of such policies.[56]

Output increases and inflation decreases in these models because the shift into domestic deposits comes from two (unproductive, from the domestic view) sources: (1) unproductive domestic resources, such as fallow land and mattress money, and (2) from foreign assets held by domestic residents. The domestic rate of saving increases as it is not crowded out by foreign saving but only augmented by the repatriation of saving originally held in the form of foreign assets.

1.4   THE NEO-STRUCTURALIST APPROACH

In discussing the Brazilian stabilisation of 1964–7, Samuel Morley (1971) shows that contractionary monetary policy carried significant 'stagflationary' effects, i.e. inflation and stagnation. The explanation of this curious phenomenon centred around the fact that working capital costs are important in Brazil and other Latin American countries. Restrictive monetary policy which raises interest rates not only has significant demand side dampening effects but also causes aggregate supply to fall as interest costs affect working capital costs. Such a view of the inflation process in Latin America, however, is not new.[57] Van Wijnbergen (1983a and 1983b), inspired by these experiences and interpretations, develops a model that incorporates the cost of working capital in aggregate supply and allows for 'curb' or black credit markets (or any other type of direct debt market with a free interest rate). Perverse price and output effects may result from interest rate liberalisation as individuals shift out of a productive asset (direct curb market loans) with no reserve requirement into time deposits. The supply of funds contracts as part of the increase in time deposits must be kept as reserves. This pushes the cost of working capital up, causing prices to increase and output to contract.

In other words, output will increase if the shift into time deposits comes mainly from currency instead of curb market loans. If, however, the shift comes mainly from curb market loans then credit decreases and output falls. The reason net credit falls in the latter situation is that curb market loans do not carry a reserve requirement, i.e. there is less intermediation in curb market loans. If interest rates are high (owing to restrictive monetary policy) and supply effects dominate the (decreased) demand effect, low levels of output will be associated with high levels of inflation.

Consider a change in deposit rates in an environment where supply effects dominate. Again, the outcome depends upon whether the shift into time deposits comes from currency or curve market loans. If it comes from currency then credit expands as do deposits; inflation decreases while output increases. This is the McKinnon–Shaw hypothesis. If, on the other hand, the portfolio shift comes mainly from curb market loans then total credit contracts, causing inflation to increase and output to contract. The shift into time deposits causes credit to decrease, pushing the curb market rate up. Firms restrict output and pass the added costs on to consumers faster than consumption and investment demand decrease, causing inflation to rise. In this light, the McKinnon–Shaw hypothesis is seen to depend upon whether the shift into time deposits comes from unproductive assets such as cash balances not used to finance working capital or real estate, or from productive assets such as curb market or free market loans. Again, the results depend on the strength of the saving effect.

Clearly this analysis is short-term in nature, as are most of the above. A long-term analysis will not be attempted here. Van Wijnbergen (1983a) extends this model to the long term. He concludes that in the stagflationary case above, time deposit rate increases may lead to slower growth and financial market stagnation. In the McKinnon–Shaw case above, in which the saving effect dominates, both output and the financial system grow.[58]

Moving to the open-economy context, the contractionary effects of devaluation in Kapur's (1983) model stem from the fact that there is an imported working capital input. Krugman and Taylor (1978) and, in a more complex model, Bruno (1979) argue that this effect may be enhanced if one starts from a position of trade balance deficit. Devaluation raises both import and export prices. If one is experiencing a trade deficit the ability of devaluation to improve this deficit depends upon far more restrictive conditions than simple 'Marshall –Lerner' conditions. Further, if the country in question has a large foreign debt outstanding, devaluation may be even less effective.[59] Devaluation may also cause a contraction in the monetary base in domestic currency terms, even though it improves in foreign currency terms. In the context of the Van Wijnbergen (1983a and 1983b) model, such a restriction in the money base will restrict credit, causing the curb market rate to increase, working capital costs to increase, inflation to increase, and output to decline.

The problem with this view is that, as in Kapur (1983), it does not account explicitly for portfolio determinants of capital flows. Buffie (1984) presents a model that retains the adverse output and price effects of credit restriction and interest rate liberalisation in Van Wijnbergen (1983a and 1983b), but devaluation is not necessarily contractionary. This stems from the fact that domestic residents hold foreign bonds. A devaluation decreases the real wage, increasing real loan demand as in the Van Wijnbergen model. Loan supply, however, may be increased as domestic residents move out of foreign assets into domestic deposits. This may result in the opposite of stagflation, where output increases and inflation falls.[60]

Finally, contractionary effects of interest rate liberalisation and devaluation might be counteracted by an appropriate increase in the domestic component of the money base or a decrease in the reserve ratio. This, at best, would allow interest rate liberalisation to be neutral with respect to inflation and output in the short run. We thus return to the question of the role of financial markets in the growth process considered as opposed to their role in stabilisation. A preliminary conclusion that could be ventured on the basis of the above analyses is that one may not be able to kill the two birds of allocative efficiency and price stabilisation with the one interest rate liberalisation stone.

1.5 TROUBLE IN THE SOUTHERN CONE

By far the most pervasive reforms along neo-liberal lines were undertaken in the Southern Cone countries of Argentina, Chile, and, especially, Uruguay. Their experience with financial liberalisation and the problems it created are well documented and hence only a brief discussion of these reforms will be dealt with here.[61] Most of the neo-liberal financial liberalisation attempts were undertaken in the context of large capital inflows from private international money centre banks. Whether the liberalisation attempts caused or were a reaction to these countries' new-found ability to borrow in international markets, the implicit conclusion of the neo-liberal argument for such policies is that free and 'unrepressed' financial markets were necessary to allocate these capital resources efficiently. The usual recipe was some combination of reducing trade barriers, opening the capital account of the balance of payments, freeing interest rates, reducing barriers to entry of financial institutions, and allowing financial 'innovation' to flourish.

Although the countries which undertook the liberalisation of financial markets followed different sequences and degrees in the implementation of these policies, the short-term problems that each economy encountered were surprisingly similar. All encountered difficulties in allocating the overabundant capital resources efficiently. In other words, they were not able to avoid a destabilising capital inflow as manifested in the 'overlending' which took place and the increased riskiness of the financial sector loan portfolio.[62] Adverse terms of trade movements, coupled with the increase in dollar interest rates, pushed these vulnerable financial structures to the brink of collapse in 1982. In each of the Southern Cone countries, the central banks intervened in one form or another to monetise nonperforming loans. Both Uruguay and Chile weathered the crisis, although at high cost and significant capital flight, while Argentina slipped back to 'financial repression' with the reinstatement of 100% required reserve ratios and a closing of the capital account.[63]

After the relative failure of trade and capital market liberalisation schemes attempted in the Southern Cone, especially in Argentina, recent work has concentrated on the timing of the different policies in a full liberalisation package. Specifically, Edwards and Van Wijnbergen (1986 and 1987) conclude that the best sequence of liberalisation would be to (gradually) liberate trade first and then free capital flows.[64] If capital flows are freed in the absence of free trade, the harmful effects of the trade distortion (restrictions) would be enhanced, thus causing a welfare loss. The government could intervene to prevent this outcome by (1) placing restrictions on the amount paid to foreign owners of capital and (2) creating an institution which would allocate investment according to 'shadow' (world) prices as opposed to the distorted internal prices.

McKinnon (1985) comes to similar conclusions concerning the liberalisation of capital inflows and outflows but based upon macroeconomic concerns. He concludes that both capital inflows and outflows should be liberated not only after trade is freed but also only after a fiscal reform is implemented. If the government uses the inflation tax to finance chronic deficits, one would want to control capital outflows to prevent erosion of the inflation tax base (the monetary base) and the consequent fiscal distress and acceleration of inflation. Further, inflation tax 'receipts' increase with the spread between deposit rates and loan rates owing to required reserves. To the extent that inflows of foreign funds reduce this spread, inflation tax revenue will fall. Hence, capital inflows should also be controlled. A 'fiscal reform' would allow the government to rely less on the inflation tax and capital flows would not be detrimental to public finance.[65]

Curiously enough, the Southern Cone country which generated the most efficient and largest financial market, Uruguay, undertook financial and trade liberalisation in exactly the opposite order to that expressed by these apologists of the liberalisation school. Uruguay fully freed its capital account before undertaking either a fiscal reform or freeing the trade account.

Why did the neo-liberal experiments in financial market opening impose such stress on financial markets and the economies as a whole? Certainly, much of the blame can be borne by the policies pursued in the Southern Cone countries to manipulate inflation expectations through the exchange rate.[66] Analyses of these exchange rate polices are in excess supply, and therefore in what follows I will try briefly to go beyond the mere analysis of policy flaws and try to discern what was lacking in the neo-liberal theory. Other explanations appear in Diaz-Alejandro (1985) and Felix (1986).

A fatal flaw in neo-liberal arguments is that debt and equity are assumed to be perfect substitutes and that firms are indifferent between them for financing projects. There is good reason to believe that this is not the case, especially in developing countries. Firstly, the differential tax treatment of interest payments, which are usually deductible as a cost of business, and dividends, which are not, will cause a bias against equity issues. Secondly, a firm can dissipate the risk of bankruptcy by issuing stock. The market, however, may see a stock issue as a signal that the firm is of lower quality, i.e. needing to lower the likelihood or socialise the cost of bankruptcy.[67] Good firms will expand operations by debt finance while poor ones will expand by issuing stock. This renders the cost of capital in equity financing higher than that of debt financing and perhaps prohibitive. Thirdly, the cost of bad management is borne to a larger degree by managers with debt financing than with equity financing. Monitoring managers is a 'public good' among shareholders and 'free-rider' problems do exist to the extent that ownership in the firm is decentralised. There will tend to be underinvestment in the monitoring of managers and, hence, equity financing is less attractive.[68] This effect is complicated further when the controlling group of a company consists of managers in the firm. Managers then have an incentive to divert resources for their own purposes, which do not necessarily correspond to those of the other stockholders which maximise the efficiency of the firm.

Capital market liberalisation will favour financial markets as opposed to stock markets. For example, stock markets in Latin American countries play a small role in financing economic activity in spite of attempts to stimulate these markets. This reinforces the supply side effects of credit rationing as the high cost of equity capital renders stock issues inviable as an alternative source of capital. Capital market liberalisation may increase the supply of credit, but interest rates may not decline significantly if there is credit rationing owing to adverse selection.[69] If banks impose high collateral requirements, perhaps in the form of compensating balances, they will tend to make riskier loans because safer borrowers are rationed out of the market by higher interest rates. An increase in resources available to banks may cause 'over-lending' to risky borrowers, which puts the solvency of the banking system in danger, especially in light of the fact that equity issues will generally not occur. Explicit or implicit deposit insurance will tend to exacerbate this tendency due to moral hazard. The recent experiences of Argentina and Chile with respect to full financial market liberalisation suggest that there is a strong possibility of a decrease in the stability of the financial system owing to liberalisation. Regulatory improvements and convergence should be clearly articulated when capital market liberalization is undertaken.

1.6   A RECONSIDERATION OF THE THEORY OF THE FINANCIAL ASPECTS OF ECONOMIC DEVELOPMENT

Implicit in much of the theoretical discussion presented above is the proposition that with a larger financial and capital market, the quality of investment will improve as a more decentralised system would be able to evaluate projects more efficiently. When unregulated financial markets do not successfully achieve allocative efficiency (defined by the equality of relative input prices and marginal rates of substitution) there is a market failure. Government intervention could improve this situation, keeping in mind the cost, through tax-cum-subsidy schemes or by creating financial market institutions that are seen as lacking (e.g. mutual funds, forced saving funds, pensions, investment banks, regional banks, etc.). Clearly, in some circumstances, these two types of policies are complementary. A tax-cum-subsidy scheme is a 'first best' policy when the market failure raises the cost of capital relative to other inputs.

Lloyd (1977) describes a 'vicious circle' in the growth process where credit demand continually increases with industrialisation, putting increasing pressure on interest rates. The high interest rates push firms to appeal to the government for cheaper funds. If subsidies are granted and the process is followed to its logical end, all sectors will become subsidised, a contradiction, resulting in further financial repression and inflation.[70] The McKinnon (1973) and Shaw (1973) proposals were meant to represent an alternative to this inconsistent policy. Unfortunately, the institutional development alternative has received scant treatment in the literature, save for a few case studies. As discussed above, financial liberalisation will not necessarily achieve efficiency objectives, let alone stabilisation objectives.

Financial repression is by definition, however, a market failure to the extent that it is not caused by government intervention. Financial repression results not only from interest rate control by government but also occurs because of lack of information, large differences in the returns on different projects, inflation, and so forth. Earlier, it was argued that one of the deficiencies of the neo-liberal models of financial growth was the fact that debt and equity were implicitly viewed as perfect substitutes. In Latin American countries this is clearly not the case. Pre- and post-reform stock markets are typically small, with few traders.[71] Firms are usually closed and family-owned, with most stock issues flowing directly to current owners. Most new projects are financed with retained earnings. As argued above, there are good reasons for firms to resist equity financing even in the face of higher interest costs on debt.

The importance of the lack of reaction of the stock market to financial liberalisation is clear in the experiences of the Southern Cone countries of Latin America (as well as Brazil, as we shall see). After interest rate liberalisation, the main vehicle for expansion of economic activity was through borrowing and not the issue of new equity. Not only did debt–equity ratios rise but also the payments on that debt, increasing the default risk of the firms in question. The stability of the financial systems of Southern Cone countries were threatened with collapse as the riskiness of bank portfolios rose significantly.

Interest rate liberalisation tends to change the initial small debt–asset ratios of firms. With higher interest rates, financial innovation is enhanced. If financial reform is undertaken with no or ineffective policies to stimulate new issues of stocks, private firms may grow without allowing a dissemination of control by contracting increasing amounts of debt. There is reason to expect, therefore, significant increases in debt–asset ratios, especially if the economy is growing as a whole.

Latin American economies, therefore, seem prone to the type of financial instability discussed in Minsky (1982).[72] The ability of firms to finance payments on their debt outstanding, in this scenario, becomes increasingly vulnerable to income or interest rate shocks.[73] If there is full indexing of debt (or even partial indexing) then firms in general may become increasingly vulnerable to external shocks such as changes in the terms of trade or foreign interest rates.[74] This will be reflected in higher interest rates in the domestic economy, which may push firms into unstable positions where they must contract new debt to meet debt service.[75] To the extent that firms (or households and government for that matter) have secured foreign debt, foreign debt crises such as the current one in Latin American may result.[76] Typical monetary and fiscal policy restraint to decrease inflation and improve balance of payments problems can be implemented only at a large cost in output reduction and unemployment during a large debt deflation process.

Unfortunately, among economists the analysis of the role of institutions in the development process is generally disdained.[77] The development of financial market institutions, however, in the Latin American context is clearly important in order to decrease financial market instability. For example, one could create tax incentives for the issuance of equity or create a strong regulatory framework that enhances the desirability of equity financing to diminish default risk. Further, if the private sector did not provide funds for the underwriting of equity securities even with tax benefits then the government might create its own institutions for such purposes. Brazilian policy makers in the early 1960s felt that such development was important for the stability of the financial system and the growth process. As we shall see, not only did they try to create a robust financial market by interest rate liberalisation through the creation of indexation but they also tried to decrease the risk of the financial system through the creation of institutions and incentives.

1.7 SUMMARY AND CONCLUSIONS

This chapter examined basic issues concerning financial growth in less developed nations. Gurley and Shaw's (1955) argument represents a strong case for the development of financial markets in fostering economic growth and development. McKinnon (1973) and Shaw (1973) extend these arguments, maintaining that both allocative efficiency and stabilisation goals can be achieved (at least in the short to medium term) by interest rate liberalisation (coupled with trade liberalisation). Interest rate liberalisation, however, does not necessarily achieve allocative efficiency in the context of the Stiglitz and Weiss (1981) model as shown above. Further, the success of using financial liberalisation for stabilisation purposes depends upon certain implicit assumptions about economic structure and behaviour. Specifically, it depends upon saving being interest-sensitive, on substitution into deposits coming from unproductive assets, and on supply effects of investment-savings relationships dominating.

The failure of interest rate liberalisation to achieve allocative efficiency stems from a market failure that is due to risk and imperfect knowledge in credit markets. This calls for a policy directed toward increasing information and a decrease in the overall default risk of financial market agents. This could be achieved through regulation or direct participation of state-owned financial institutions in the market. The inability of interest rate liberalisation to achieve stabilisation objectives raises questions about the appropriateness of using financial policies for this end and about the appropriate mix of interest rate, monetary, fiscal, and exchange rate policies to achieve stabilisation goals. The analysis suggests that economic structure should be considered (especially the financial structure of firms and other agents) during the design of stabilisation policies.

Difficulties after financial liberalisation has taken place were briefly examined, with special emphasis on instabilities resulting from interest and exchange rate indexation and financial innovation. This brings up an important question: should LDCs promote financial growth during development efforts in spite of these difficulties? The position taken here is yes. The reasoning is the following. The demand for financial services increases with development[78] by both surplus and deficit agents. Financial intermediaries tailor their assets and liabilities to the tastes of their customers. It seems this basic characteristic of financial institutions and markets is sometimes forgotten by economists. In this sense, when financial markets are institutionally dynamic, financial growth, if correctly regulated, could play a decisive role in the ability of an economy to adjust (or not adjust) to a changing economic environment.

A theory that allows for the calculation of a reasonable optimal path between the comparative static points of 'financially repressed' and 'financially deepened' for an economy is still lacking. It is clear from the above analysis that there is room for the development and use of institutions as policy instruments in such a theory. This opinion may be looked at as a sort of 'infant industry' argument for the financial sector. Post-1964 Brazilian financial policy was formulated in this tone by the development and use of government financial institutions, for better or for worse, as policy instruments. Examining the Brazilian case in such detail will allow for the sketching out of such a policy.

2 Development with Inflationary Finance: 1945–63

2.1 INTRODUCTION

The period 1945–63 in Brazil is sometimes referred to as the period of easy import substitution. Until 1961, when the ability to industrialise through import substitution industrialisation had ended, industrialisation was financed to a large extent through inflation. Domestic firms were protected by selective exchange controls and the 'law of similars' which allowed high tariff barriers to be erected on competing products.[1] In general, firms financed long-term investment with the inflated retained earnings from protection, while financing working capital through short-term bank credit.[2] Industrialisation proceeded by initially developing consumer durable production. The short-term and medium-term financial system grew up around consumer durables where commercial banks discounted the accounts receivable or 'duplicatas' of firms needing working capital. This system was complemented by the appearance of the bills of exchange (letras de cambio) market. Vertical integration was promoted by the generous application of the law of similars, the encouragement of multinational corporations to operate in Brazil, and direct government production in heavy industries such as steel, petroleum, transportation, and public utilities.[3]

Table 2.1 shows that domestic private savings grew as a percentage of GDP. Ness (1972) presents empirical evidence that domestic saving was positively related to the inflation rate over this period.[4] The fact that savings as a percentage of GDP remained relatively high in the face of accelerating inflation and high growth rates (see Table 2.2) loosely confirms the proposition that inflation acted as the vehicle for transferring saving to the retained earnings of firms, a process that has come to be referred to as 'forced savings'.

The financial structure of firms corresponding to this type of industrialisation strategy left output and prices very sensitive to changes in the cost of working capital. This will be shown below. It

Table 2.1   Brazil: Saving as a Percentage of GDP, 1947–64

	Gross private saving	Government current account	Current account of balance of payments	Total saving
1947	9.55	4.14	1.89	15.58
1948	11.24	4.01	0.43	15.68
1949	7.97	4.08	1.02	13.07
1950	9.43	2.72	–0.76	11.40
1951	11.37	4.67	2.84	18.88
1952	11.42	3.63	3.74	18.50
1953	12.72	0.97	–0.10	15.55
1954	14.79	3.58	1.20	19.77
1955	13.49	1.90	0.14	15.53
1956	14.02	0.79	–0.08	14.73
1957	14.32	1.47	1.34	15.13
1958	8.02	4.38	1.37	13.77
1959	10.44	4.61	1.83	16.88
1960	7.87	5.21	2.59	15.47
1961	14.89	1.71	1.30	17.90
1962	14.33	0.16	3.08	17.57
1963	14.95	0.65	1.52	16.90
1964	15.95	0.48	–5.04	11.39

Source: Fundação Getulio Vargas—IBGE.

also tended to be inflationary because the government's activities necessitated large amounts of capital resources with a limited ability to tax. This situation was complicated by two laws dating back to the 1930s: (1) the usury law, which set the nominal interest rate ceiling at 12%, and (2) the gold exchange clause, which effectively ruled out the index-linking of financial assets because it allowed only transactions in domestic currency at its legal value.[5] Since the government could not use tricks (except for the Bank of Brazil) to get around these ceilings as commercial banks and the finance companies (the so-called 'financeiras') could, the demand for government bills and bonds disappeared completely by 1963 as inflation went far above 12% and real interest on these securities became very negative. In sum, 'non-inflationary' finance of government activities, e.g. taxation and the placement of government bonds, was not a viable alternative for the Brazilian government, given the institutional and political framework of the period. Heavy reliance on monetary expansion fed inflation, which deteriorated tax revenue (as people delayed payments), which led to more money expansion.

Table 2.2   Brazil: Real Growth and Inflation Rates, 1948–64

	Real growth	Inflation[a]
1947	1.8	6.3
1948	9.5	9.2
1949	5.6	9.0
1950	5.0	13.4
1951	5.1	19.8
1952	5.6	10.3
1953	3.2	15.1
1954	7.7	30.3
1955	6.8	13.1
1956	1.9	19.2
1957	6.9	12.5
1958	6.6	12.2
1959	7.3	37.7
1960	6.7	30.9
1961	7.3	38.1
1962	5.4	53.2
1963	1.6	73.5
1964	3.1	91.6

Source: Centro de Contas Nacionais—Fundação Getúlio Vargas and *Conjuntura Economica*.

Referring again to Table 2.1, we see that the government showed current account surpluses throughout this period. Monetary expansion came mainly through government deficits on capital account. It was therefore the government's ambitious investment objectives which led to money creation. It became clear by the end of the period that method of government finance would have to change.

Import-substitution industrialisation is necessarily inflationary, for many reasons. For example, high tariff policy shifts the internal terms of trade in favor of industry. The expansion in demand for industrial goods translates into an enhaced demand for inputs not previously produced domestically. If the country faces foreign exchange constraints, the supply bottleneck pushes input prices upward. The general increase in the retained earnings of industrial firms leads to *ex post* supply increases as investment increases. The limitations of inflationary finance are felt when the social cost of incremental finance is higher than the marginal product of investment. Notice that this definition of the limitation of the import substitution process does not assume that the marginal product of investment is falling. The limitation becomes binding only as the cost of finance for society as a whole grows faster than output (or better profits).[6]

Figure 2.1

Period	0	1	2	3
Receipts	0	0	$R_0(1+\Pi)^2$	$R_0(1+\Pi)^3$
Payments	C_0	$C_0(1+\Pi)$	$C_0(1+\Pi)^2$	$C_0(1+\Pi)^3$
Profit	$-C_0$	$-C_0(1+\Pi)$	$(R_0-C_0)(1+\Pi)^2$	$(R_0-C_0)(1+\Pi)^3$

Many have criticised the choice of such a financial mechanism for development. The following quote from Werner Baer points to the institutional constraints facing the government when the explicit decision to industrialise was taken.

> . . . in a relatively underdeveloped country, with inexperienced, inefficient, and generally backward bureaucracies, with an under-developed and inefficient tax system, the inflationary method would, on the whole, be the more efficient in the short run.[7]

As industrialisation proceeds, larger amounts of working capital are needed to finance the existing stock of fixed capital (i.e. to allow fixed capital to be fully utilised). Further, inflation itself puts pressure on working capital needs. One can see this by the use of the following (overly) simple exercise.[8] Suppose a firm must purchase goods and services today in order to sell produced goods two periods in the future. Its temporal income statements will be as follows (abstracting from financial costs). R_0 is the real value of receipts in terms of period 0 currency, C_0 is real payments or cost, and Π is the one period inflation rate. All are assumed constant over the four periods studied, i.e. the firm can pass all of Π on into prices. Working capital is borrowed over the first two periods of production and then paid back in later periods. The real present value (in period 0) of the total flow of profits over the four periods is $2(R_0 - C_0) - 2C_0$, which is unaffected by the inflation rate. The nominal amount of working capital demand in the first two periods is a positive function of the inflation rate. If we allow for interest costs that vary with the inflation rate, there will be more deficit periods than in this example and hence the amount of nominal working capital demand will be higher.[9]

Douglas Gale captures the essence of what happens in capital markets which are imperfect when faced with higher nominal borrowing demand:

Inflation causes a reduction in the real value of the manufacturer's indebtedness and this increase in net wealth ought, in some sense, to have counted as income. Had there been some way to realise this income, he would have been able to meet his interest payments without difficulty. If he had had access to a perfect capital market or if his banker had paid more attention to present values than current profits, he would have borrowed to meet the interest payments. In practice, capital markets are highly imperfect and a banker who is asked to lend increasingly large amounts to a firm which, if inflation continues, will always have a negative cashflow, will certainly decline to do so. Present values have little meaning when capital markets are imperfect. Again, if there existed a perfect capital market for equity, it might be possible, by issuing new shares, to capitalise the value of the reduction in real indebtedness but this too is not observed in practice.[10]

It is in this context that the financial structure used in import substitution industrialisation (hereafter referred to as ISI) broke down in Brazil. As inflation increased, the working capital needs of firms increased. Lending was choked off as banks could no longer attract deposits to finance loans, nor could they increase interest rates fast enough to ration demand. If the nominal value of working capital loans does not keep pace with the nominal demand for working capital loans (which increases in the short run approximately as fast as inflation), the economy will move into an inflationary recession. Many economists at the time projected a recession for 1963–4 because working capital increases did not keep pace with inflation.[11] Table 2.3 confirms this prognosis. Working capital grew faster than prices from 1959 to 1961, although the difference was decreasing. The inflation rate caught up with working capital increases in 1962 and surpassed them in 1963.

Term sales become increasingly important with industrialisation owing to a growing urban population and division of labor. It becomes increasingly difficult to finance working capital through ploughed-back profits. Corporations in Brazil were closed to outside investors, owned by families, which was the natural outcome of the

Table 2.3   Brazil: Working Capital Increases and the Inflation Rate
(Percentage Changes)

	Working capital	Inflation	Volume of business[a]
1959	34.8	30.4	+11
1960	34.0	31.7	+7
1961	48.2	45.7	+5
1962	50.7	50.7	—
1963	68.3	78.2	−13

[a] (Level of working capital)/price index
Source: *Conjuntur Economica*, February, 1965.

Table 2.4   Brazil: Privately Owned Corporate Financing of Investment in
Manufacturing, 1959–62

Self-financing			Outside sources		
Total	Undistributed profits	Depreciation	Total	Equity capital	Other
43.2	46.4	6.8	56.8	8.2	48.6

Source: United Nations, ECLA, *The Process of Industrial Development in
Latin America*, No. 66.11g4 (New York: United Nations, 1966), Table 35.

import-substitution industrialisation strategy. It may be argued that
the choice of ISI was also conditioned by this type of corporate
ownership structure and ISI tended to strengthen it. Owners seemed
to value control of the firm more than the present discounted value
of any extra profits from a higher degree of equity finance.[12]

The latter came mainly from the selling of new shares to existing
owners. Hence, any investment not financed by undistributed profits
was generally underwritten by the contraction of new debt. Table 2.4
shows that equity capital financed only 8.2% of investment over the
period 1959–62 while undistributed profits accounted for 43.2% and
debt accounted for 48.6%.

The growing demand for working capital strained the Brazilian
financial system. The government appeased the consequent illiquidity of firms through money creation at the rediscount window (the
Brazilian monetary authorities discounted private paper). Monetary
expansion led to increased inflation and further increases in working
capital demand. Firms increased their debt-to-equity ratios at a very
quick pace, especially towards the end of this period.

Table 2.5   Brazil: Average Debt to Equity and Debt to Total Asset
Ratios, 1954–63

	Debt–equity ratio	Debt–asset ratio
1954	1.41	0.59
1955	1.34	0.57
1956	1.05	0.49
1957	1.23	0.55
1958	1.37	0.58
1959	1.43	0.59
1960	1.41	0.59
1961	1.71	0.63
1962	1.95	0.66
1963	2.12	0.68

Source: Calculated from data appearing in *Conjuntura Economica*.

Table 2.5 presents average debt-to-equity ratios and debt-to-total-asset ratios for Brazilian corporations from 1954 to 1983. The debt-to-equity ratio increased from 1.41 in 1954 to 2.12 in 1963, while the debt–asset ratio rose from 0.59 in 1954 to 0.68 in 1963. A better indicator of what firms were doing are the marginal debt–equity and marginal debt–asset ratios. These are presented in Table 2.6. The marginal debt–equity ratio increased from 1.68 in 1985 to 4.24 in 1963. The marginal debt–asset ratio increased from 0.63 in 1954 to 0.81 in 1963. Finally, Table 2.7 shows that the growth in working capital borrowing outstripped other sources of working capital financing, especially as the economy went into recession in 1963. By this time the financial structure of Brazilian firms had become extremely fragile.

In sum, the general economic environment in the period 1961–3 indicates that the costs of maintaining the inflationary mode of finance had become large relative to alternatives, e.g. tax and debt financing. Increases in working capital demand increased the illiquidity of firms, which ultimately put pressure on the rediscount window of the monetary authorities. Monetary expansion led to inflation and increased illiquidity.[13] As we shall see, this put severe pressure on the marginal borrowing costs of firms, especially in light of the fact that individuals increasingly avoided holding financial assets as inflation accelerated. Effective borrowing costs were more flexible upward than interest rates accorded to those who invested in financial assets. Financial institutions, namely commercial banks,

Table 2.6   Brazil: Marginal Debt–Equity and Debt–Asset Ratios, 1955–63

	Marginal debt/Equity	Marginal debt/Assets
1955	1.68	0.63
1956	1.01	0.50
1957	3.17	0.76
1958	2.94	0.74
1959	2.32	0.70
1960	2.28	0.70
1961	4.23	0.81
1962	3.81	0.79
1963	4.24	0.81

Source: Calculated from data appearing in *Conjuntura Economica.*

Table 2.7   Brazil: Percentage Changes in Investment, Self-financed
Working Capital, and Borrowed Working Capital, 1961–3

	1961	1962	1963
New fixed investment	30.0	123.9	33.7
Self-financed working capital	55.0	71.6	1.9
Borrowed working capital	111.0	70.1	83.7

Source: *Conjuntura Economica.*

could use tricks such as compensating balances and advance collection of interest. Firms tried to increase their debt-to-equity ratios, which led to the appearance of the (legal and parallel) bills of exchange market. Further, owing to the institutional financial arrangements for working capital loans (discussed below) and the higher debt–equity ratios, prices became very sensitive to interest rates. In the eyes of many economists, a reform that forced a lowering of the debt–equity ratio of firms, allowing a positive real return to financial assets, and that took pressure off the monetary authorities to expand the money supply, was necessary.[14]

The decision to carry out the reforms, contrary to the arguments of McKinnon (1973) and Shaw (1973), can be seen as complementary to the import-substitution industrialisation process, not a substitute for it. The acute increase in working capital demand between 1961 and 1963 presupposes the existence of an established and growing industrial base and increasingly sophisticated lines of marketing and distribution for traditional and agricultural products. Industrialisation and the diversification of the productive structure of an economy necessitate the dissemination of term contracts and with them an enhanced demand for financial capital. Inflationary finance is viable at the early stages of this process, after which a more sophisticated financial system is needed.[15] Unfortunately, given the fact that firms had increased their debt–equity ratios to a large extent before the reforms, the costs of such reform would be high in terms of foregone output growth.

2.2   THE 'DUPLICATA' DISCOUNT AND THE BILLS OF EXCHANGE MARKET

Import-substitution industrialisation moves in stages, which started in the Brazilian case with the production of consumer durables then spread backwards toward heavier industry.[16] The financial market structure naturally followed this pattern of development. It should come as no surprise that the most dynamic sector of the Brazilian financial system was directed toward financing consumer durables and concentrated on short- to medium-term credit. The only active source of long-term credit was the National Economic Development Bank (BNDE) created in the early 1950s. Other types of financial institutions, such as insurance companies and savings banks, played relatively small roles.[17] Investment banks concentrated their efforts on the financing of consumer durables. Table 2.8 shows the relative importance of different institutions in the extension of credit in 1966.

Consumer durable loans, which actually represented the main source of working capital for firms, was initially extended through the commercial banks' discounting of accounts receivable or 'duplicatas'. The operation consists of firms, which sold goods to customers on term, selling their accounts receivable to commercial banks at a discount. The commercial banks are then partially responsible for the collection of the debt from the buyer of the goods. The firm borrowing the money receives not only a loan but also a collection service from commercial banks. Consequently, commercial banks became the main agents responsible for the collection of debts and taxes. The commercial bank minimises default risk of loans in this way because its ultimate payment is directly matched by the collateral embodied in the goods and services sold on term. The maturity of this loan rarely exceeds 180 days. The popularity of this type of credit operation is illustrated by the fact that the duplicata discount is still a main source of working capital.

Table 2.8   Brazil: Credit to the Private Sector, 1966 (Percentage of total)

Short-term credit

Commercial and development banks	48.9
Bank of Brazil and CACEX	20.1
Finance companies	9.7
Savings banks	2.6
National Cooperative Credit Bank (BNCC)	0.2
Social welfare institutes and insurance companies	0.2
Total short-term credit	81.7

Long-term credit

National Economic Development Bank (BNDE)	8.1
Bank of Brazil	5.6
FINAME	1.1
Savings banks	2.3
National Housing Bank (BNH)	0.8
National Cooperative Credit Bank and others	0.2
Social welfare institutes and insurance companies	0.2
Total long-term credit	18.3

Source: Mario H. Simonsen (1969): 'Inflation and the Money and Capital Markets of Brazil' in H. S. Ellis, ed., *The Economy of Brazil* (Berkeley: University of California Press), p. 139.

Data relating the effective interest rates charged to the borrower in these transactions are not available for the following reasons. Since the discounting of duplicatas by a bank represents a credit operation in the legal sense, it was subject to the usury law. It should be noted that the usury law did not stipulate whether the 12% interest rate represented simple or compound interest. Hence, banks could increase the effective rate on loans simply by shortening the maturity of a loan with a tacit promise to refinance it when it came due. For example, a 1-month loan at 1% per month (12% annual simple interest) would legally earn 12.68% annually.

Clearly, the practice of shortening of the maturity structure of loans in order to increase effective interest rates alone can only be severely limited. The increased administrative costs as the maturity becomes smaller will be prohibitive. The practice is powerful, however, when used in conjunction with the following non-interest devices for increasing effective rates: (1) compensating balances, (2) making service charges, and (3) the payment of interest and service charges when the loan is contracted instead of at maturity. In Brazil, all four of these devices gave banks a good bit of flexibility in changing effective interest rates.

The following example should show the extent to which these practices allowed banks to ration credit with higher interest rates. Suppose the bank discounts a duplicata with n months to maturity. The nominal (simple) interest charged for n months is $i(n/12)$, where i is the annual (simple) interest rate, which usually equalled the legal ceiling of 12% per year, plus any service charge. When banks receive the interest and service charge on the date the loan is contracted and a proportion cb must be set aside in the form of compensating balances, the effective annual interest rate, i^*, is calculated according to the following formula:

$$i^* = \left(1 + \frac{\frac{n}{12}i}{1 - \frac{n}{12} - cb}\right)^{\frac{12}{n}} - 1 \qquad (2.1)$$

Notice that the effective interest rate will increase as n decreases, i increases, and cb increases. Table 2.9 shows annual effective interest rates for a 90-day duplicata discount with compensating balance rates of 0.10, 0.20, and 0.30, respectively, using equation (2.1) above. The interest rates and service charges are those that were charged by the Banco do Estado de Minas Gerais during this period and represent rates generally charged in the market.[18] Table 2.10 shows effective real rates of interest.

Clearly, it was within the commercial banks' powers to keep loan rates above the inflation rate. It should be noted, however, that as inflation accelerated it became increasingly difficult for banks to maintain positive real loan interest rates. Further, when inflation decreased, real effective interest rates would become quite large. These institutional rigidities caused the inflation expectation component of a Fisherian interest rate equation to act as if expectations were formed in a severely adaptive way.[19] There has been no rigorous explanation of this behaviour, which is usually being attributed to 'institution inertia' or other vague concepts. A more reasonable explanation of interest rate stickiness lies in the fact that this type of credit operation resembles a customer market where fixed price behaviour is rational under certain circumstances.[20]

Table 2.9   Brazil: Effective Commercial Bank Loan Interest Rates with Compensating Balances on 90-Day Discounts (Annual Rates)

	Interest rate	Service charge	Effective interest with compensating balance rates of:		
			0.10	0.20	0.30
1946	12.0	1.5	16.5	18.8	21.9
1947	12.0	1.5	16.5	18.8	21.9
1948	12.0	1.5	16.5	18.8	21.9
1949	12.0	1.5	16.5	18.8	21.9
1950	12.0	2.0	17.2	19.6	22.8
1951	12.0	3.0	18.6	21.2	24.6
1952	12.0	6.0	22.8	26.1	30.5
1953	12.0	6.0	22.8	26.1	30.5
1954	12.0	6.0	22.8	26.1	30.5
1955	12.0	8.0	25.7	29.5	34.5
1956	12.0	10.0	28.7	33.0	38.7
1957	12.0	12.0	31.9	36.6	43.1
1958	12.0	12.0	31.9	36.6	43.1
1959	12.0	12.0	31.9	36.6	43.1
1960	12.0	15.0	36.7	42.3	50.0
1961	12.0	18.0	41.6	48.3	57.4
1962	12.0	24.0	52.4	61.2	73.4
1963	12.0	24.0	52.4	61.2	73.4

Source: Interest rates and service charges from the Banco do Estado de Minas Gerais (formerly Banco Mineiro de Produção) as reported in Antonio M. Silveira (1971): *Studies of Money and Interest Rates in Brazil*, Ph.D. Dissertation, Carnegie-Mellon University, published in Portuguese by Edições Multiplic. These interest rates and service charges were generally used by all commercial banks during the period.

Interest rate rigidity tended to make inflation stabilisation difficult, especially in terms of monetary policy. If the government was able to temporarily lower the inflation rate, lending rates would turn sharply higher in real terms, which would put severe pressure on the working capital of firms, especially those with weak financial positions. Political pressure was put on the monetary authorities, as shown below, to ease the firms' liquidity problems. Increased monetary expansion led to higher inflation. As we shall see, one of the most persuasive arguments for introducing indexed debt obligations was that their real interest rates would remain constant and not rise precipitously when stabilisation was attempted.

The problem, then, was not that commercial banks could not

Table 2.10 Brazil: Effective Real Commercial Bank Loan Interest Rates

| | Inflation | Effective real interest rates at compensating balance rates of: | | |
		0.10	0.20	0.3
1947	6.5	9.4	11.6	14.5
1948	9.2	6.7	8.8	11.6
1949	9.0	6.9	9.0	11.8
1950	13.4	3.4	5.5	8.3
1951	19.8	−0.1	1.2	4.0
1952	16.3	5.6	8.4	12.2
1953	15.1	6.7	9.6	13.4
1954	30.3	−5.8	−3.2	1.5
1955	13.1	11.2	14.5	18.9
1956	19.2	8.0	11.6	16.4
1957	12.5	17.2	21.4	27.2
1958	12.2	17.6	21.8	27.5
1959	37.7	−4.2	−0.8	3.9
1960	30.9	4.4	8.7	14.6
1961	38.1	2.5	7.4	14.0
1962	63.2	−6.6	−1.2	6.3
1963	73.5	−12.2	−7.1	−0.1

Source: See Table 2.9 and *Conjuntura Economica.*

increase interest rates in line with inflation, but that they could not easily increase the rates paid to their deposits. Table 2.11 shows that as inflation accelerated, the ratio of time deposits to total deposits fell dramatically. Further, total deposits in real terms stagnated after 1958. Resources were being shifted to other parts of the financial market and into land and goods. As Table 2.12 shows, real commercial bank loans to the private sector fell as deposits declined significantly toward the end of the period. The explanation for the shift out of time deposits is that interest notes on commercial bank deposits were limited to 6% annually. Demand deposits stayed relatively constant in real terms because they were needed for transactions. This led commercial banks to compete for deposits by increasing the number of agencies and services offered to depositors. Table 2.13 presents the growth of commercial bank agencies over the period. The higher inflation rates meant disintermediation with higher profit rates and a large increase in unit costs for the commercial banking sector.

The inability of commercial banks to remunerate depositors gave

Table 2.11   Brazil: Demand and Time Deposits, 1951–64 (1953 Cruzeiros)

	Demand deposits Value	% of total	Time deposits Value	% of total	Total
1951	63.3	75.6	20.5	24.4	83.8
1952	66.7	76.6	18.7	23.4	85.4
1953	62.9	80.1	15.6	19.9	78.5
1954	60.5	80.7	14.5	19.3	75.0
1955	66.7	83.8	12.9	16.2	79.6
1956	65.6	85.7	10.9	14.3	76.5
1957	88.3	87.9	12.2	12.1	100.5
1958	84.7	89.4	10.1	10.6	94.8
1959	92.7	91.3	8.9	8.7	101.6
1960	95.1	90.2	10.3	9.8	105.4
1961	88.3	91.7	8.0	8.3	96.3
1962	100.0	94.9	5.4	5.1	105.4
1963	90.3	95.0	4.7	5.0	95.0
1964	84.2	96.4	4.1	4.6	88.3

Source: Banco Central do Brasil, *Boletim*, and Mario H. Simonsen (1969), op. cit., p. 142.

Table 2.12   Brazil: Real Credit Extended by Commercial Banks, 1951–64 (Millions of 1953 Cruzeiros)

	Value	Change (%)
1951	73,833	
1952	75,135	1.8
1953	70,641	–6.0
1954	67,575	–4.3
1955	69,344	2.6
1956	67,577	–2.6
1957	81,606	20.8
1958	76,682	–6.0
1959	76,768	0.1
1960	82,988	8.1
1961	72,737	–12.6
1962	74,734	3.0
1963	65,225	12.7
1964	61,062	–6.4

Source: Mario H. Simonsen (1966), op. cit.

Table 2.13   Brazil: Commercial Bank Agencies, 1951–65

	Total agencies	Change (%)
1951	4,036	
1952	4,036	0.0
1953	4,358	7.9
1954	4,528	3.9
1955	4,036	–10.9
1956	4,257	5.5
1957	4,628	8.7
1958	4,857	5.0
1959	5,135	5.7
1960	5,270	2.6
1961	5,629	6.8
1962	6,128	8.9
1963	6,545	6.8
1964	6,826	4.3
1965	7,283	6.7

Source: Banco Central do Brazil, *Boletim.*

rise to the appearance in 1959 of the Sociedades de Credito, Financiamento e Investimento (the so-called 'financeiras' or finance companies) and the bills of exchange market. Finance companies set up what were called 'participation funds', allowing them to intermediate between individuals and firms in profit sharing. The return to the investor was legally considered 'profits', although the participation was closer to a debt. They also floated bills of exchange on the stock market at a discount which were also considered legally as profits. In this way finance companies sidestepped the usury law. It allowed them to pay investors an 'interest rate' which could better follow inflation. Table 2.14 presents average annual nominal and real returns on bills of exchange over the period.[21] Clearly, bills of exchange were a more desirable asset than deposits, although their return did not keep pace with inflation.

The credit operations with the finance companies were also based upon the discounting of duplicatas, but in a modified form. A firm would sell duplicatas to the finance company at the discount price, which was the price the purchaser of the goods would pay if he paid cash.[22] The finance company would pay for the duplicata with bills of exchange. These could be sold on the stock market at a discount, which more or less matched the discount on the duplicatas. The finance companies became partially responsible for the payment of

Table 2.14   Brazil: Annual Average Interest Rates Received by the
Holders of Bills of Exchange and Time Deposits

| | Time deposits | | Bills of exchange | |
	Nominal	Real	Nominal	Real
1960	4.3	–19.3	21.0	–6.4
1961	4.3	–23.9	26.3	–7.9
1962	3.8	–31.6	29.5	–14.9
1963	3.5	–41.0	35.0	–23.1
1964	3.0	–45.9	43.9	–24.5
1965	2.8	–34.4	36.0	–13.3
1966	1.9	–26.2	30.4	–5.5
1967	1.7	–20.7	31.3	2.3
1968	3.7	–16.6	29.6	4.3
1969	4.3	–13.7	28.4	6.2

Source: Donald Syvrud (1972): 'Estrutura e Política de Juros no
Brasil—1960–70' in *Revista Brasileira de Economia*, Vol. 26, No. 1, p. 130.

the bill of exchange at maturity and was therefore responsible for
monitoring the creditworthiness of the firms borrowing in this
market.[23] As in the case of commercial bank loans, default risk was
minimised, although inflation risk was not. The finance companies'
income came from the spread of the operation, which included
administrative fees accruing to themselves and their brokers.[24] Table
2.15 shows average nominal and real interest rates on loans financed
by bills of exchange. Notice that these interest rates acted similarly to
those of commercial bank loans presented earlier, becoming very
negative when inflation accelerated, benefiting borrowers at the
investors' cost, and very positive when inflation declined, hurting
borrowers and benefiting investors, as happened for example in 1965.
Note also that the spread was large on such transactions, but nowhere
near as large as the spread enjoyed by commercial banks. Table 2.16
shows nominal and real growth of finance credit operations. Real
growth of finance credit is high in all years except 1963 as a result of
the deceleration of inflation.

The pressure placed on commercial banks both on the liability
side with the flight from deposits and on the asset side with the
increase in the demand for working capital, coupled with the usury
law, led to financial innovation which took the form of the bills of
exchange market. Structural deficiencies, which did not disappear
with financial liberalisation, led to large spreads enjoyed by financial
institutions on their *de facto* credit operations. A good portion of the

Table 2.15   Brazil: Nominal and Real Interest Rates on Loans Financed
by Bills of Exchange

	Nominal interest Rate	Real interest Rate	Nominal spread
1960	41.0	9.9	21.0
1961	52.0	10.9	26.0
1962	60.0	5.5	30.5
1963	70.6	–2.8	35.6
1964	81.2	–4.9	37.3
1965	79.0	14.1	43.0
1966	71.5	24.1	41.1
1967	49.0	16.1	17.7
1968	46.2	17.7	16.6
1969	44.2	19.3	15.8

Source: Donald Syvrud (1972), op. cit., pp. 123–5.

spread was due to taxes collected at the source. The high costs of this type of intermediation led to the appearance of a parallel or black credit market for bills of exchange. Bills of exchange, duplicatas, and promissory notes were sold directly to the investor on the stock market, allowing firms to sidestep the large spreads.[25] Since no financial intermediary monitored the quality of debtors in this market, investors received a risk premium. This partially explains why interest rates in this market were substantially higher than those on paper co-signed by a finance company.[26] These higher interest rates led to a very high growth rate for this market, which became at least as large as the official market by 1964.[27]

Significant resources were used to subvert the usury law. The revocation of this law was an extremely sensitive political issue, as evidenced by the fact that the 1964–6 reforms did not remove it from law. In this light, the Brazilian government's stance on the usury law seems paradoxical as the government-owned commercial bank, the Bank of Brazil, issued its own bills of exchange starting in 1963. Until then it had also issued import bills in order to finance purchases of imported goods by monopolistic firms which had been granted import licenses. These bills usually carried rates of return higher than those on bills of exchange.[28] The issue of bills of exchange by the Bank of Brazil was quickly abandoned amid private sector objections to having to compete with a government commercial bank for funds. Nonetheless, it seems clear that the government viewed the usury law

Table 2.16   Brazil: Nominal and Real Growth in Credit Extended by
Finance Companies, 1960–5

	Nominal growth	Real growth
1960	450.0	320.2
1961	84.0	33.2
1962	268.0	140.2
1963	70.0	–2.1
1964	192.0	52.4
1965	158.0	71.2

Source: Mario H. Simonsen (1966), op. cit.

as outdated by the mere fact that the Bank of Brazil had been
allowed to deal in import bills and bills of exchange.

2.3   THE STRUCTURE OF THE BRAZILIAN MONETARY AUTHORITIES: 1945–64

The distinguishing feature of the Brazilian monetary authorities
before 1964 is that there did not exist an independent central bank
per se. As we shall see, the reforms of 1964–5 did not completely
change this aspect of the monetary policy decision process. The
power to create base money was divided between the Treasury, the
Bank of Brazil, and the Superintendency of Money and Credit
(SUMOC), without an effective coordinating agent. SUMOC and its
advisory council were originally created for this purpose, but in
actuality did not enjoy executive power. The fact that the Bank of
Brazil was both a commercial bank and a lender of last resort made it
extremely susceptible to any borrowing pressure put on its rediscount
window (the Carteira de Redesconto) from the private sector and
from the Treasury (whose paper was ultimately handled by the
'amortization window', or the Carteira de Amortização). As inflation
accelerated toward the end of the period, the monetary policy decision mechanism went into disarray, with the three organs acting
independently to expand the monetary base.

Owing to the usury law, the demand for treasury bills disappeared
as inflation accelerated. The only treasury bills bought by the private
sector were those purchased by commercial banks to be held in lieu of
required reserves. Monetary policy was carried out through the use
of the discount window and changes in the reserve ratio. As de-

Table 2.17   Brazil: Sources of Expansion and Contraction in the
Monetary Base (Cr$ Millions)

	1957	1958	1959	1960	1961	1962	1963	1964
A. Domestic accounts								
1. Treasury	38.4	14.0	−30.5	75.4	128.9	215.6	432.6	748.4
2. State and municipal governments	−1.4	−0.5	−0.5	−0.8	−2.0	0.2	−2.5	−10.9
3. 'Autarquias': other public entities	−5.3	−4.0	−3.2	−15.1	−33.7	−13.9	−35.5	−209.0
4. Private sector loans and deposits	11.8	21.7	8.7	35.3	45.3	118.6	175.5	252.0
5. Commercial loans and deposits	−18.9	8.6	28.1	−9.8	−31.2	−92.6	−180.4	−233.9
6. Own resources	−4.3	−7.7	−7.1	−9.0	−19.9	−33.9	−72.7	−125.3
7. Other accounts	−1.5	−1.9	66.1	−9.9	8.3	44.5	50.9	75.5
Total	8.8	35.2	5.4	67.7	95.0	238.7	367.7	496.6
B. Foreign accounts								
Total	3.3	−13.1	27.8	−18.6	2.1	−56.5	—	−70.3
C. Currency in circulation outside the monetary authorities								
Total	5.5	22.1	33.2	49.1	98.0	182.2	343.7	566.9

Note: Positive numbers signify an expansion in the monetary base and negative numbers a contraction.
Source: Mario H. Simonsen (1966), op. cit., p. 94.

scribed below, the rediscount window became the primary source of expansion (but not contraction) of the monetary base. The only policy tool used actively to restrict the growth in the money supply was raising the reserve ratio, but this was of limited effectiveness. Between 1951 and 1964, the compulsory reserve ratio on demand deposits increased from 4% to 28%.[29]

Table 2.17 shows that the two main sources of expansion of the monetary base were the Treasury and rediscounts to the private sector. The Treasury was able to finance deficits completely by monetary expansion because of the functional relationships developed with its financial agent, the Bank of Brazil. Any excess monetary value of checks written against the Treasury's accounts at the Bank of Brazil over the amount held in those accounts was passed on to the rediscount window. These debts were then passed to the amortisation window, whose function it was to amortise the Treasury's debt outstanding. Hence, any new lending by the amortisation window was translated directly into money creation. This source of monetary expansion proceeded relatively unfettered. Similarly, rediscounts to the private sector were relatively uncontrolled as they were subject to the usury law and credit had to be restricted by credit controls.

SUMOC, as mentioned above, had originally been created (in 1945) as a Central Bank and its advisory council was to act as the coordinator of monetary policy. Brazilian monetary policy could only be effective if a comprehensive credit policy was imposed. As SUMOC did not enjoy executive privilege, this was virtually impossible. The necessity for credit policy, as opposed to pure 'monetary' policy, arose from two sources. The first was that when inflation increased past the nominal interest rate ceiling imposed by the usury law, the rediscount window became a cheap source of funds because there existed no mechanism for increasing the cost of funds to the borrower. The second is the fact that private-sector time and demand deposits at the Bank of Brazil were necessarily part of the monetary base. Hence, that portion of the monetary base on the liabilities side of the consolidated balance sheet of the monetary authorities was endogenous. In order to control the monetary base, one had to control the growth in the assets of the monetary authorities, i.e. credit. It should be noted that the reforms of 1964–5 did not change this institutional aspect of monetary policy, but only the manner in which credit policy was articulated.

The exact relationship between the monetary base and the money supply (here described as currency in circulation plus demand and time deposits or M_2) can be described in the following way.[30] The monetary base (B), representing the liabilities of the consolidated balance sheet of the monetary authorities, is equal to compulsory reserves (R^c), voluntary reserves (R^v), demand and time deposits at the Bank of Brazil (D^{bb}) and currency in circulation (C):

$$B = R^v + R^c + D^{bb} + C \qquad (2.2)$$

The money supply consists of currency in circulation and total time and demand deposits (D), which in turn are made up of time and demand deposits at the Bank of Brazil and time and demand deposits at commercial banks (D^{bc}):

$$M = D^{bb} + D^{bc} + C = D + C \qquad (2.3)$$

Using equations (2.1) and (2.2), it can be shown that the relationship between the money supply and the monetary base is the following:[31]

$$M = \left[\frac{1 + c}{r^v + r^c + d^{bb} + c} \right] B = mB \qquad (2.4)$$

where $r^v = (R^v/D)$ is the proportion of total voluntary (free) reserves of commercial banks to total demand and time deposits, $r^c = (R^c/D)$ is the proportion of required commercial bank deposits to total deposits, $d^{bb} = (D^{bb}/D)$ is the ratio of demand and time deposits at the Bank of Brazil to total deposits, and c is the ratio of currency to deposits.

The money multiplier, m, is sensitive not only to those factors (which in many studies are assumed constant) in typical money multiplier formulations, e.g. r^v, r^c, and c, but also to the fraction of total deposits held at the Bank of Brazil. Hence, monetary base and the money multiplier are endogenous. This fact underscores the importance of coordinated credit policy in the monetary programming exercises of the Brazilian monetary authorities. The institutional framework of the Brazilian monetary authorities lacked the centralised executive power under which such financial programming could be coordinated.

2.4 SUMMARY AND CONCLUSIONS

We have looked at the Brazilian financial system during the period leading up to the reforms. It was characterised by policy-directed import substitution industrialisation. Industrialisation was financed primarily by money creation, which allowed policy makers to sidestep the restrictions of Brazil's underdeveloped capital market. Although the capital market did not constrain growth in the early stages of ISI, it proved to be a binding constraint towards the end of the process. This argument differs from typical exhaustion theories of ISI in that it concentrates on the financial aspects of growth and not on the size of demand relative to growing minimum scales of production.

Financial market growth was limited by the usury law and also by the financial structure of firms. The financial innovations that took place toward the end of the period would probably have occurred even in the absence of a usury law, but at a smaller cost. Because marginal borrowing occurred in semi-legal markets for the more financially sound firms and on parallel markets for financially weak firms, monetary authorities could not adequately monitor the balance sheet positions of firms. The precipitous increase in debt–equity ratios left the economy extremely sensitive to any attempt at price stabilisation. Any restriction in credit would push a good portion of firms into the parallel bills market for credit. The competition for credit in this market would push interest rates to such a level that many firms would fold, causing a large contraction in output. Because most interest costs were (in good portion) passed on into higher prices, the credit squeeze would have to be rigorously adhered to for a long period of time for inflation to subside. Further, any financial market reforms, such as interest rate liberalisation or financial asset indexation, might come at a significant social cost if effective interest costs to firms were not kept at reasonable levels.

As mentioned above, many felt a reduction in debt-to-equity ratios of firms was necessary for price stability and long-term growth. If this was achieved only by credit reduction then the cost in output reduction would be large. A reform that would minimise output loss would necessarily dynamise the stock market, making stock issue an attractive way for firms to raise capital or retire debt. As we shall see, a major emphasis of the 1964–5 reforms was to reduce the above-mentioned barriers to the use of the stock market as a main source of funds.

Finally, for financial market development to succeed, the institutional structure of the monetary authorities would have to be made compatible with coordinated monetary programming. The ultimate success of the reforms would depend upon the degree to which each of these objectives was achieved, which clearly entailed trade-offs between them.

3 The Reforms of 1964–5

3.1 INTRODUCTION

The financial reforms initiated in 1964 had three basic objectives: (1) improve allocative efficiency of capital markets, (2) design an institutional structure which would allow the implementation of selective credit policy, and (3) establish institutions that would facilitate inflation stabilisation. In many instances, these objectives were not mutually compatible. For example, creating strong primary and secondary markets for equities is difficult in the face of restrictive monetary policy. Further, selective credit programmes made, at times, anti-inflationary monetary programming difficult, if not politically impossible. In other cases, the initial measures did not achieve the original objectives and stronger measures were implemented. This chapter outlines the initial objectives of the reformers, the initial reforms, and the resulting structure of the financial system.

As discussed in Chapter 2, there had been severe disintermediation in the period immediately prior to the 1964 military coup. Specifically, the combination of interest rate ceilings and inflation caused a flight from financial assets, resulting in a severe contraction in real credit. Insurance policies, mortgages, and other forms of long-term financial obligations disappeared from the market, which caused a decline in investment across sectors. Firms starved for working capital were increasingly forced to seek financing in the legal and illegal bills of exchange market. The National Economic Development Bank (BNDE) was the only source of long-term financing but had limited resources and, hence, limited credit programmes, the recipients of which were selected on 'non-economic' (non-market) criteria. The only sector that seems to not have suffered extraordinarily in terms of credit allocation was agriculture. If one considers, however, that the rural sector was suppressed owing to the import-substitution industrialisation policies of the prior period, the subsidised credit programmes can be seen as a measure to compensate agriculture for its past burden. The recipients of these funds were mainly large landowners.[1] As argued in later chapters, the pacification of politically strong groups which were from time to time discriminated against by certain economic policies was in most cases the *raison d'être* for the creation of subsidised credit programmes.

The Castello Branco administration emphasised the need to increase financial savings and facilitate a real credit expansion. Not only did it feel that real interest rates would have to become positive and that inflation would have to be quickly brought under control, but it also considered that institutional reform was a *sine qua non* for sustainable economic growth.[2]

It should be noted that although the administration felt that positive interest rates were necessary, the usury law was not repealed. It chose instead to get around it by creating government indexed bonds and allowing the private sector to deal in indexed financial obligations. The choice to subvert the law rather than to repeal it is difficult to explain. Syvrud (1972) offered the following:

> The only answer I can find to this question is that the usury law in Brazil, as in so many other countries, is based on religious as well as social and economic traditions, that the authorities found it preferable to circumvent rather than confront this law.[3]

However, a better explanation emerges from the fact that, paradoxically, the main beneficiaries of the usury law were the politically powerful commercial banks. As we saw in Chapter 2, commercial banks were very profitable under the usury law as long as they could count on a reliable source of funds. Banks easily got around the usury law *vis-à-vis* their loans, while interest on their liabilities was more or less effectively restricted by it. As long as inflation did not accelerate in an unstable way, commercial banks enjoyed a favoured position in financial markets. Political pressure from commercial banks was substantial in explaining the continuation of the usury law. This argument will appear again later when we discuss why the private sector resisted the use of indexed loan obligations.

Financial asset indexation was perhaps the most significant institutional development to result from the 1964 reforms. Hence, in this book a complete chapter (Chapter 5) has been reserved for the role of financial asset indexation in Brazilian financial markets and the subject will not be discussed again until then.

3.2   FINANCIAL MARKET REFORMS

The reforms of 1964 concentrated on institution building in areas in which it was felt that market failure existed. Two objectives seem to have implicitly motivated the resulting nature of these institutions: (1) to ameliorate market failure and (2) to create an apparatus for selective credit policy. Further, the design of the reforms emulated the U.S. financial system in that institutions were meant to specialise in their respective portion of the market. As we shall see, the actual functioning of the market was more akin to the European system owing to the large amount of conglomeration that occurred in the 1970s, promoted by government policy. The original segmentation of the market coupled with economic policy led to a large compartment-alisation of the market in spite of its growth.

Capital market reforms after 1964 proceeded mainly through the introduction of three laws. The Housing Finance System (SFH), with its central institution, the National Housing Bank (BNH), was created by Law 4380 of 1964. The 'Bank Reform Act' (Law 4595 of 1964) created the Central Bank (BCB) which substituted for SUMOC, redefined the Bank of Brazil's role as a monetary authority (discussed below), expanded the functions and programmes of the BNDE and transformed the extinct SUMOC council into the National Monetary Council (CMN) which was to coordinate monet-ary and financial policy. The 'Capital Markets Law' (Law 4728 of 1965) created 'open capital companies' and provided firms with fiscal incentives to issue common stock. Forced-savings funds which were financed with social-security-type taxes were created in the late 1960s and early 1970s to provide additional capital resources for both financial and equities markets. As mentioned above, financial index-ation was created in 1964 with the floating of Adjustable National Treasury Obligations (ORTNs). Finally, as described in the introduc-tory chapter, a scheme for facilitating the inflow of foreign loans and capital was created, embodied in BCB Resolution 63.

3.3 THE HOUSING FINANCE SYSTEM AND THE NATIONAL HOUSING BANK

Credit allocated to housing construction disappeared with the accel-eration of inflation in the early 1960s. This, however, was not the only source of market failure in the housing market. A major portion of the Brazilian populace could not meet the collateral requirements for mortgages. The Housing Finance System (SFH) with its 'central bank', the National Housing Bank (BNH), was set up to allow lower-income groups to have access to credit with which to purchase their 'own house' ('casa propria').[4] Also, it was meant to promote a recovery in housing and sanitary construction, which was badly needed in urban centers.

The SFH is comprised of the Federal Savings Banks (Caixas Economicas Federais), the State Savings Banks (Caixas Economicas Estaduais), the Housing Credit Societies (Sociedades de Crédito Imobiliário) and the Savings and Loan Associations (Associações de Poupança e Emprestimo). The first two types of institution are owned by the federal and the state governments, respectively.

The state and federal caixas economicas' main source of funds is the inflation-indexed passbook savings account (caderneta de poupança). Changes in indexing rules and maturities of the cadernetas profoundly affect their desirability and, hence, the ability of the caixas (and other institutions which offer cadernetas) to finance housing construction.

The private savings and loan institutions and mortgage credit institutions create indexed deposits, which compete with the cadernetas. The BNH's main source of funds is the forced-savings fund, the Time for Service Guarantee Fund (FGTS), which was created in 1966. Another source was indexed housing bonds, which gradually declined in importance over the period.

  The liabilities of the SFH, e.g. the cadernetas de poupança, FGTS, and other types of indexed deposits, comprise the main form in which workers hold their savings other than durable goods. The use of these funds is coordinated by the BNH under the guidance of the National Monetary Council (CMN).[5] Housing credit policy is very important to workers, as their ability to finance the purchase of a home and the return on their financial saving depends upon it. Consequently, a well-articulated lobbying system has grown up around the BNH and SFH, which includes construction unions (SECOVI), industrial unions, and other financial institutions.

Two characteristics of the SFH deserve comment. The first concerns its ability to stem market failure. The risk that pushed collateral requirements to prohibitive levels became balance sheet risk, which could not be diversified for either the lender or the borrower, depending on the indexing rule for loans. If mortgages to workers are indexed in a way that fully reflects inflation rates while wages are not, it is only a matter of time before the borrower is pushed into default. If the loan is indexed to wages while the liabilities of the financial institutions are indexed to the inflation rate, the financial institution will lose on such transactions. These difficulties have plagued the SFH since its inception, as is evidenced by the frequent changes in housing finance rules and the fact that the SFH reached virtual bankruptcy by the early 1980s.

The second salient feature of the SFH is that there exists a direct relationship between the SFH's liabilities and workers' consumption patterns. If there is doubt about the future determination of the volume of housing credit and interest rates or about the return on the cadernetas, workers may increase consumption of other goods such as consumer durables. The failure to determine housing credit policy in early 1986 explains in part the boom in consumption of consumer durables that followed the imposition of the so-called 'Cruzado Plan'.[6] Hence, SFH policy has important ramifications for inflation stabilisation policies.

3.4   SHORT-TERM CREDIT INSTITUTIONS

As in the prior period, consumer durables consumption financing and working capital are extended by commercial banks and the credit, finance, and investment societies or 'financeiras'. The reforms of 1964–6, however, regulated the financeiras in a more complete way. Direct credit to consumers was created in 1966 and attempts were made to limit access of other institutions such as investment banks to this type of activity. As we shall see below, these attempts were generally frustrated. The financeiras were also allowed access to one of the special funds set up at the BNDE, the Special Agency of Industrial Financing (FINAME).[7] Finally, after the conscious policy of promoting conglomeration, most financeiras are now associated with one of the large financial conglomerates.

The Caixas Economicas Federais also function in this market, concentrating their loans on financing consumer durables such as automobiles and electric appliances. Finally, so-called 'sales promoters' (promotores de vendas) act as a liaison between the financeiras, the consumers, and the stores. They contract to guarantee intermediate financial contracts and are allowed to float exchange bills on behalf of borrowers.[8]

Commercial banks maintained a prominent position in financial markets, although competition from non-bank intermediaries diminished their importance to a certain extent after the reforms. They are still the main source of working capital for industry, commerce, and agriculture. Specialisation in this sector came with the reforms with commercial banks being pushed mainly into short-term finance. Owing to increased competition, commercial banks created new liabilities such as certificates of deposit and repurchase agreements, and diversified the services they offered into such areas as bill collection, tax collection, payroll services, payments of public services, etc. It should be noted that funds collected as taxes proved over time to be a cheap and significant source of funds, especially as inflation accelerated toward the end of the period. Specifically, these funds (referred to as 'float') did not have to be remitted to the government for periods of up to 15 days. During the float period, they could be invested in short-term securities or repurchase agreements at no cost to banks other than transactions costs.

3.5 MEDIUM- AND LONG-TERM CREDIT INSTITUTIONS

The National Economic Development Bank (BNDE) remained the main institution extending medium- and long-term credit. The reforms, however, increased its role by creating a series of special funds designed to serve different sectors of the economy. The most important fund resulting from the reforms was FINAME, as mentioned earlier. The BNDE's funds stem from two forced savings funds: the Programme of Social Integration (PIS) and the Public Employees Financial Reserve Fund (PASEP, originally at the Bank of Brazil). The BNDE conducts selective credit policy according to the norms determined by the National Monetary Council (CMN) through the network of public and private development banks that was set up with the 1964–6 reforms.

The main publicly owned development banks subordinate to the BNDE are: (1) the Bank of the Northeast (BNB), created in 1952, which works directly with the Superintendency of Northeastern Development (SUDENE) under the Ministry of the Interior; (2) the Bank of Amazônia (BASA), created out of the defunct Credit Bank of Amazônia in 1966, which works directly with the Superintendency of Amazônia (SUDAM) under the Ministry of the Interior; (3) the National Bank of Cooperative Credit (BNCC), created in 1966, whose main funds stem from the cooperative tax imposed on all operations performed by credit cooperatives; (4) the Regional Development Bank of the Extreme South (BRDE), created in 1962, which mainly relends funds from the special funds set up at the BNH, BNDE, Bank of Brazil, and Central Bank; and finally (5) the state development banks owned and operated by the different states of the country.[9]

Private investment banks were created in 1966 in order to perform the tasks of underwriting private securities, providing long-term credit by relending foreign funds (under resolution 63) and public funds, and the management of stock and bond portfolios. Unfortunately, these banks concentrated more on short-term financing (consumer durable, working capital, and indexed bonds) than on the extension of long-term credit.

3.6 INSTITUTIONAL INVESTORS

Institutional investors do not represent a large portion of the Brazilian capital market. They held approximately 3.2% of all financial assets in 1982.[10] The main institutional investors are: (1) private pension funds; (2) fiscal investment funds; (3) insurance societies; (4) investment mutual funds; and (5) foreign investment societies. The Central Bank imposes quantitative restrictions on the different assets that each of these investors may hold. This greatly decreased the quality of the investment instrument each could offer the general public, which presumably hindered their growth.[11]

Fiscal investment funds refers to mutual funds created by the Brazilian government during the reforms. Financeiras, brokers, and investment banks could create fiscal mutual funds in which taxpayers could invest in lieu of paying taxes up to certain limits. These funds are mainly directed at channelling resources to the Northeast, to be managed by the BNB and SUDENE, and to the Amazon, to be managed by BASA and SUDAM.

3.7 EQUITIES MARKETS

The structure of equities markets was earmarked for reforms in what some have termed an attempt at 'agrarian reform in capital markets'.[12] A good portion of the Capital Markets Law of 1965 was devoted to nurture the growth of equities markets and to expand the degree of general public participation in corporate ownership. The objective was to increase the flow of funds to firms through the sale of equities as opposed to debt, the reasoning for which was outlined in the last chapter. This, the reformers felt, would lead to stable prices, fortify the financial positions of firms, and change the ownership structure of firms from one of a closed and family nature to one of general public ownership.

'Open capital companies' (SCAs) were created in 1964. Firms that qualified for SCA status would be exempt from a special surtax on distributed profits. An SCA had to issue negotiable stock, a certain proportion of which would be held by the general public. The latter would have to be at least 30%. Finally, the number of public share-holders and the proportion of voting shares held by the public were to expand to certain levels over time.[13]

The voting shares requirement proved politically sensitive and was resisted by firms. Central Bank Resolution 16 lowered the initial voting share requirement and seriously reduced the necessity of an SCA to expand continuously its sales to the public.[14]

The legislation which created SCAs and the subsequent revisions attempted to achieve two possibly contradictory goals: (1) to increase the funds acquired by firms through issues of equities and maintain their liquidity, and (2) decentralise and expand 'control' of corpora-tions. Trubek (1971) outlines this possible contradiction:

> The main emphasis of this confusing regulation was on creating a trading market. The authors of Resolution 16 were little concerned with the impact of outside stockholders on management or in affecting 'control'. For them, democratisation of capital meant merely placing of a certain percentage of equity shares in the hands of the public, and maintaining the liquidity of shares. The inadequacy of this concept quickly became apparent.[15]

Simonsen (1965) suggested that the limited rights of minority shareholders was a large obstacle to the compatibility of these two objectives.[16] Until these rights became explicitly defined or an insti-tution was created that would improve information about firms, there would also be demand side reluctance to the holding of equities.

In 1968, Central Bank Resolution 106 changed the qualification requirements for SCA status and offered additional incentives to become an SCA. The new eligibility requirements were as follows: (1) 20% of SCA common stock would be issued to the general public; (2) the percentage of common stock shareholders would have to increase over time to 49% of stock outstanding; and (3) conditions of negotiability of shares were to be maintained.[17] The new tax benefits were the following: (1) the deductibility from income taxes of part of the purchase of new shares in SCAs by individuals up to 50% of gross income; (2) the profit distribution taxes of 15% were to hold for SCAs rather than the 25% for other types of firms; and (3) SCAs were exempt from the surtax on distributed profits and were allowed to deduct a portion of dividend payments from gross income.[18] As we shall see later in this study, these conditions were again revised in 1976.

In 1964, a special fund was also created, called the 'Fund for the Democratization of Corporate Capital' (FUNDECE). This fund was ultimately to perform the task indicated by its name, but it initially served as a source of working capital during the 1964–7 working capital crisis. Firms found themselves decapitalised after the prior period's rapid inflation because they valued assets at historical cost and not at replacement cost, which caused them to distribute 'illusory profits'.[19] FUNDECE in its early years did more to recapitalise companies than to change their ownership. This was because FUNDECE gave firms the right to issue new stock to existing shareholders in an amount that exactly matched the loan it extended.[20] Another incentive was Central Bank Resolution 21, which allowed funds received from the sale of indexed government bonds to be channelled to firms to finance working capital.

The initial incentives for the development of equities markets were deemed insufficient to make the stock market active. This was due to the working capital crisis of 1966. The causes of the crisis were twofold: (1) a tight monetary policy for inflation stabilisation made credit extremely expensive,[21] and (2) the undercapitalised nature of Brazilian firms described above. Further, to protect assets against inflationary erosion, firms invested heavily in real estate, machinery, and buildings, which are highly illiquid. A good proportion of firms faced severe difficulties in financing working capital needs.[22]

The policy makers' perception that the creation of SCAs, FUNDECE, and Resolution 21 had been insufficient led to the creation of 157 funds, named after Decree Law 157 in 1967. These forced saving fiscal mutual funds allowed taxpayers to purchase securities in lieu of paying a percentage of their income taxes.[23] Finally, a special fund, the Fund for the Development of Capital Markets (FUMCAP) was created in 1972 to finance the underwriting of equity, debt, and convertible debentures, sponsored by the BNDE, Federal Savings Bank (Caixa Economica Federal), the International Finance Corporation, and USAID.[24]

3.8   A SUMMARY OF SPECIAL PROGRAMMES AND FUNDS

As mentioned above, the reforms created a series of special credit programmes and funds designed to channel resources to sectors of the economy deemed important by policy makers. This section merely lists each of these funds.[25]

A. Funds and programmes managed by the Bank of Brazil
 1. FAD: the German Development Fund.
 2. FDI: Industrial Development Fund.
 3. FUNDRIA: Industrialisation of Agriculture, Livestock, and Fisheries Fund.
 4. FIRAE: Foreign Branch Financing.
 5. FIRUN: Capital Goods and Services Import Financing.
 6. FIMEO: Equipment and Machinery Financing.
 7. FIREX: Industrial Financing with Foreign Loans (resolution 63).
 8. PRODESAR: Storage Infrastructure Development Programme.
 9. FDU: Urban Development Fund.
10. EXIMBANK: U.S. Goods Import Financing.
11. PCAS: Warehouse and Silo Construction Programme.

   The Bank of Brazil extends credit from these funds through the use of four loan windows or 'carteiras':
1. Carteira de Credito Geral (CREGE): conducts short- and medium-term credit operations with the commercial sector and medium- and long-term credit operations with industry.
2. Carteira de Credito Rural (CREAI): conducts medium- and long-term operations with the rural sector (primary goods).
3. Carteira de Comercio Externo (CACEX): finances exports.
4. Carteira de Cambio (CAMBIO): conducts foreign exchange operations.

B. Funds and programmes managed by the BNDE
 1. FINAME: Special Industrial Financing Agency.
 2. FRE: Economic Retooling Fund.
3a. FIPEME: Small and Medium Size Enterprise Finance Programme, which later became.
3b. POC: Joint Operations Programme.
 4. FUNTEC: Technology and Scientific Research and Development Fund.
 5. FMRI: Industrial Modernisation and Reorganisation Fund.

6. FUNGIRO: Special Working Capital Fund.
7. PIS: Program for Social Integration.
8. PASEP: Public Employees Financial Reserve Fund.
9. PIB-NE: Northeastern Industry Financial Support Programme.
10. FMRC: Commercial Modernisation and Reorganisation Fund.
11. PEB: Development Bank Loan Programme.
12. PRODOESTE: Centre-West Development Programme.
13. PROVALE: Special Vale do São Francisco Programme.
14. FUMCAP: Capital Market Development Fund.

FINAME became a wholly owned subsidiary of the BNDE shortly after its creation. Further, in 1974 three new BNDE owned subsidiaries were created: (1) Brazilian Mechanics (Mecânica Brasileira, S.A. or EMBRAMEC), (2) Basic Inputs Financing and Participations (Insumos Básicos, S.A. Financiamentos e Participações or FIBASE), and (3) Brazilian Investments (Investimentos Brasileiros, S.A. or IBRASA). These companies were meant to invest in stocks and debentures of preferential status. They were merged in 1982 to form BNDESPAR (BNDES Participações).

C. Funds and programmes managed by the Central Bank
1. FNRR: National Rural Refinancing Fund.
2. FUNDAG: Special Agricultural Development Fund.
3. FINEX: Export Finance Fund.
4. DUNEBE: Cattle Development Fund.
5. FUNAGRE: Agricultural Export Fund.
6. FUNDECE: Fund for the Democratisation of Corporate Capital.
7. FIBEP: Productive Goods Import Financing.
8. FINSOCIAL: Social Investment Fund.
9. Canadian Wheat.
10. U.S. Wheat.
11. Two-step loans.
12. FUMCAP: Capital Market Development Fund.
13. PROTERRA: North and Northeast Land Redistribution and Agroindustry Fund.

3.9 STRUCTURAL CHANGES IN BRAZILIAN FINANCIAL MARKETS, 1964–85

The structure of the Brazilian financial system changed significantly after the reforms of 1964–7. Table 3.1 shows the shares of different financial institutions in loans to the private sector over the period. The first noteworthy trend is that the share of the monetary system declined from 86.3% of loans to the private sector in 1963 to 37.6% in 1985 while over the same period the non-monetary system grew from 13.7% to 62.4%. One of the main consequences of the reforms was that the Brazilian financial system became increasingly diversified in terms of the source of credit. Since Chapter 5 concentrates on indexed financial assets and Chapter 6 on financial conglomerates and then explores in detail how the liability structure of the financial system changed, the liability structure of the financial system is not looked at in this chapter. Suffice it to say that monetary liabilities of the financial system became relatively less important compared with non-monetary liabilities, including indexed instruments.

The participation of the institutions that comprised the monetary sector showed a few distinct trends. The participation of publicly owned commercial banks other than the Bank of Brazil fell over the period from 39.27% of total loans to the private sector in 1963 to 5.33% in 1985. The Bank of Brazil's participation generally fell throughout the period from 33.31% of total loans to the private sector in 1963 to 10.93% in 1985, although it experienced a mild recovery between 1974 and 1980 during the Second Naticnal Development Plan (PND-II).[26] The participation of private commercial banks was somewhat unstable, but a clear pattern can be discerned from the data. Private commercial bank participation generally increased during recessions—from 13.72% of total loans to the private sector in 1963 to 16.52% in 1966 and from 10.60% in 1981 to 21.35% in 1985—while it generally fell during economic recoveries and booms—from 15.75% in 1967 to 0.68% in 1980.

The experience of the non-monetary sector, the more dynamic of the two, displayed some salient trends. The most obvious is the large growth in the participation of the Housing Finance System (SFH). It should be noted that net lending from the BNH understates the importance of this institution, as loans to other SFH institutions are not included. Net lending from the BNH showed erratic behaviour, oscillating around 3% of total loans to the private sector. Both the Federal and State Caixas Economicas showed an increase in participation: Federal Caixa Economica loans increased from 3.78% of the total in 1963 to 14.71% in 1985, while over the same period State Caixa Economica loans showed a dramatic increase from 0.04% of total loans to the private sector to 15.72%. Tavares and

Table 3.1   Brazil: Structure of Loans to the Private Sector by Lender, 1963–85 (Percentage of Total)

Monetary system

	Bank of Brazil	Other state-owned commercial banks	Private commercial banks	Total commercial banks
1963	33.31	39.27	13.72	86.3
1964	32.08	38.61	15.31	86.0
1965	27.55	39.93	14.52	82.0
1966	28.58	33.20	16.52	78.3
1967	25.26	33.29	15.75	74.3
1968	22.71	30.54	13.15	66.4
1969	23.45	27.80	12.65	63.9
1970	22.02	26.97	12.84	58.4
1971	22.31	24.65	10.24	57.2
1972	19.70	23.68	9.72	53.1
1973	19.05	21.15	9.80	50.0
1974	21.72	19.26	10.12	51.1
1975	22.79	18.14	10.17	51.1
1976	23.34	17.05	9.91	50.3
1977	22.95	17.08	10.07	50.1
1978	20.91	17.96	10.33	49.2
1979	20.89	18.49	10.72	50.1
1980	20.14	18.18	10.68	49.0
1981	16.37	18.65	10.60	45.1
1982	13.43	10.52	17.07	41.0
1983	12.52	6.64	16.74	35.9
1984	9.52	5.85	20.50	35.9
1985	10.93	5.33	24.35	37.6

Source: Banco Central do Brasil, *Boletim*.

Carvalheiro (1985) estimate the increase in the participation of the SFH in total lending to the private sector to have increased from 0.3% in 1963 to nearly 33% in 1981.[27] Clearly, the SFH proved to be one of the most dynamic credit sectors in the post-reform financial system in spite of the difficulties mentioned in prior sections.

The participation of the credit and finance companies (the 'financieras') generally grew throughout the period, from 3.25% in 1963 to a peak of 15.05% in 1973 (the last year of the so-called 'miracle'), contracting to 5.16% in 1981 and finally recovering to 10.49% by 1985. Investment banks showed a similar but less accentuated pattern, increasing from 1.32% in 1966 to a peak of 12.62% in 1973, then contracting slightly and stabilising around 10% between 1974

Table 3.1   cont.

Non-monetary system

	Financeiras (Public and Private)	Investment banks (public and private)	BNH[a]	Federal Caixas Economicas	State Caixas Economicas
1963	3.25	—	—	3.78	0.58
1964	5.57	—	0.00	2.80	0.90
1965	9.90	—	0.27	2.92	1.89
1966	10.65	1.32	0.74	4.01	1.48
1967	9.92	4.60	1.85	3.75	1.39
1968	12.53	5.41	3.33	3.76	1.31
1969	10.32	7.62	4.48	3.47	1.59
1970	11.98	8.32	5.62	4.66	1.91
1971	12.63	9.59	5.78	4.88	1.97
1972	12.90	12.62	3.94	5.11	1.88
1973	15.05	12.70	3.10	5.90	2.10
1974	12.08	10.95	2.49	6.85	2.25
1975	10.37	10.90	2.05	7.82	2.45
1976	8.45	9.99	1.94	8.55	3.28
1977	7.14	10.23	2.10	8.38	3.29
1978	7.62	10.16	2.29	8.03	3.40
1979	6.89	10.63	2.44	7.23	3.29
1980	5.56	10.91	3.01	8.11	3.21
1981	5.16	11.14	3.73	9.06	3.40
1982	8.90	9.24	0.91	10.01	4.17
1983	10.50	8.77	4.11	13.17	5.05
1984	11.04	9.98	3.71	13.68	4.75
1985	10.49	8.43	3.61	14.71	4.07

[a] Net lending which equals total lending minus loans to intermediate financial institutions.

and 1981 and finally falling to 8.43% by 1985.

Finally, the BNDE system's participation increased throughout the period from 6.5% of total credit to the private sector to 12.3% by 1981 (as calculated by Tavares and Carvalheiro (1981)).[28] Net lending from the BNDE, as in the case of the BNH, understates its importance in the financial system. Net lending from the BNDE was erratic, decreasing from 6.01% in 1963 to 2.52% in 1967, then increasing to 7.40% by 1969, then decreasing to 2.05% in 1973, then increasing to 8.13% by 1982, then abruptly declining to 2.35% by 1985. Lending from the state development banks showed itself to be generally increasing from 0.08% in 1963 to a peak of 4.01% in 1981, then falling to 3.02% by 1985.

Table 3.1   cont.

Non-monetary system

	BNDE[a]	State development banks and BNCC	Real estate credit societies and savings and loans	Total
1963	6.01	0.08	—	13.7
1964	4.51	0.22	—	14.0
1965	3.35	0.40	—	18.0
1966	2.97	0.50	0.04	21.7
1967	2.52	0.46	1.18	25.7
1968	3.43	1.14	2.65	36.1
1969	7.40	1.26	3.43	36.1
1970	3.99	1.21	3.91	41.6
1971	2.78	1.33	4.49	42.8
1972	2.16	1.64	6.66	46.9
1973	2.05	1.80	7.30	50.0
1974	4.20	2.30	7.73	48.9
1975	5.43	2.69	7.29	48.9
1976	6.21	3.68	7.95	49.7
1977	6.54	3.39	8.83	49.9
1978	6.81	3.45	9.04	50.8
1979	6.79	3.39	9.28	49.9
1980	6.48	3.52	10.30	51.0
1981	6.70	4.01	11.69	54.9
1982	8.13	3.75	13.24	59.0
1983	2.36	3.11	17.04	64.1
1984	2.54	2.13	16.30	64.1
1985	2.35	3.02	15.72	62.4

[a] Net lending which equals total lending minus loans to intermediate financial institutions.

Table 3.2 shows loans to the private sector as a percentage of GDP. Total loans to the private sector generally increased over the period as a percentage of GDP, from 19.1% in 1963 to a peak of 56.1% in 1978, then fell back to 38.1% by 1985. The importance of the financial system in financing economic activity seems to have increased substantially over the period. The non-monetary sector showed the most significant growth in this process, increasing from 2.6% of GDP in 1963 to a peak of 31.5% in 1982, then falling slightly to 23.6% by 1985. Loans from the monetary system, on the other hand, grew more slowly between 1963 and 1981, from 16.5% of GDP to 22.6% of GDP. After the collapse of foreign lending to Brazil in 1982 and the imposition of a restrictive credit policy between 1981

Table 3.2   Brazil: Loans to the Private Sector by Lender as a Percentage of GDP

	Private commercial banks	Monetary system	Non-monetary system	Total
1963	7.5	16.5	2.6	19.1
1964	6.9	15.4	2.5	12.9
1965	6.6	13.5	2.9	16.4
1966	5.1	12.1	3.3	15.4
1967	6.3	14.2	4.9	19.1
1968	7.4	16.2	8.2	24.4
1969	7.7	17.7	10.0	27.7
1970	7.8	18.6	13.2	31.8
1971	8.9	20.6	15.4	36.0
1972	9.9	22.1	19.4	41.6
1973	9.9	23.4	23.5	46.9
1974	9.7	25.6	24.5	51.1
1975	10.0	28.2	27.0	55.2
1976	9.3	27.4	27.2	54.6
1977	9.4	27.5	27.5	55.0
1978	10.4	27.6	28.5	56.1
1979	10.6	27.7	27.6	55.3
1980	8.6	22.5	23.4	45.9
1981	9.2	22.6	26.7	49.3
1982	9.1	21.9	31.5	53.4
1983	7.6	16.3	29.1	45.5
1984	8.7	15.2	27.1	42.3
1985	8.2	14.5	23.6	38.1

Source: Banco Central do Brasil, *Boletim*, and Fundação Getulio Vargas, *Contas Nacionais*.

and 1984, the participation of the monetary system fell drastically from 21.9% of GDP in 1982 to 14.5% in 1985. Although part of the monetary system, commercial banks were relatively impervious to the expansions and contractions of the monetary system, having a relatively stable loan-to-GDP ratio that ranged from 8% to 10%. This fact seems to suggest the continued importance of bank financing in relation to economic activity, especially, as argued throughout this study, in terms of working capital finance. This clearly has relevance to the efficacy of monetary and credit policy, which is discussed in other chapters.

Table 3.3 shows nominal and real growth rates of credit to the private sector. Real credit growth was high from 1965 (30.3% per year) through 1973 (35% per year), ranging from 20% per year to

Table 3.3   Brazil: Nominal and Real Credit Growth to the Private Sector,
1965–85

	Nominal change (%)	Real change (%)
1965	75.2	30.3
1966	36.0	−1.6
1967	66.9	33.5
1968	81.8	44.9
1969	49.9	23.3
1970	45.6	22.1
1971	54.2	29.1
1972	51.8	31.2
1973	56.0	35.0
1974	55.9	15.8
1975	56.8	21.2
1976	57.9	7.9
1977	51.0	8.8
1978	47.4	4.7
1979	66.3	−6.1
1980	74.8	−16.8
1981	91.9	−1.7
1982	96.6	−1.6
1983	145.8	−21.0
1984	203.4	−6.3
1985	247.6	7.2

Source: Banco Central do Brasil, *Boletim*.

around 45% per year, excluding the outlier recession year of 1966.
After the first oil shock in late 1973, real credit growth fell to 15.8%
per year in 1974, owing mainly to the acceleration of inflation. Real
credit growth declined but was still positive until the second oil shock
of 1979, when real credit growth became significantly negative. Real
credit to the private sector fell by 6.1% in 1979, 16.8% in 1980, 1.7%
in 1981, 1.6% in 1982, 21% in 1983, and 6.3% in 1984. A monetary-
policy-led recovery during the second half of 1985 led to 7.2% growth
in real credit in 1985.

Lastly, the increasing importance of the financial sector in the
productive economy can be seen from Table 3.4. The financial
sector's participation in national income increased from 3.2% in 1959
to 8.6% in 1980. In other words, the financial sector doubled in its
participation in national income between 1960 and 1980, which
showed it to be the most dynamic sector of the Brazilian economy in
the post-reform era.

Table 3.4   Brazil: Participation in National Income by Sector

	Agriculture	Industry	Services		Total
			Commerce	Financial intermed.	
1949	24.9	26.0	12.4	3.7	49.1
1959	19.2	32.6	14.4	3.2	48.2
1965	15.9	32.5	15.1	4.4	51.6
1966	13.3	33.5	15.2	5.0	53.2
1967	12.8	32.5	14.8	5.1	54.7
1968	11.7	34.7	15.3	5.0	53.6
1969	11.1	35.8	15.5	5.6	53.1
1970	10.1	35.9	15.6	5.7	54.0
1971	10.4	35.7	15.8	6.1	53.9
1972	10.5	36.1	16.1	6.3	53.5
1973	11.3	36.6	16.6	6.2	52.0
1974	11.5	37.9	17.3	6.0	50.6
1975	11.0	37.1	17.1	6.5	51.9
1976	12.8	35.7	16.8	7.6	51.6
1977	14.9	34.2	16.7	8.1	50.9
1978	13.5	33.4	16.1	8.4	53.1
1979	13.3	32.4	15.6	9.0	54.2
1980	13.0	34.0	16.1	8.6	53.0

Source: Fundação Getulio Vargas, *Contas Nacionais.*

The post-reform financial system increased in importance both in terms of financing economic activity and in its participation in national income. It also became increasingly diversified as the non-monetary sector of financial markets came to dominate the financial system over the period. One consequence of this growth is that contractions in credit growth fell disproportionately on the monetary sector, which is typical when financial innovation occurs. This was due to the fact that credit policy is imposed by credit controls on the Bank of Brazil and other publicly owned commercial banks. Private commercial banks, however, seemed relatively untouched by either expansions or contractions in overall credit in terms of their participation in loans to the private sector.

3.10   THE STRUCTURE OF BRAZILIAN MONETARY AUTHORITIES

One of the main objectives of the 1964 reforms was to create a process of decision making which would foster growth with stable prices. The 1964 reforms created a whole apparatus of state financial institutions whose actions were controlled by the monetary authorities, outlined each year in the monetary budget. The scope of policy formulated by the monetary authorities grew over the period into most sectors and hence the monetary budget was extremely important in terms of a policy instrument. The power wielded by the monetary authorities in terms of the formulation of economic policy was at times close to absolute, not only owing to the breadth of their decisions, but also because the monetary budget did not need congressional approval.

As described in the prior chapter, the pre-reform structure of the monetary authorities fostered money creation rather than control. There existed no Central Bank *per se*, as the functions of a central bank were divided between the National Treasury, SUMOC, and the Bank of Brazil (BB): the Treasury could legally issue currency; SUMOC was the 'normative' monetary and exchange rate policy organ, but did not enjoy executive power over the other monetary authorities; the BB acted both as the 'Bank of the Treasury' and as the lender of last resort for the financial system (viz. the Carteira de Redescontos and the Carteira de Mobilização Bancária), as well as acting as a commercial bank and investment bank.[29, 30] The combination of high inflation rates and the lack of a cohesive financial policy network were seen as a main obstacle to economic growth.

An important aspect of the reforms was that the BB's role as a monetary authority was not diminished but actually increased as the legislation forced it to act as a monetary authority and not simply as a commercial bank.[31] Hence, the peculiar money creation and money multiplier relationships outlined in the previous chapter did not change as a result of the reforms.[32] Further, an account called the 'conta de movimento' or movement account was set up for the BB at the newly created Central Bank. The existence of this account effectively meant that the Central Bank would maintain BB reserves at certain levels. Any shortfall in BB receipts in relation to payments was ultimately monetised, because the Central Bank would replenish the decline in BB reserves.[33] Later, state banks (e.g. Banco do Estado de São Paulo or BANESPA, Banco do Estado de Rio de Janeiro or BANERJ, etc.) were granted the so-called 'saque especial' or special 'special withdrawal right'. This effectively gives state banks their own 'conta de movimento'.[34] Hence, the inflationary bias the BB instilled in the financial system in the past was not diminished but enhanced.

The reforms created the National Monetary Council (CMN),

which was to have executive power over the other public financial institutions created or regulated by the reforms, e.g. the Central Bank, the BNH, the BB, the Caixas Economicas, and the subordinate financial institutions. The CMN prepares and approves the so-called 'monetary budget' and also determines 'out-of-budget' resource allocations that do not appear in the monetary budget. The existence of the monetary budget is somewhat peculiar, as it exists simultaneously and independently of the two other government budgets, the fiscal budget and the state enterprise budget. Its existence stems from the fact that, as discussed in previous chapters, the liabilities of the monetary authorities have a large endogenous component. Hence, successful monetary programming must be effectuated through credit policy. Each year, the monetary authorities must forecast changes in its assets and liabilities.[35] With the BB acting as both a commercial bank and a monetary authority, the large state-run system of intermediation set up with the financial reforms, special funds, minimum price guarantees, coffee operations, export and import credit, lending to the Treasury, state enterprise, and the private sector, and later the creation of dollar (432) accounts at the Central Bank (see the introductory chapter) all directly or indirectly affecting the monetary base and the monetary multiplier, monetary programming through the monetary budget is a difficult task.[36] Clearly, the monetary budget became the main instrument of strategic economic development policy through the use of selective credit policy. Further, such policy could be put into place without the consent of congress. Unfortunately, the existence of the so-called 'off-budget' items and the BB's 'conta de movimento' render published accounts of the monetary budget unreliable at best.

The creation of base money and the objectives of the monetary budget can be looked at the following way. As mentioned above, the identities developed in the previous chapter for the monetary base and money multiplier still applied in the period 1964–85, because the BB's status as a monetary authority was not diminished. Hence, the following analysis complements the previous one. The consolidated balance sheet of the monetary authorities appears in Table 3.5. The financial institutions and programmes created by the reforms enter this simplistic balance sheet under the heading of special assets and liabilities. Changes in the monetary base are determined as the difference of the change of the monetary authorities assets and non-monetary liabilities:

Table 3.5   Brazil: Consolidated Balance Sheet of the Monetary
Authorities[38]

Assets	Liabilities
(a) International reserves	(h) Monetary base
(b) Loans to the national treasury	(1) currency
(c) Government bonds	(2) demand deposits (excluding
(d) Loans to the private sector	Treasury deposits)
(e) Loans to state and municipal	(3) commercial bank reserves
governments, 'autarquias', and	deposited at the Central
other public entities	Bank
(f) Special assets	(i) Non-monetary liabilities
(g) Rediscounts and other loans to	(1) national Treasury deposits
commercial banks	(2) time deposits
	(3) 432 accounts (as of 1977)
	(4) foreign loans
	(5) special liabilities
	(6) net other accounts

$$\Delta B = \Delta A_{MA} - \Delta NM_{MA} \qquad\qquad (3.1)$$

where B is the monetary base, A_{ma} are the assets of the monetary
authorities and NM_{ma} are the non-monetary liabilities of the monetary authorities. The endogenous component of the monetary base is
mainly NM_{ma}, because as it includes time deposits at the Bank of
Brazil and the 432 deposits in dollars at the Central Bank described in
the introductory chapter. Forecasting the behavior of identity (3.1) is
the prime objective of the monetary budget.

The CMN became the main organ of economic policy decisions in
Brazil during the period 1964–74, as credit programmes were put into
place and became the main instrument of strategic economic plan-
ning. During this period the activities of the Interministerial Price
Council (Conselho Interministral de Preços or CIP), the Industrial
Development Council (Conselho de Desenvolvimento Industrial or
CDI), and the Customs Policy Council (Conselho de Politica
Aduana) were all coordinated by the CMN.[37] As the Second National
Development Plan (PND-II) was put into effect starting in 1974, the
CMN fell into to a passive role as the newly created Economic
Development Council (CDE) took over as the main source of econ-
omic policy. When a stabilisation policy was undertaken in 1976, the
CMN once again assumed the central position of economic policy.

Finally, with the disappearance of foreign lending to Brazil in 1982 and the consequent severe stabilisation programme which was undertaken, decision making became even more centralised because most policy was formulated by a small subset of the CMN (called the 'conselhinho' or little council), mainly over the phone.[39]

As Table 3.6 shows, the size and members of the CMN have changed since 1964. The core of the CMN is comprised of the Minister of Finance (who is the president of the CMN), the Minister of Planning, the Minister of Industry and Commerce, the president of the Bank of Brazil, the president of the BNDE, and the President of the Central Bank. Other public institutions have been represented, as well as those employed outside government entities. The size as well as the character of the CMN's members has changed in line with the chronology outlined above: the total number of members grew from 12 in the period 1965–9 to 15 in 1973, falling to 10 in the period 1974–7 and growing to 24 in 1981.

3.11   SUMMARY AND CONCLUSIONS

The reforms of 1964–6 created a giant mechanism for government intermediation in financial markets. Many of the programs and savings funds described above were essential to the large growth experienced by the Brazilian economy in the years to follow. But, as we shall see, much of the intermediation was financed by the inflation tax in spite of the fact that these reforms were meant to allow flows of resources by more direct and less socially undesirable means. The core problem is that many items that enter the monetary budget are actually fiscal ones, and hence financed through the monetary authorities' accounts, i.e. by inflation. Unfortunately, indexing only imperfectly mitigates the undesirable effects of inflation and also creates problems of its own.

Although the institutional structure fostered growth and allowed policy makers control in promoting strategically important sectors, the inflationary bias in the system rendered stabilisation more and more difficult as the system matured. As Mario H. Simonsen, ex-Minister of Finance and Planning, put it:

Summing up, for a determined Minister of Finance, backed enough by the President of the Republic, the money supply can be managed as a quasi exogenous variable. . . . For a less determined

Table 3.6   Brazil: The Composition of the National Monetary Council, 1964–84[a]

January 1965–December 1960	January 1970–September 1972
Minister of Finance	Minister of Finance
Minister of Planning	Minister of Planning
Minister of Industry and Commerce	Minister of Industry and Commerce
President of BB	President of BB
President of BNDE	President of BNDE
President of Central Bank	President of Central Bank
4 other government members	Minister of the Interior
2 civilians	Minister of Agriculture
	4 other government members
	2 civilians
Total 12	Total 14
1973	1974–7
Minister of Finance	Minister of Finance
Minister of Planning	Minister of Planning
Minister of Industry and Commerce	Minister of Industry and Commerce
President of BB	President of BB
President of BNDE	President of BNDE
President of Central Bank	President of Central Bank
Minister of Interior	President of BNH
Minister of Agriculture	3 civilians
President of BNH	
President of Caixa Economica Federal (CEF)	
3 other government members	
2 civilians	
Total 15	Total 10

[a] The Minister of Finance acted as President of the CMN throughout the period (and continues to do so) except for the brief period from April 1979 to August 1979 when the Minister of Planning took on the Presidency.

Minister of Finance. the monetary budget is a mere piece of formality, since it can be revised at any moment by the National Monetary Council. . . . In a word, the system is too flexible and too exposed to political pressures.[40]

Table 3.6   cont.

1978	1979–80
Minister of Finance	Minister of Finance
Minister of Planning	Minister of Planning
Minister of Industry and Commerce	Minister of Industry and Commerce
President of BB	Minister of Interior
President of BNDE	Minister of Agriculture
President of Central Bank	President of BB
President of BNH	President of BNDE
President of the Stock Market	President of Central Bank
Council (CVM)	President of BNH
3 civilians	President of CEF
	President of CVM
	President of CACEX
	President of IRB
	8 civilians
Total 11	Total 21
1981–4	The 'Conselhinho' or small council (1981–4)
Minister of Finance	Minister of Finance
Minister of Planning	Minister of Planning
Minister of Industry and Commerce	Minister of Industry and Commerce
Minister of Interior	Minister of Interior
Minister of Agriculture	Minister of Agriculture
President of BB	President of BB
President of BNDE	President of Central Bank
President of Central Bank	2 civilians
President of CEF	
President of BNB	
President of BASA	
President of CVM	
President of IRB	
President of CACEX	
9 civilians	
Total 23	Total 9

Sources: Jorge Vianna Monteiro (1982): *Fundamentos de Política Pública* (Rio de Janeiro: IPEA), p. 187; Monteiro (1983a): 'Mecanismos Decisórios da Política Economica no Brasil,' in *Revista IBM*, No. 16, p. 25.

4 The Development of Equities Markets: 1964–85

4.1 INTRODUCTION

Creating robust primary and secondary markets for stocks and bonds was the dominant objective of the reforms of 1964–7. The reasoning behind the reforms and the initial attempts at reform were outlined in Chapters 2 and 3. The economic crisis of 1963–4 saw firms become extremely illiquid. Policy makers felt that firms relied too heavily on (marginal) borrowing to finance any increase in productive activity. The fact that firms valued assets on a historical basis, as opposed to a market basis, combined with inflation to decapitalise them. This resulted in inadequate provisions for depreciation showing up as 'illusory profits'.[1] The small market for equities, comprised of both the stock exchanges and the almost non-existent 'over-the-counter' market (mercado de balcão), was seen as a barrier to the stronger capitalisation of domestic firms through stock issue. Further, the closed nature of firms and their reluctance to dilute control made the issue of common stock extremely rare, thus stunting the development of a primary issues market.[2]

The reforms embodied in the 'Capital Markets Law' and the associated regulatory standards were meant to change this scenario. Firstly, by the creation of 'open capital companies' and the granting of tax benefits, firms were encouraged to open their capital in an effort to achieve 'democratic capitalism'. Secondly, the changes in accounting regulations on the adjustment of assets and liabilities for inflation would keep firms from declaring 'illusory profits' incurred during the prior period. Thirdly, the creation of public and private investment banks, originally with an eye toward the U.S. model, would allow specialisation in the underwriting of new stock issues. Fourthly, the creation of public and private mutual funds would allow access by all investors to securities markets.

This chapter seeks to describe the post-reform events and policies in order to better understand the difficulties that confronted Brazilian policy makers in developing active stock markets. As will be clear, securities markets after the late 1960s were dominated by sales of indexed government bonds in the so-called overnight market (SELIC). The main conclusion of this chapter is that the policies to develop securities markets were moderate failures when gauged by the original goals of the policy makers. These goals, however, were overambitious. The reforms planted the seeds of a strong securities market. The necessity of creating a strong and 'decentralized' market for equities, however, still remains, and any new capital market reforms must focus again on this issue.

The chapter is organised as follows. The first section gives a historical overview of the Brazilian experience with security market development. The second provides an interpretation. The third outlines the tax structure of capital markets and firm finance. The fourth section looks at the performance of the '157 funds' while the fifth examines the role of the BNDES. The final section summarises the chapter and draws some conclusions.

4.2   HISTORICAL EXPERIENCE: 1964–85

The data contained in Tables 4.1–4.5 reveal a good deal of information about the recent Brazilian stock market experience. The stock market had a brief and frenzied growth from 1968 to 1972, which culminated in a large crash in 1972. As can be seen from Tables 4.1 and 4.2, the real percentage change in the Rio de Janeiro price index was 0.5% in 1966, 39.4% in 1967, 172% in 1969, 40% in 1970, and 180.9% in 1971, while the real percentage change in the São Paulo stock price index was 123% in 1969, 25.8% in 1970, and 123.7% in 1971. Starting in 1972, the Rio stock exchange index did not register a significant real increase until 1985. Although the São Paulo stock exchange fared slightly better, it only showed a significant recovery starting in 1984. Not only did prices increase significantly during the period 1968 to 1972 but volume did as well. Tables 4.3–4.5 chronicle the change in volume in both Rio and São Paulo. The combined increase in real volume was 42.5% in 1967, 23.2% in 1968, 389.1% in 1969, 54.0% in 1970, and 372.3% in 1971. Again, changes in real volume were mostly negative from the crash of 1972 until 1984.

The causes for the tremendous upsurge in stock volume and prices from 1968 through 1971 were: (1) the easing in monetary policy in 1968 (described in the Introduction), and (2) the reforms surrounding

Table 4.1   Brazil: Rio de Janeiro Stock Exchange Index (IBV[a]), 1966–85

Year	IBV	Change in IBV (%)	Inflation rate[b]	Real change in IBV[c] (%)
1966	8.6		38.2	
1967	10.8	25.6	25.0	0.5
1968	18.9	75.0	25.5	39.4
1969	62.4	230.2	21.4	172.0
1970	105.0	68.3	19.8	40.5
1971	350.1	233.4	18.7	180.9
1972	265.2	–24.3	16.8	–35.1
1973	206.8	–22.0	16.2	–32.9
1974	198.2	–4.2	33.8	–28.4
1975	309.5	56.2	30.1	20.0
1976	385.4	24.5	48.2	–16.0
1977	450.8	17.0	38.6	–15.6
1978	550.1	22.0	40.5	–13.1
1979	573.2	4.2	76.8	–41.1
1980	1,215.7	112.1	110.2	0.9
1981	1,738.6	43.0	95.2	–26.7
1982	4,591.8	164.1	99.7	32.3
1983	10,602.3	130.9	211.0	–25.8
1984	20,533.0	93.7	223.8	–40.2
1985	130,134.0	533.8	235.1	89.1

[a] The IBV (Indice de Bolsa de Valores) is a non-value weighted stock market index similar to the Dow Jones Average.
[b] Measured by the General Price Index (IGP-DI), *Conjuntura Economica*
[c] Let Π be the annual inflation rate and $\hat{\imath}$ be the percentage change in the stock index. The real percentage change is calculated as $[(1 + \hat{\imath})/(1 + \Pi)] - 1$.
Source: Banco Central do Brasil: *Boletim*.

the 'Capital Markets Law' combined with the creation of the fiscal '157' mutual funds (described in Chapter 3). The initial provisions of the Capital Markets Law, e.g. creating open capital companies, etc., did not induce firms to readily seek stock markets in their efforts to recapitalise, nor did investors display interest in stocks. The government then created the '157' fiscal mutual funds, which allowed individuals to invest in stock mutual funds in lieu of paying portions of their income tax. These came on stream during a period when monetary policy was relaxed. The stock market reacted with extremely strong growth, outstripping the administrative and regulatory capacity of the system.

A more interesting question deals with the causes of the stock

Table 4.2   Brazil: São Paulo Stock Exchange Index (BOVESPA[a])

Year	BOVESPA	Change in BOVESPA (%)	Inflation rate[b]	Real change in BOVESPA[c] (%)
1968	157		25.5	
1969	426	171.3	21.4	123.5
1970	642	50.7	19.8	25.8
1971	1,712	166.7	18.7	124.7
1972	1,307	−23.7	16.8	−34.6
1973	1,166	−10.8	16.2	−23.2
1974	1,187	1.8	33.8	−23.9
1975	1,855	56.3	30.1	20.1
1976	2,384	28.5	48.2	−13.3
1977	2,974	24.7	38.6	−10.0
1978	3,898	31.1	40.5	−6.7
1979	4,498	15.4	76.8	−34.7
1980	9,064	101.5	110.2	−4.1
1981	11,656	28.6	95.2	−34.1
1982	27,575	136.6	99.7	18.5
1983	79,161	187.1	211.0	−7.7
1984	488,675	517.3	223.8	90.6
1985	2,926,000	498.8	235.1	78.7

[a] The IBV (Indice de Bolsa de Valores) is a non-value weighted stock market index similar to the Dow Jones Average.
[b] Measured by the General Price Index (IGP-DI), *Conjuntura Economica*
[c] Let Π be the annual inflation rate and $\hat{\imath}$ be the percentage change in the stock index. The real percentage change is calculated as $[(1 + \hat{\imath})/(1 + \Pi)] - 1$.
Source: Banco Central do Brasil: *Boletim*.

market crash. The usual explanations place the blame on unbridled speculation, the lack of sufficient operationally and regulatory infra-structure which could avoid abuses of the newly created trading environment, and lack of knowledge on the part of the investor.[3] Although these factors did play an important role, the movement in the stock market was also very sensitive to changes in the regulation of fiscal incentives, especially the 157 funds. The rules of the game regarding 157 funds continually changed until they were completely phased out in the early 1980s. A full discussion of the performance of 157 funds follows later in this chapter. One should note, however, that a major modification occurred in June of 1970. At the time, the minimum maturity of participation in the fund was increased from two years to allowing only a 30% withdrawal at the end of the second year, a 50% withdrawal in the third year and the remaining 20% in the fourth year.[4] This gave the funds more immediate resources but

Table 4.3   Brazil: Volume of Stock Traded on the Rio de Janeiro Stock Exchange

Year	Volume (CR$ millions)	Change in volume (%)	Inflation rates	Real change in volume (%)	Volume in millions of stocks	Change in volume (%)
1966	100					
1967	175	75.0	38.2	40.0		
1968	252	44.0	25.0	14.7		
1969	1,598	534.1	25.5	422.3		
1970	2,943	84.2	21.4	53.7		
1971	14,140	380.5	19.8	304.8	2,689	
1972	7,706	−45.5	18.7	−53.3	1,911	−28.9
1973	6,924	−10.1	16.8	−22.7	2,219	16.1
1974	6,475	−6.5	16.2	−30.1	2,446	10.2
1975	15,690	142.3	33.8	86.3	4,540	85.6
1976	17,021	8.5	30.1	−26.8	5,655	24.6
1977	22,990	35.1	48.2	−2.5	9,307	64.6
1978	29,409	27.9	38.6	−9.0	14,240	53.0
1979	45,310	54.1	40.5	−12.9	24,749	73.8
1980	190,315	320.0	76.8	99.8	54,411	119.9
1981	453,310	138.2	110.2	22.0	86,830	59.6
1982	669,531	47.7	95.2	−26.0	87,833	1.2
1983	939,161	40.3	99.7	−54.9	256,646	192.2
1984	6,820,360	626.2	211.0	124.3	650,963	7.0
1985	68,341,405	902.0	223.8	199.0	2,087,805	220.7
			235.1			

Source: Banco Central do Brasil: *Boletim.*

Table 4.4 Brazil: Volume of Stock Traded on São Paulo Stock Exchange

Year	Volume (CR$ millions)	Change in volume (%)	Inflation	Real change in volume (%)	Volume (millions of stocks)	Change in volume of stocks (%)
1966	51		38.2			
1967	94	84.3	25.0	47.5		
1968	164	74.5	25.5	39.0		
1969	872	431.7	21.4	338.0		
1970	1,615	85.2	19.8	54.6		
1971	11,413	606.7	18.7	495.4	2,414	
1972	10,299	-9.8	16.8	-22.7	3,461	43.4
1973	10,928	6.1	16.2	-8.7	4,791	38.4
1974	7,707	-29.5	33.8	-47.3	3,288	-31.4
1975	10,987	42.6	30.1	9.6	4,346	32.2
1976	11,040	0.5	48.2	-32.2	5,338	22.8
1977	14,706	33.2	38.6	-3.9	7,759	45.4
1978	23,551	60.1	40.5	14.0	12,687	63.5
1979	41,419	75.9	76.8	-0.5	22,460	77.0
1980	92,217	122.6	110.2	5.9	39,474	75.8
1981	121,076	31.3	95.2	-32.7	99,096	151.0
1982	389,144	221.4	99.7	60.9	200,877	102.7
1983	1,860,406	378.1	211.0	53.7	499,921	148.9
1984	11,417,927	513.7	223.8	89.5	1,412,850	182.6
1985	65,269,809	471.6	235.1	70.6	6,367,166	350.7

Source: Banco Central do Brasil: *Boletim*.

Table 4.5   Brazil: Volume of Stock Traded on the Rio de Janeiro and
São Paulo Stock Exchanges

Year	Volume (CR$ millions)	Change in volume (%)	Inflation	Real change in volume (%)
1961	12.4		38.1	
1962	34.1	175.0	53.2	79.5
1963	76.3	123.8	73.5	29.0
1964	111.5	46.1	91.9	–23.8
1965	206.5	85.2	34.5	37.7
1966	151	–26.9	38.2	–47.1
1967	269	78.1	25.0	42.5
1968	416	54.6	25.5	23.2
1969	2,470	493.8	21.4	389.1
1970	4,558	84.5	19.8	54.0
1971	25,553	460.6	18.7	372.3
1972	18,005	–29.5	16.8	–39.7
1973	17,852	–0.8	16.2	–14.7
1974	14,182	–20.6	33.8	–40.6
1975	26,677	88.1	30.1	44.6
1976	28,061	5.2	48.2	–29.0
1977	37,696	34.3	38.6	–3.1
1978	52,960	40.5	40.5	–0.0
1979	86,729	63.8	76.8	–7.4
1980	282,532	225.8	110.2	55.0
1981	574,386	103.3	95.2	4.1
1982	1,058,675	84.3	99.7	–7.7
1983	2,799,567	164.4	211.0	–15.0
1984	18,238,287	551.5	223.8	101.2
1985	133,611,214	632.6	235.1	118.6

Source: Banco Central do Brasil: *Boletim*.

inhibited investor demand. The beginning of the stock market crisis corresponded closely to the first withdrawal date following this modification. Additionally, 157 funds were instructed to increase investment in primary issues from at least a third to 50% of resources in May of 1971. The combination of these regulatory changes had a strong contractionary effect on the overly robust secondary stock market.

The secondary market for stocks has recovered only in the early 1980s from the 1972 crash. The main objective of the reforms in 1964, however, was to stimulate the primary market for stock issue. Fostering robust secondary markets was meant to be a means to this long

Table 4.6   Brazil: Primary Market Issues as a Percentage of Total Saving, 1965–77 (Constant Cr$ Millions[a])

	Savings applied to subscription of publicly offered stocks registered at the Central Bank	Total savings applied to capital formation[b]	Savings in new stock issue as a percentage of capital formation savings
1965	557	187,307	0.30%
1966	313	179,335	0.17%
1967	1,118	151,037	0.74%
1968	5,586	197,642	2.83%
1969	4,164	276,206	1.51%
1970	3,962	268,529	1.48%
1971	7,178	303,491	2.37%
1972	7,078	343,580	2.06%
1973	4,128	456,710	0.90%
1974	1,885	502,928	0.37%
1975	1,381	416,502	0.33%
1976	1,568	448,362	0.35%
1977	1,865	479,390	0.39%
Total	40,783	4,211,019	0.97%

[a] In 1978 prices, deflated by the wholesale price index, IPA-DI, from *Conjuntura Economica*.
[b] Net private saving plus government saving.
Sources: Banco Central do Brasil, *Boletim*; *Conjuntura Economica*; and Comissão de Valores Mobiliários (1979): *Sistema de Intermediação de Valores Mobiliários: II. Evolução Histórica*, p. 103.

term goal. Tables 4.6 and 4.7 give some indication of the role primary equity issues on the stock exchanges have played in generating savings used in capital formation. As a consequence of capital market reforms, savings in new stock issues as a percentage of domestic saving rose from a paltry 0.3% in 1965 to 2.83% in 1967, levelling off to around 2% in 1972. After the stock market crash of 1972, this percentage again fell below 0.5%. There was a mild recovery in the primary issues market as a source of investment saving in the 1980s, during which the percentage of domestic saving for investment hovered around 1.5%.[5] Further, new stock issues as a percentage of total stock market volume were (and are) extremely small, around 7% to 8%. Despite the large number of fiscal and credit incentives for firms to issue stock on the exchanges as open capital companies, firms resisted becoming open capital companies and using stock issues as an important source of capital.

Table 4.7   Brazil: Primary Market Issues as a Percentage of Total Saving, 1980–5 (Constant Cz$ Millions[(a)])

	Savings applied to subscription of publicly offered stocks registered at the Central Bank	Total savings applied to capital formation[(b)]	Savings in new stock issue as a percentage of capital formation savings
1980	96.566	6,091.24	1.57
1981	35.858	5,861.33	0.61
1982	57.644	4,643.68	1.24
1983	37.232	3,750.25	0.99
1984	78.161	5,070.61	1.54
1985	87.120	6,033.87	1.44
Total	392.581	31,450.98	1.25

[(a)] In March 1986 prices, deflated by the wholesale price index, IPA-DI, from *Conjuntura Economica.*
[(b)] Net private saving plus government saving.
Sources: Banco Central do Brasil, *Boletim*; *Conjuntura Economica.*

4.3   AN INTERPRETATION

Should one interpret these numbers as indicating a total failure of the reforms in relation to the stock market? If one judges by the original objectives of the reformers, the reforms were indeed a failure. One should note, however, as Table 4.9 shows, that equity markets do not play the role of a direct supplier of investment capital in any nation, including the industrialised nations. Hence, the reformers were doomed to failure because their expectations of the role of equities markets as a direct source of investment capital were much too optimistic (based upon international standards). The lack of a strong direct role for equities markets, however, does not mean that investment decisions are not conditioned by equities markets. Stock markets are markets primarily for control and not for savings. A theory of how stock markets affect investment behaviour must be based upon how they signal information and affect the control structure (as well as the financial structure), rather than upon how they channel investment capital. We will return to this subject later in this chapter.

The data in Table 4.9 further reveal that Brazil's market for equity provides a relatively large amount of resources to firms when one considers all stock subscriptions by corporations (public offering plus direct subscription by existing stockholders), because the new

Table 4.8   Brazil: Primary Issues as a Percentage of Total Volume on the Rio and São Paulo Stock Exchanges

1980	12.13%
1981	4.72%
1982	7.98%
1983	5.17%
1984	5.39%
1985	2.73%

Source: Banco Central do Brasil, *Boletim.*

Table 4.9   Stock Issues as a Percentage of GNP, 1970–83 (Yearly Averages)

	1970–3	1974–9	1980–3
Brazil[a]	4.75	2.41	1.52
Brazil[b]	0.43	0.11	0.18
Austria[a]	0.82	0.40	0.36
Belgium[a]	1.60	1.35	1.45
Canada[a]	0.51	1.39	1.95
Denmark[a]	2.00	1.58	2.66
Finland[a]	3.74	2.69	1.36
France[b]	0.97	0.65	0.90
Greece[b]	0.38	0.30	0.14
Japan[a]	1.38	0.72	0.74
Luxembourg[a]	0.61	0.67	0.22
Netherlands[a]	0.11	0.15	0.13
Norway[a]	1.00	0.83	0.78
Portugal[a]	3.94	1.03	n.a.
Spain[a]	2.82	1.87	0.95
Sweden[a]	0.38	0.75	1.37
Switzerland[a]	2.57	1.74	0.78
United Kingdom[b]	0.47	0.66	0.60
United States[b]	1.01	0.57	1.20
West Germany[a]	0.53	0.42	0.41
Average	1.50	1.01	0.89

[a] New stock subscription by all corporations.
[b] New stock issues by public offering.
Source: OECD *Financial Statistics*, IMF *International Financial Statistics*, *Conjuntura Economica*, and Domingos de Gouveia Rodrigues (1985): 'O Porte dos Mercados de Ações e Debêntures: Brasil Versus Países Industrializados,' in *Revista Brasileira de Mercado de Capitais*, Vol. 11, No. 33, Jan.–March, p. 57.

Table 4.10   Brazil: Primary Market Issues of Stock, 1980–5 (Cr$ Millions)

	Ordinary		Preferred		Total		
	Number of shares	Value	Number of shares	Value	Number of shares	Value	Number of issues
1980	6,274	10,141	13,719	24,140	19,993	34,281	123
1981	11,663	14,682	8,651	12,427	20,314	27,109	78
1982	17,091	40,446	24,219	44,060	41,310	84,506	82
1983	23,502	53,714	40,018	90,895	63,520	144,609	72
1984	125,740	271,505	367,566	710,978	493,306	982,483	120
1985	458,380	1,055,990	895,835	2,585,607	1,354,215	3,641,597	119

Source: Banco Central do Brasil, *Boletim*.

Table 4.11   Brazil: Structure of Primary Market Issues of Stock, 1980–5
(As a Percentage of the Total)

	Ordinary		Preferred	
	Number of shares	Value	Number of shares	Value
1980	31.4	30.0	68.6	70.0
1981	57.4	54.2	42.6	45.8
1982	41.4	47.9	58.6	52.1
1983	37.0	37.1	63.0	62.9
1984	25.5	27.6	74.5	72.4
1985	33.8	29.0	66.2	71.0

Source: Table 4.9.

issues–GNP ratio is well above the average for this sample of countries. However, the importance of stock subscriptions declined significantly in the post-reform era from 4.75% of GNP in 1970–3 to 1.52% of GNP in 1980–3. Clearly, as the process of financial innovation progressed in the post-reform era, firms increasingly preferred to underwrite expansion through borrowing in lieu of increasing equity (even to existing stockholders).

The amount of resources transferred to corporations in the form of publicly offered issues, i.e. through the sale of control, was relatively minuscule and decreasing over the post-reform era. Further, of the small volume of new stock issues, preferred shares (with no voting rights) tend to dominate. Tables 4.10 and 4.11 show the composition during the 1980s of primary stock issue. In only one year between 1980 and 1985 were common stock issues larger than preferred stock issues.

Clearly, Brazilian firms were reluctant to relinquish control in spite of the fiscal incentives and forced-savings funds created by the 1964–6 reforms to spur equity financing, in addition to the BNDES system's role as a minority shareholder and underwriter of new stock issues, which will be discussed below. Why would firms resist relinquishing control? The discussion in Chapter 1 suggests three reasons why debt and equity are not good substitutes: (1) differential tax treatment, (2) stock issue signalling higher risk, and (3) more effective control of managers by banks through monitoring.

Some evidence, although not extensive, indicates that the second and third explanations may hold in the Brazilian case. Brito and Touriel (1980) show that the controlling interest in Brazilian firms owns, on average, 65% of voting shares and that around 70% of the administration of firms is made up of members of the controlling interest.[6] Further, private corporations have resisted protecting minority shareholders and divulging clear and honest information. The relative transparency of publicly owned corporations compared with private sector explains in part the fact that trade in both the primary and secondary markets in Brazil is dominated by the stock of publicly owned enterprises. Tables 4.12–4.14 show that the participation of the five largest state-owned open capital companies and all state-owned corporations have had a high and growing participation in the volume of transactions in the secondary market for stocks. State enterprise dominance on the primary market has been even more pronounced as the percentage of new subscriptions issued by public enterprise averaged 65% of total new issues between 1971 and 1976.[7] In spite of the relatively strong position public enterprise has in the domestic market for equities in Brazil, equity sold by these firms contributed only 2% of external financing in the 1970s.[8]

Because of the dominance of public enterprise in Brazilian capital markets, many have argued that these firms have an 'unfair' advantage and new issues of stock suppresses demand for private sector stocks.[9] In other words, the participation of these mixed companies crowds out private firms from the primary market for equities by increasing the cost of equity financing for private firms. Consequently, state enterprise primary issues were suspended in the late 1970s.

The implication of this argument is that if only the public enterprise participation in the stock markets would contract, private sector firms would then be able to use the market for equities as a viable source of financing. Ness (1978) finds otherwise.[10] He bases his

Table 4.12   Brazil: Participation of the Five Largest State Enterprises in
Stock Market Transactions, 1970–4[a] (Cr$ Millions)

	Total value of transactions	Participation of five largest public enterprises[b]	%
1970	1,570	268	17.1
1971	9,108	2,560	28.1
1972	10,284	2,175	21.1
1973	10,912	2,571	23.6
1974	7,081	2,930	41.4

[a] For the São Paulo Stock Exchange.
[b] Includes state-owned open-capital companies Petrobrás, Banco do Brasil,
Siderurgica Nacional, Vale do Rio Doce, and ACESITA.
Source: Bolsa de Valores de São Paulo: *Annual Report* and José Roberto
Mendonça de Barros and Douglas H. Graham (1978): 'The Brazilian Miracle
Revisited: Private and Public Sector Initiative in a Market Economy,' *Latin
American Research Review*, Vol. 13, No. 2, p. 21.

Table 4.13   Brazil: Participation of the Five Largest State Enterprises in
Stock Market Transactions, 1973–7[a] (Cr$ Millions)

	Total value of transactions	Participation of five largest public enterprises[b]	%
1973	18,743	5,688	30.4
1974	14,077	6,191	44.0
1975	27,471	15,749	57.3
1976	29,146	15,198	52.1
1977	33,255	19,837	59.6

[a] Includes all stock exchanges.
[b] Includes the state owned open capital companies Petrobrás, Banco do
Brasil, Siderurgica Nacional, Vale do Rio Doce, and ACESITA.
Source: Comissão Nacional de Bolsas de Valores: *Relatório Annual* and
Walter L. Ness, Jr. (1978): 'A Empresa Estatal no Mercado de Capitais,'
Revista Brasileira de Mercado de Capitais, Vol. 4, No. 12, p. 364.

conclusions on the following facts. Firstly, the return to the holder of
public enterprise stock is relatively high.[11] Investor interest today
depends upon the success of prior investors. Secondly, state enterprises do not show an exceptional return on equity. Clearly, if state
enterprises are abnormally favoured in equity markets, they should
command a high price–earnings ratio. This, however, is not borne

Table 4.14   Brazil: Total Participation of Private and State-owned Open-capital Companies in Stock Market Transactions, 1973–7[a]
(Cr$ Millions)

	State enterprises	%	Private national and multinational corporations	%	Total
1973	5,985	31.9	12,758	68.1	18,743
1974	6,522	46.3	7,555	53.7	14,077
1975	16,106	58.6	11,365	41.4	27,471
1976	15,649	53.7	13,497	46.3	29,146
1977	20,397	61.3	12,858	38.7	33,255

[a] Includes all stock exchanges.
Source: Comissão Nacional de Bolsas de Valores: *Relatório Annual* and Walter L. Ness, Jr. (1978): 'A Empresa Estatal no Mercado de Capitais,' *Revista Brasileira de Mercado de Capitais*, Vol. 4, No. 12, p. 364.

out by the facts.[12] Thirdly, public enterprise stock shows a large amount of risk, whether it is measured by the so-called 'beta' coefficient or by the variance of daily returns.[13] The high risk of public enterprise stock should inhibit stockholder interest. Finally, Ness (1978) finds that state enterprise stock does not hold a speculative advantage over private sector stock because the turnover of public enterprise stock as a proportion of total stock in the hands of the public is relatively small compared with that in the case of private corporations. For example, stock turnover rates for public firms in 1977 was 4% as opposed to 14% for private enterprise.[14] The main implication of these stylised facts is that stock of private and public sector firms are not good substitutes. If public enterprise stock was not traded in the market, the most probable outcome would be for investors to shift their portfolios toward financial assets other than private sector stocks.

Did the private sector firm stocks replace public enterprise stock in primary and secondary markets? State enterprise stock clearly still dominates the secondary markets. In 1984, 62.2% of the spot market volume in the Rio de Janeiro stock exchange dealt in state enterprise stocks, while in 1985 state enterprise stock accounted for 71.7% of the volume. Further, the top five public enterprises (Petrobrás, Banco do Brasil, Siderurgica Nacional, Vale do Rio Doce, and ACESITA) increased their dominant share of the market.[15] As for the primary market, we must determine whether or not there was a decrease in the value of primary market issues as well as the amount of savings transferred to the firms through this market. When we refer back to Tables 4.6 and 4.7, the percentage of capital formation savings in the form of new stock issues seems to have risen slightly in the period 1980–5 as compared with 1965–77 although the averages for each period are not significantly different in a statistical sense. The percentage of total volume on the Rio de Janeiro and São Paulo stock exchanges comprised of primary issues (Table 4.8) dropped dramatically from 12.13% in 1980 to 2.73% in 1985, even in the face of a strong growth in real volume on these two exchanges (Table 4.5). The implication is that private sector corporations are averse to using the primary issues market for raising capital. Even when the alleged source of their difficulties in using primary markets disappeared with the suspension of primary stock issues by state corporations, private sector firms did not rush to issue new stock.

If state enterprise does not command privileged advantages in Brazilian stock markets, what can explain the dominance of the stock of these firms on the primary and secondary markets? Ness (1978) explains this phenomenon as due to the sheer size of public enterprise. Magliano Filho (1986) takes this line of reasoning a step further. He shows that public enterprises distribute a higher proportion of earnings than do private firms. Hence, he concludes that public sector firms take advantage of their size and ability to borrow in foreign and domestic credit markets as well as their ability to draw on the financial resources of the state to finance these higher dividend payments. Therefore, state enterprise commands a competitive advantage over private enterprise by subsidising shareholders through decapitalising state-held firms. Not only does this conclusion assume highly irrational behaviour on the part of state enterprise owners and managers but it also does not stand up to the preceding analysis. Firstly, the value of the enterprises would reflect the lower value of investments. Secondly, foreign and domestic creditors, especially the former, would have to be completely ignorant of how these firms use funds lent to them. Typically, the control problems posed by state enterprises in Brazil lie in the tendency of managers to manage the firm as if it was a private concern and not to subsidise shareholders.[16] Perhaps Magliano Filho's (1986) proposition reflects more the use of public enterprise dividend policy to force private sector firms to increase their own dividend payments as opposed to gain a competitive edge in credit markets.

Some economists, most notably Mario Henrique Simonsen, argued that the initial 'failure' (1967–76) of the reforms in equity markets was due mainly to the lack of a mechanism for protecting minority shareholders' rights.[17] These rights are especially important when it is considered that minority investors, especially in stocks of firms which are not traded, are interested in receiving dividends. Firm managers, especially if they are one and the same as the controlling interest in the firm, have a higher interest in reinvesting retained earnings as opposed to distributing profits in the form of dividends.[18] This creates a 'moral hazard' problem, especially when ownership is diffused.[19] The failure of the reforms, therefore, was due to private sector managers not declaring large enough dividends. After some debate, the Comissão de Valores Mobiliários (CVM) was created in 1976 (Law 6.385) in the guise of the U.S. Securities Exchange Commission along with the new corporations law (a Lei de Sociedades Anônimas, Law 6.404).[20]

The corporations law of 1976 allowed open capital companies to issue two thirds of the equity outstanding in the form of preferred stock with a set minimum dividend. The old legislation allowed firms to offer up to one half of their equity in the form of preferred shares. In other words, minority shareholders would have the regularity of dividend payments protected in exchange for their voting rights.[21] The problem with this law was that inflation quickly outstripped its ability to protect the dividends of minority shareholders. Specifically, the law stated that owners of preferred stock had the right to receive 25% of profit in a certain year. These dividends, however, could be paid over twelve months and, as such, the real value of these dividends would erode faster the higher the inflation rate and the longer the period over which dividends were paid out. The law also permitted open capital companies to have one third of their equity outstanding in the form of common stock, and a controlling interest was defined as holding at least 50% of common stock or 16.7% of all equity.[22] Consequently, as the data show, the effects of the law on the stock exchange was limited through the early 1980s.

In conclusion, the most reasonable explanations for the lack of a vigorous market for corporate control are the tax structure and the problems associated with private sector control. Public sector participation in equities markets created a vehicle for investment in such instruments. Until the moral hazard problems inherent in the highly concentrated ownership structure of the Brazilian private sector are reduced by a more decentralised ownership structure, broad-based growth in this market will not occur. Unfortunately, the process seems to be a vicious circle. A strong stock market cannot exist without decentralised ownership but decentralised ownership will not be possible without strong equities markets. However, as discussed later in this chapter, progress has been made in interesting larger segments of society to invest in stocks, although the market is still dominated by publicly owned firms. As interest increases and the administrative efficiency of the market improves, perhaps firms will become more willing to dilute control by opening their capital. One clear conclusion remains—the removal of state enterprise stock from the market or a complete divestiture of the state from productive enterprises will not generate in the short or medium terms a large growth in equities markets. In fact, such a move would likely inhibit further growth in the market for corporate control unless foreign investors are allowed more participation in the market.

4.4   THE TAX STRUCTURE OF FINANCIAL INSTRUMENTS

A full chronology of the tax legislation concerning financial markets between 1964 and 1985 would make a large volume and therefore such an attempt will not be made here. Suffice it to say that the tax structure of financial markets and firms has undergone numerous modifications. A number of characteristics of the tax structure have been maintained over the period: (1) a propensity to favour debt financing rather than equity financing, (2) a propensity to use withholding or 'at-the-source' taxes, and (3) an increased difficulty in maintaining the size of the tax base. Before turning to these questions, I will briefly outline the tax structure of Brazilian financial markets as of 1986.

Table 4.15 outlines the basic tax rates on different financial instruments. As stated in prior chapters, dividends and payments on debentures are subject to double taxation, whereas debt instruments are taxed only once.[23] The tax structure, however, has a few built-in incentives. Longer maturities tend to be taxed at a lower rate, which creates a marginal incentive to stretch out maturity structure.[24] By virtue of the monotonic shortening of the maturity structure of debt instruments over the last twenty years, the effects of this tax structure have been swamped by the effects of inflation.[25] Secondly, open capital companies are marginally favoured over closed capital companies in gross taxation. One should bear in mind that these gross tax rates do not clearly reflect the level of fiscal burden,

Table 4.15   Brazil: Financial Market Tax Structure (February 1986)

Instrument	Payment and term	Investor type	Gross taxation rates
Open market	Floating rate paid daily	Individual or corporation	Withholding at the source of 35% or 45% depending upon maturity
Fixed-rate CDs (bearer or nominative), bills of exchange, acceptances, bank deposit receipts	Fixed rate paid periodically or on a discount basis	Individual or corporation	Withholding at the source of 35% on gain
Savings accounts	Monetary Correction plus 6%, no specific term	Individual or corporation	Tax exempt. Individuals may qualify for tax incentives
Mutual funds (nominative)	Variable based upon portfolio return	Individual	Tax exempt
		Corporation	Income tax net income tax paid by the fund
Corporate equity not purchased on margin (bearer or nominative)	Variable based upon capital gains and dividends	Individual	Shares traded on exchanges exempt of capital gains or held for more than 5 years; dividend withholding of 23% for open-capital companies and 25% for closed-capital companies, not deductible from income tax
		Corporation	Capital gains taxed on (biannual) tax statement, dividends paid by open-capital companies to open-capital companies taxed only at year-end tax statement; dividends paid to closed-capital companies by open-capital companies pay 23% withholding at the source

Table 4.15   cont.

Instrument	Payment and term	Investor type	Gross taxation rates
Gold (nominative)	Variable based on international prices and exchange rate	Individual or corporation	Capital gains taxed at year end statement or on 6-month statement if profits exceed 20,000 OTNs (Obrigações do Tesouro Nacional, now replaced by BTNFs, Bonus do Tesouro Nacional Fiscais)
Debentures (bearer and nominative)	Fixed rate plus income from premiums or discounts	Individual	Interest, premiums, and discounts subject to withholding at the source
	Variable term variable, final term 2 years	Corporation	Interest, premiums, and discounts subject to withholding at the source, non-deductible expense; real earnings excluded from taxable profits

Source: Coopers and Lybrand (1986): *Profile of Banking and Finance in Brazil* (São Paulo: Coopers and Lybrand), pp. 64–5.

especially in the case of firms, because they do not incorporate the fiscal incentives. The net fiscal stimulus to opening capital, for example, is much larger than the 2% difference in tax rates on dividends.

The use of withholding taxes at the source reflects the difficulty that Brazilian fiscal authorities have in assessing the taxable income of individuals and businesses and the need on the part of the Brazilian government to reduce revenue collection lags. Increasing assessment problems partially reflect the increased tendency of individuals to resist taxes. The government's need to reduce collection lags is due to the fact that real tax receipts tend to fall as individuals delay payment during high and increasing inflation.[26]

Another important development since the 1964–7 reforms is the reappearance of bearer bonds ('titulos ao portador'). Again, this partially reflects tax resistance. The tax structure in 1986 marginally penalised the holders of bearer bonds. The new tax legislation of 1988 increased withholding taxes significantly on bearer securities compared with nominative ones.[27]

How large an effect does the tax structure have on the capital structure of firms? This question clearly requires an empirical answer. Unfortunately the data needed to test such effects is either confidential or scarce. One clear conclusion is that the substantial fiscal incentives for firms to open capital have not led to the 'democratic capitalism' envisioned by the designers of the reforms in the 1960s. The reasons for this are both microeconomic, related to control, and macroeconomic, related to inflation, inflation uncertainty, and policy.

4.5 THE PERFORMANCE OF DECREE LAW 157 FUNDS

The Brazilian government created Decree Law 157 fiscal mutual funds in February 1967 in order to help firms recapitalise and create a vigorous market for corporate equities as discussed in Chapter 3. Decree Law 157 effectively became extinct in 1983 and the existing 157 funds were converted or absorbed into the mutual fund system in August 1985.[28] The administration of the funds was undertaken initially by financial market intermediaries of all types. In 1975, administration of the funds was limited by law to investment banks and brokers. Finally, in 1978, the administration of the funds was limited to the investment banks.

The idea of allowing individuals and firms to buy existing and new issues of equity of open capital companies in lieu of paying income taxes was extremely novel. The limited success of the programme in getting capital markets to become a leading sector in the development process has been amply chronicled above and in previous chapters. Therefore, the following will review only briefly the Brazilian experiment with using the tax system to promote the opening of corporate capital.

The regulation of the funds reveals a learning process on the part of investors and fund managers as well as changes in the objectives of the government. This learning process concerned the attracting of resources, the maturity structure, and the diversification of portfolios. Subscription to the funds from 1967 to 1972 was done through the purchase of Equity Purchase Certificates (Certificados de Compra de Ações or CCAs) from the financial institution which managed the funds or put money in a CCA account at an investment bank. The investor would then deduct this amount from his or her income tax statement.[29] Between 1972 and 1978, the CCA voucher issued by the Federal Revenue Secretary augmented the CCA system. The investor received the CCA voucher directly and would submit it to the institution of choice along with the funds. In 1978, the CCA voucher was eliminated and the investor could opt for 157 funds in his or her income tax statement.

As noted in the discussion of the stock market, the maturity structure of withdrawals extended a number of times over the period. Between 1967 and 1970, the maturity was two years. From 1970 to 1974, only 30% could be withdrawn after two years, 50% after three years, and the rest in the fourth year. Finally, between 1974 and 1982, 50% could be withdrawn only after the fifth year and the rest after the sixth year.[30]

The diversification parameters mandated by the government for the funds reflected the policy makers' wishes to have firms open their capital. The legislation put into effect in 1978 limited the quantity of a single firm's stock in the portfolio of a fund to 4%. It also limited the equity holdings of a fund to 10% of the capital of the firm. The portfolio had to hold equity from at least forty firms. Finally, each fund was limited to the purchase of 10% of any new issue, while the DL 157 system as a whole could only purchase up to 50% of the public offering of stocks.[31]

The original objective of the reformers was to fortify (first and foremost) the primary market for equities. The regulation of the 157 funds reflected this concern in the first part of their history. Between 1969 and 1974, two-thirds of the funds had to be applied in the acquisitions of equities on primary markets, except during a small interlude from May 1970 to May 1971. Over the course of that year, the 157 funds could apply two-thirds of their funds in secondary markets.[32] Further, between 1971 and 1974, 157 funds were required to use at least 20% of new funds in the acquisitions of small and medium-sized open capital companies. After 1974, the focus on the primary securities market dissipated, with the increase of the maximum percentage of new funds applied on the exchanges from 25% to 40%.[33] As of 1978, the regulation was revised in such a way as to not discriminate in favour of primary markets. The focus had clearly shifted to developing the exchanges, because the main stipulation of the regulation was that at least 80% of 157 fund resources were to acquire Brazilian-owned private corporations.

Table 4.16 illustrates the participation of institutional investors in equities markets, as measured by the net injection of resources. Clearly, the sum total of public sector entities dominated intermediation in this market. 157 funds clearly contributed substantially in relative terms to the capitalisation of firms through primary markets.

Table 4.17 shows comparative data for the 1981–5 period. 157 funds clearly diminished in importance compared with the prior period. These funds were merged into the mutual funds system in July 1985. Tables 4.18 and 4.19 show the participation in primary and secondary markets for the periods 1969–72 and 1975–80. A noticeable shift from strong participation in primary markets and weak participation in secondary markets to the opposite occurred between these periods, reflecting the change in legislation discussed above. For example, 157 funds contributed on average 37.9 per cent of the funds for public offer new issues over the 1976 to 1977 period, while this participation fell on average to 15.4 per cent in the 1978 to 1980 period. On the other hand, 157 fund participation in secondary markets increased from an average of 6.17 per cent in the 1969–72 period to 25.3 per cent in the 1976–80 period.

The inability of 157 funds to provide efficient intermediation in equities markets, however, contributed to their extinction. The rates of return on 157 funds were extremely disappointing compared with other assets. Table 4.20 indicates that 157 funds showed lower rates of return relative to other assets and inflation. Brito and Neves (1984), using a variation on the capital asset pricing model, found that 157 funds over the period were extremely poor in terms of absolute returns, relative returns and risk.[34] Further, the administration of 157 funds was not consistent across funds—those which performed well in one period did not necessarily perform well in the next period.[35] If we compare 157 funds with mutual funds, 157 fund performance was not significantly different from mutual fund performance between 1977 and 1978 but seemed to deteriorate in the period 1979–81.[36]

The poor performance of 157 funds was related to another stylised fact—the increasing concentration of 157 funds in investment banks linked to commercial banks in a conglomerate.[37] Further, the worst-performing funds showed the highest growth rates over the period, which pointed to large operational inefficiencies in the management of such funds. The reason given by the CVM for the extraordinary growth of poorly performing funds at conglomerate subsidiaries was the saving in transactions costs of clients who did other business with the conglomerate and the general lack of investor interest in the stock market during this period.[38] In this sense, 157 funds failed at increasing investor knowledge and interest in holding equities as opposed to other assets. The more recent increase in interest in the stock market came only after the 157 funds were phased out in 1985.

4.6   MUTUAL FUNDS AND VENTURE CAPITAL COMPANIES

The legislation creating mutual funds was outlined in Chapter 3 and therefore will not be dealt with here. Both mutual funds and venture capital companies have played a very limited role in Brazilian equities markets. According to Tables 4.16 and 4.17, investment by mutual funds (including foreign investment funds) grew significantly from 1969 to 1972, then fell dramatically from 1973 onwards until around 1982. From 1982 to 1985, mutual funds became one of the most dynamic institutional investors in equities markets.

Mutual funds underwent a few transformations during the period. In 1984, 157 funds were absorbed by the mutual funds system. Further, the mutual investment fund system was split by the creation of fixed investment or money market mutual funds and stock mutual funds. The former can invest up to 10% of total assets in stocks while the latter can invest no less than 70% of assets in stocks. The total assets of the stock mutual funds in January 1986 was Cr$18,428,120 as compared with the fixed-return mutual funds, whose assets totalled Cr$1,852,869.

Brito and Neves (1984) found that the performance of mutual funds during the period 1977 to 1981 was disappointing. However, in contrast to 157 funds, the performance of mutual funds was consistent and their risk–return performance improved substantially over the period. A process of consolidation and learning envisioned by the reformers of 1964–7 came to fruition only some twenty years later. Finally, individuals showed interest in investing on a voluntary basis *vis-à-vis* mutual funds and these funds are now a strong force in equities markets.

Venture capital companies, other than the subsidiaries of the BNDES, play a minuscule and embryonic role in Brazilian capital markets. What differentiates a venture capital company from a holding company is that typically the holding company owns a controlling interest in the firm while a venture capital company does not. Unfortunately, data on participation companies in Brazil are scarce. Montezano (1983) circumvented this problem to a degree by conducting interviews with managers of five out of the six existing participation firms as of 1980 and a few observations can be made based upon his findings.[39] Firstly, Brazilian private sector venture capital companies have mainly taken the form of 'participation companies'.[40] These participation companies, in general, are not

Table 4.16   Brazil: Net Investment of Institutional Investors in Equities Market, 1969–79 (Cr$ Millions)

	1969	1970	1971	1972	1973	1974	1975	1976	1977	1978	1979
157 Funds	88	129	88	238	788	884	440	1,243	1,923	1,421	3,890
Foreign investment funds	—	—	—	—	—	—	92	148	82	118	—
Mutual funds	234	243	1,999	461	-309	-374	-473	-481	-305	-187	-287
Insurance companies	—	—	—	—	—	—	155	613	989	1,522	2,907
FINOR	—	—	—	—	—	—	—	1,666	1,655	2,171	1,377
FISET— tourism	—	—	—	—	—	—	—	81	46	-40	-23
FISET— fishing	—	—	—	—	—	—	—	70	11	-10	-9
EMBRA-MEC	—	—	—	—	—	—	91	410	343	580	905
IBRASA	—	—	—	—	—	38	311	293	388	59	—
FIBASE	—	—	—	—	—	15	40	87	76	219	497
State development banks	—	—	—	—	—	10	10	31	126	46	235
Bank of Brazil	52	-33	-36	40	2	4	191	239	1,020	1,304	28
BNDES	—	—	—	4	—	—	40	16	—	-91[a]	—
PIS/ PASEP	—	—	—	—	—	—	—	122	—	-81[a]	36
Public sector	1,319	1,399	3,316	3,638	4,195	6,244	8,683	15,788	17,012	15,721	9,242
Total Nominal	1,915	1,971	6,011	4,767	5,290	7,537	10,550	22,831	26,143	25,158	25,752
Real[b]	30,290	26,026	65,903	44,683	43,073	47,688	52,267	80,067	64,236	44,578	25,752

[a] Only 11 months.
[b] 1979 cruzeiros deflated by the IPA-DI of the Fundação Getúlio Vargas.
Source: Marcos Fernandes Machado (1982): 'Um Balanço dos Incentivos Fiscais do DL 157: Evolução, Situação Atual e Aspectos Críticos,' in *Revista Brasileira de Mercado de Capitais*, Vol. 8, No. 22, p. 7.

venture capital companies *stricto sensu* in that they not only provide financial support in the equity and 'quasi-equity'[41] markets, but also provide financial and other assistance to small, medium, and large corporations for installing initial capacity, expansion, and refinancing.[42] Further, Brazilian participation companies tend to lean toward being holding companies rather than pure venture capital companies

Table 4.17   Brazil: Net Investment of Institutional Investors in Equities Market, 1981–5[a] (Cr$ Millions)

	1981	1982	1983	1984	1985
157 funds	42,050[c]	62,102	505,222	2,202,741	3,272,302[d]
Foreign investment funds	692	808	10,995	52,740	402,654
Mutual funds (fixed income and stock funds)[d]	N.A.	229	35,400	198,252	16,413,103
Insurance companies	13,916	30,199	96,562	305,889	1,680,000
Pension funds (private open and closed)	N.A.	67,315	655,800	3,560,076	24,930,061
Total Nominal	N.A.	160,653	799,262	6,319,698	46,698,120
Real[b]		19,558	28,228	94,276	214,007

[a] Total figures in this table understate the full value because they do not include public sector intermediary activities compared with Table 4.16.
[b] 1979 cruzeiros deflated by the IPA-DI of the Fundação Getúlio Vargas.
[c] Estimated.
[d] Includes only the period December 1984 to July 1985 when DL 157 funds were merged into the mutual fund system. Mutual fund data also include the sum of stock purchases by both fixed income (money market) mutual funds and mutual stock funds, which were separated in 1984.

and usually are not open capital companies.[43] Finally, participation company investment strategies are sensitive to government fiscal incentives and subsidy programmes.

4.7   THE ROLE OF THE BNDE

In the early 1970s, Brazilian policy makers felt creating public sector venture capital companies through the BNDE system necessary to fill the void left by the private sector. As mentioned in previous chapters, the BNDE created its subsidiaries Investimentos Brasileiros S. A. (IBRASA), Mecânica Brasileira S. A. (EMBRAMEC),

Table 4.18   Brazil: Participation of Decree Law 157 Funds in Primary
Markets (Cr$ Millions)

	157 funds subscriptions	Registered subscription for public offering	Total subscriptions	Participation (%) of 157 funds in	
				Public offer	Total
1969	110.3	463.7	1,965.8	23.8	5.6
1970	162.4	408.4	2,130.8	39.8	7.6
1971	269.2	2,192.5	6,245.5	12.3	4.3
1972	55.8[a]	405.4	5,396.2	13.8	1.0
Average	149.4	867.5	3,933.5	17.2	3.8
1975	69.0	341.6	12,222.9	20.2	0.5
1976	514.9	1,373.0	21,180.5	37.5	2.4
1977	923.5	1,413.5	24,246.3	38.3	3.8
1978	1,385.4	9,362.7	30,309.2	14.8	4.6
1979	2,108.2[b]	15,142.9	28,198.6	13.9	7.5
1980	6,019.2	34,281.5	N.A.	17.6	N.A.
Averages					
1976–7	719.2	1,393.2	22,713.2	37.9	3.1
1978–80	1,746.8	19,595.7	29,253.9	15.4	6.1

[a] First 11 months.
[b] Data from 44 funds from the Anuário da Bolsa de Valores de São Paulo. In 1978, all subscription registrations came to be registered at the newly created CVM, which used a set of criteria different from those of the Central Bank.
Source: Marcos Fernandes Machado (1982): "Um Balanço dos Incentivos Fiscais do DL 157: Evolução, Situação Atual e Aspectos Críticos," in *Revista Brasileira de Mercado de Capitais*, Vol. 8, No. 22, p. 15.

and Insumos Básicos S. A. (FIBASE) in order to play the role of the heretofore non-existent venture capital companies.[44] They were meant to play a leading role in capitalising small and medium-sized companies and to promote the so-called 'democratization of capital' repeatedly mentioned in this study. The targeted sectors were those in import substitution industries and those which showed promise in developing new technologies.[45] The system was to do this by taking a minority interest in firms by investing in equities—mainly preferred shares—and convertible debentures.[46] IBRASA's main role was to promote broad-based ownership of corporations and therefore provide resources to open capital companies whose stock was traded on

Table 4.19   Brazil: Participation of Decree Law 157 Funds in Secondary
              Markets (Cr$ Millions)

	157 exchange purchases	157 exchange sales	157 total transactions	Volume on BVRJ plus BOVESPA	Participation (%) of 157 funds
1969	75.8	75.3	148.1	2,461.0	6.02
1970	178.1	211.8	389.7	4,558.0	8.55
1971	431.1	611.9	1,043.0	25,553.0	4.08
1972	530.0	1,008.0	1,538.0	18,005.0	8.54
Average	303.7	476.7	779.7	12,644.2	6.17
1976	1,618.7	2,414.7	6,033.4	28,061.0	21.5
1977	5,284.4	3,699.5	8,983.9	37,696.0	23.8
1978	7,349.6	6,494.4	13,844.0	52,960.0	26.1
1979	13,839.0	10,872.1	24,711.1	86,431.0	28.5
1980	20,813.5	16,812.1	37,625.6	141,176.4	26.6
Average	10,181.0	8,058.6	17,032.9	63,652.7	25.3

Source: Marcos Fernandes Machado (1982): 'Um Balanço dos Incentivos
Fiscais do DL 157: Evolução, Situação Atual e Aspectos Críticos,' in *Revista
Brasileira de Mercado de Capitais*, Vol. 8, No. 22, p. 15.

the stock exchanges or in companies that presented significant signs
that they would open their capital in the future. The holding time for
IBRASA's minority share position initially was to be from three to
five years. Later, IBRASA bought shares in companies that were
leaders in their respective sectors.[47] EMBRAMEC and FIBASE
were meant to supply capital resources to firms producing in the
capital goods and basic input sectors, respectively.[48] Although it was
not the primary objective of these two subsidiaries, both also promoted the opening of capital. In 1982 the three firms were merged into
one corporation, BNDES Participações (BNDESPAR).[49]

Initially, IBRASA, EMBRAMEC, and FIBASE (and then
BNDESPAR after 1982) concentrated on investing in temporary
ownership in that they would take a minority position in firms and
then divest their position in the medium term. Over the period, their
effective role changed to being sources of subsidised credit through
transferring resources to firms *via* buying stocks with repurchase
agreements (sometimes mandatory) and relending of BNDE funds.[50]
Further, these subsidiaries became important sources of technical
and managerial consulting for the firms involved. By concentrating

Table 4.20   Brazil: Rates of Return to Decree Law Funds 157 Relative to
Stock Markets and Inflation

	Rate of return				
DL 157 funds[a]	IBV[b]	IBOVESPA[c]	IPBV[d]	ORTN[e]	Inflation[f]
1972	−38.7	−46.0	−23.7	—	15.3	15.7
1973	−9.1	−22.0	−10.8	—	12.8	15.5
1974	−5.2	−4.0	1.8	—	33.3	34.5
1975	16.1	38.7	56.3	45.0	24.2	29.4
1976	38.1	17.0	28.5	29.0	37.2	46.3
1977	52.3	27.0	24.7	38.0	30.1	38.8
1978	20.9	22.3	31.1	54.7	36.2	40.8
1979	20.7	46.0	42.0	33.1	47.2	77.2
1980	25.2	44.9	45.7	44.0	50.8	110.2

[a] As measured by the ANBID (Associação Nacional de Bancos de Investimento).
[b] The General Index of Profitability of the Rio de Janeiro Stock Exchange.
[c] The Index of Profitability of the São Paulo Stock Exchange.
[d] The General Price index of the Rio de Janeiro Stock Exchange.
[e] The Rate of Return on ORTN (Obrigações do Tesouro Nacional).
[f] As measured by the wholesale price index, IGP-DI of the Fundação Getúlio Vargas.
Sources: Marcos Fernandes Machado (1982): 'Um Balanço dos Incentivos Fiscais do DL 157: Evolução, Situação Atual e Aspectos Críticos,' in *Revista Brasileira de Mercado de Capitais*, Vol. 8, No. 22, p. 15; ANBID; *Conjuntura Economica*.

on the leading firms in each sector, BNDE system venture capital favoured medium to large corporations, often to the detriment of small firms.

Tables 4.21 and 4.22 show the BNDE holdings in enterprises in nominal and real terms. The BNDE real holdings in BNDESPAR stayed relatively constant over the period. Table 4.23 shows BNDESPAR's nominal and real holdings in other corporations. The real value of its holdings grew from 1981 to 1983 but stagnated thereafter. This probably reflects the Brazilian public sector cuts in investment expenditure. Table 4.24 shows BNDESPAR's nominal and real financing levels. Real underwriting activities grew dramatically in real terms from 1981 to 1985. Finally, Table 4.25 shows BNDESPAR's nominal and real net profits. BNDESPAR's real profits were negative except for 1981. They deteriorated dramatically during 1986.

These subsidiaries took on another role in Brazilian financial

Table 4.21   Brazil: BNDE Equities Holdings, 1980–6 (Cr$ Millions)

	BNDE[b]	EMBRAMEC	IBRASA	FIBASE	BNDESPAR[a]	Total
1978	30,958	3,146	3,444	9,788	16,378	47,330
1979	46,688	5,355	7,021	14,306	26,682	73,370
1980	77,845	8,323	10,602	22,658	41,583	119,428
1981	156,622	19,505	19,557	70,007	109,069	265,651
1982	532,926				186,853	719,779
1983	2,210,106				453,960	2,664,066
1984	6,903,350				1,303,860	8,207,210
1985	24,449,992				4,442,776	28,892,768
1986	32,083,323				3,683,067	35,766,384

[a] BNDESPAR was created in 1982 out of EMBRAMEC, IBRASA, and FIBASE.
The numbers before 1982 are the totals for these three companies.
[b] Net of holdings in BNDESPAR.
Source: BNDE: *Relatório*.

Table 4.22   Brazil: BNDE Equities Holdings, 1980–6 (Cr$ Millions[c])

	BNDE[b]	EMBRAMEC	IBRASA	FIBASE	BNDESPAR[a]	Total
1978	22,320	2,268	2,483	7,057	11,808	34,124
1979	21,868	2,508	3,288	6,701	12,497	34,365
1980	18,209	1,947	2,480	5,300	9,727	27,936
1981	17,120	2,174	2,182	7,802	12,155	29,606
1982	30,216				10,594	40,811
1983	49,512				10,170	59,682
1984	43,236				9,110	57,346
1985	52,482				9,536	62,018
1986	28,299				3,278	31,832

[a] BNDESPAR was created in 1982 out of EMBRAMEC, IBRASA, and FIBASE.
The number before 1982 are the totals for these three companies.
[b] Net of holdings in BNDESPAR.
[c] Deflated by the wholesale price index (IPA-DI) of *Conjuntura Economica*.
Source: BNDE: *Relatório*.

markets in conjunction with another BNDE subsidiary, the Fundo de Modernização e Reorganização Industrial (FMRI). They provided financial and administrative support to companies in financial distress. Intervention took the form of financing the following: (1) merger, incorporation, association, or liquidation of the firms, (2) administrative reorganisation through studies concentrating on updating the control, information and decision-making systems, (3) reformulation of the productive process including plant and equipment for modernising the productive system and developing new products, (4) bolstering working capital to adequate levels, and (5)

Table 4.23   Brazil: BNDESPAR Equities Holdings, 1981–6[a]
(Cr$ Millions[b])

	Nominal	Real
1981	157,097	17,508
1982	348,317	19,862
1983	1,011,173	22,653
1984	3,363,012	23,498
1985	11,553,541	24,800
1986	31,333,541	27,887

[a] BNDESPAR was created in 1982 out of EMBRAMEC, IBRASA, and FIBASE. The number before 1982 are the totals for these three companies.

[b] Deflated by the wholesale price index (IPA-DI) of *Conjuntura Economica* in 1977 cruzeiros.

Source: BNDE: *Relatório.*

liquidating liabilities including obligations with the government.[51] These activities of the BNDE subsidiaries worked against the main objective of being a source of venture capital not only by diverting the attention of the managers of these firms from supporting potentially productive open capital companies but also by creating an incentive to take on too much risk at the government's expense.

Evaluating BNDESPAR's performance as a venture capital company from the data presented above is complicated by the conflicting roles taken on by the subsidiary. The fact that BNDESPAR lost money in the early 1980s reflects Brazil's balance of payments problems and the inflation stabilisation plans. However, Brito and Touriel (1980) question BNDE's ability to select firms when underwriting stock issues. They demonstrate that firms financed by BNDE showed larger-than-average declines in net worth over the 1974 to 1976 period compared with open capital companies whose stock was publicly offered through registration at the Central Bank.[52] The poor profit showing of BNDESPAR in Table 4.25 reflects this fact. Further, BNDE-held corporations showed higher degrees of leverage and therefore a higher default risk than did the other companies.[53] On the other hand, BNDE-held firms showed a slightly lower concentration of ownership both in absolute terms and in the hands of directors of the firms.[54]

In sum, the evidence indicates that BNDESPAR did not perform well as a venture capital company in terms of investing in firms with low debt–equity ratios, although high debt–equity ratios may not necessarily reflect a poor balance sheet, and in firms with poor profit performance.

Table 4.24   Brazil: BNDESPAR Financing (Stocks), 1981–6[a]
(Cr$ Millions[b])

	Nominal	Real
1981	21,963	2,448
1982	32,459	1,851
1983	220,783	4,946
1984	2,382,636	16,648
1985	8,502,781	18,251
1986	12,068,960	10,741

[a] BNDESPAR was created in 1982 out of EMBRAMEC, IBRASA, and FIBASE. The number before 1982 are the totals for these three companies.
[b] Deflated by the wholesale price index (IPA-DI) of *Conjuntura Economica* in 1977 cruzeiros.
Source: BNDE: *Relatório*.

Table 4.25   Brazil: BNDESPAR Net Profits, 1981–6[a] (Cr$ Millions[b])

	Nominal	Real
1979	−512	−240
1981	65	7
1982	−30,403	−1,734
1983	−121,149	−2,714
1984	−619,453	−4,328
1985	−545,706	−1,171
1986	−10,571,289	−90,398

[a] BNDESPAR was created in 1982 out of EMBRAMEC, IBRASA, and FIBASE. The number before 1982 are the totals for these three companies. These data include the accounting adjustment (monetary correction) which subtracts any excess inflation adjustment of liabilities over assets from profits.
[b] Deflated by the wholesale price index (IPA-DI) of *Conjuntura Economica* in 1977 cruzeiros.
Source: BNDE: *Relatório*.

4.8   SUMMARY AND CONCLUSIONS

This chapter reviewed developments in Brazilian equities markets with an eye toward evaluating the reforms initiated in the late 1960s. The main objectives of the reformers were: (1) to create robust markets for equities, (2) to transform equities into a major vehicle for transferring resources to firms, (3) and to change the structure of ownership of the private sector firms from closed, family-owned-and-run firms to corporations with a large number of owners whose stock was traded vigorously on stock exchanges.

The first objective seems to have been achieved, because Brazil now has the largest and most sophisticated market for equities in Latin America. The growth in Brazilian equities markets took much longer than the policy makers originally foresaw and required a large degree of intervention by the state not only to create instruments and institutions (e.g. Decree Law 157 funds) that did not exist but also in underwriting the acquisition of stock. What seems to have happened is a long-drawn-out process of learning by doing, culminating at long last in the early 1980s in a significant increase in investor interest in the stock market. On the other hand, public enterprise stock dominates both primary and secondary markets which, it was argued here, reflects the lack of faith in private sector control of open capital companies. Public sector intervention was not always undertaken in an efficient manner. However, the public sector did foster the learning process. Clearly, as the private sector develops institutions and financial instruments that are dynamic in these markets, the public sector should withdraw and take a more regulatory than active role. The lack of private sector firms stepping into the primary market for securities after the withdrawal of public sector open-capital companies, however, indicates that a large scale 'privatization' programme through quick divestiture will in all likelihood hinder further development of the market for equities in Brazil.

The reforms of the early 1960s did not render the stock market a primary source of investment capital. This objective, however, was unrealistic, because the market for equities does not play this role in developed countries, let alone in underdeveloped ones. Markets for equities affect investment decisions to the extent that they change managers' incentives to invest. The role of a stock market in the economic growth process should be evaluated by assessing how it affects the control of the enterprise (e.g. the managers' incentives) rather than by the amount of capital resources transferred to firms through the stock market.

Changing the ownership structure of corporations proved to be the most difficult nut to crack. Unfortunately, it represents the most important barrier to the growth and functioning of the stock market. Private sector firms resisted opening their capital in spite of generous fiscal incentives, access to subsidised credit, and regulation. As argued here, public enterprise supplanted the paucity of true private, open capital companies. Until private sector firms are willing to dilute control and effective protection is extended to minority shareholders, full development of the market for equities will not be attained in Brazil.

5 The Indexation of Financial Assets

5.1 INTRODUCTION

The military government that took power in 1964 concentrated initially on reducing the inflation rate. This was attempted through 'gradualist' policies which were thought more appropriate for a fragile economy that could not absorb a 'shock treatment' stabilisation programme.[1] Admitting that inflation would not fall instantaneously to low levels, the Castello Branco administration, specifically Minister of Finance Octávio Gouvêia de Bulhões and Minister of Planning Roberto de Oliveira Campos, concentrated on minimising distortions which had been caused by inflation, especially in financial markets.[2] The main innovation was the creation of indexed bonds, Adjustable Obligations of the National Treasury (ORTNs), which were followed by other indexed assets. As Table 5.1 shows, indexed financial assets came to dominate financial markets over the period 1964–85 increasing from 4.7% of non-indexed assets in 1965 to around two times the size of non-indexed assets in 1985.

Index-linking of financial assets (hereafter referred to as indexed bonds) to the inflation rate (or the exchange rate) has received much attention in recent theoretical and empirical studies. The Brazilian case is especially interesting because Brazil's system of indexation is the most extensive in the world.

The main desirable aspect of the existence of indexed bonds is that it allegedly eliminates inflation risk, and hence should lower the risk premium component of interest rates.[3] In other words, the cost of borrowing declines with the use of indexation. Baer and Beckerman (1980), looking at the Brazilian case, observe that this type of argument in favour of indexing is formulated in a partial equilibrium context.[4] They argue that although risk on certain transactions does decline, it does not disappear but is merely redistributed elsewhere in the system.[5] More specifically, as indexation becomes increasingly widespread, interest rate risk is transformed into balance sheet risk.

Once indexation was created by the Brazilian government, the proportion of *ex post* indexed assets to total assets of the financial

Table 5.1   Brazil: Indexed and Non-indexed Financial Assets, 1965–85
(Cr$ Billions)

	Indexed assets[a]	Indexed assets[b]	Non-indexed[a] assets	Indexed[a] / Non-indexed	Indexed[b] / Non-indexed
1965	0.472	0.472	10.047	0.047	0.047
1966	1.488	1.488	11.592	0.128	0.128
1967	2.896	3.525	18.201	0.159	0.194
1968	5.163	7.065	27.188	0.190	0.260
1969	9.967	13.578	36.265	0.275	0.374
1970	14.672	20.712	48.784	0.301	0.425
1971	19.953	30.304	74.809	0.267	0.405
1972	30.425	48.195	112.023	0.272	0.430
1973	44.815	73.553	171.936	0.261	0.428
1974	75.630	25.961	216.001	0.350	0.583
1975	138.153	219.204	327.122	0.422	0.670
1976	225.320	364.029	459.210	0.491	0.793
1977	338.695	572.235	682.615	0.496	0.830
1978	509.300	889.657	1,034.269	0.492	0.860
1979	871.949	1,532.389	1,701.272	0.512	0.900
1980	1,740.362	2,960.503	2,597.702	0.670	1.140
1981	4,911.163	7,658.740	4,785.460	1.263	1.600
1982	13,134.220	19,236.150	9,055.077	1.451	2.124
1983	41,630.300	58,597.260	27,721.700	1.502	2.114
1984	156,805.500	212,590.552	87,254.700	1.797	2.436
1985	590,600.700	790,741.491	363,936.000	1.623	2.173

[a] Excludes stocks of indexed forced savings funds.
[b] Includes stocks of indexed forced savings funds.
Source: Banco Central do Brasil, *Boletim*.

system tended to grow over the period. The question therefore arises: if indexed bonds are undesirable, why did the Brazilian financial system become increasingly indexed, especially in light of the fact that the private sector strongly resisted contracting indexed liabilities? It seems that there is substantial demand for indexed bonds but no private sector supply. Once the government created indexed bonds, the private sector had to create their own to compete for funds, although grudgingly. This chapter describes how that process took place.

Finally, as individuals increasingly use a constant-purchasing-power unit of account, the economy loses its *numéraire* good, the price level becomes indeterminate, and the inflation rate becomes unstable.[6] All modern hyperinflations have been characterised by the flight to a constant-purchasing-power unit of account, which in most cases has been the U.S. dollar.[7] In other words, inflation feedback mechanisms are strengthened.[8]

5.2   THE DESIRABILITY OF INDEXED BONDS

This section is devoted to investigating the desirability of indexed bonds. Although many economists, including Milton Friedman and James Tobin,[9] have advocated the use of indexed bonds, their use by governments and especially by private sector firms has been extremely limited. Even in the Brazilian case where the government has created financial asset indexing, the private sector has been loath to offer bonds or to contract loans with indexing clauses. The institutional and historical reasons for this will be discussed later in the chapter. This section, however, looks at possible theoretical points of resistance on both the demand and the supply sides.

In an inflationary environment, it seems reasonable for individuals to prefer to hold assets that do not lose their purchasing power to inflation. If *ex ante* inflationary expectations, however, are always fulfilled with certainty then *ex post* indexed bonds will be redundant and will not be necessary. Obviously, such certainty about future inflation rates does not exist, especially in Brazil, and, at a casual glance, indexed bonds occupy an important place in individual wealth portfolios.

Fischer (1985) suggests that the seemingly large potential demand for indexed bonds may not be as large as one might think.[10] He comes to this conclusion through the use of a model which assumes that risk-averse individuals hold equity, nominal bonds,[11] and indexed bonds and maximise returns over time. *Ex ante* expected real returns on nominal bonds are negatively correlated with inflation, while the correlation between *ex ante* expected real returns on equity and inflation is indeterminate.[12] If investors believe that inflation helps earnings and capital gains, they may hedge against equities by buying nominal bonds in case of lower-than-expected inflation rates. As nominal bonds are demanded, they may command a premium and firms may prefer to issue nominal bonds because the cost of funds will be lower than in the indexed bond case.

This argument does not seem appropriate in the Brazilian case because the equities market played a small role during the period 1964–85. Indexed bonds would be preferred to nominal bonds and would thus command a lower interest rate. Another source of demand side resistance to indexed bonds might stem from set-up costs (e.g. education of investors, etc.), which would become economically feasible at high inflation rates or if uncertainty about inflation or borrowers' solvency was large. This explanation fits the Brazilian case very well. The purchase of indexed bonds by the public was initially resisted, owing to a preference for investing in the legal and illegal bills of exchange market. Not until a large firm, the Mannesman Group, defaulted on their illegal bills of exchange outstanding in 1967 was there a significant shift into indexed bonds.[13] Once these fixed costs were overcome, it seems that a strong demand for indexed bonds was present in Brazil. Claudio Contador (1976) shows statistically that indexed bonds became a significant asset after 1967 owing to their high elasticities of substitution with other assets.[14]

The supply side of the market for indexed assets is more complicated. Kleiman (1985), among others, argues that firms will prefer to issue indexed bonds because they will reduce the risk of inflation being below the expected rate, i.e. they will reduce the risk of making a higher than expected real interest payment.[15] Hence, the risk discount to firms borrowing by issuing indexed bonds will be smaller and firms will be willing to borrow more at each nominal interest rate. Combined with the optimistic demand profile for indexed bonds described above, their introduction should cause an expansion of credit as both supply and demand increase (shift outward in nominal interest rate and credit volume space).

Levhari and Liviatan (1977)[16] and Beckerman (1979),[17] on the other hand, come to the conclusion that borrowers will tend to prefer to issue nominal bonds over indexed bonds (assuming risk aversion) to reduce the risk attached to the firm's future wealth. This is achieved by the reduction of future real interest payments through inflation. Thus, nominal bonds are used as (1) a hedge against the loss of wealth if large money balances are held, (2) a hedge against a decreased return on equity if one believes that inflation affects the firm's stock in a negative way, and (3) a hedge against losses in real income due to inflation.

A possible problem with this argument is that it ignores the tax system and the effect that tax assessment has on the market value of the firm. According to Stanley Fischer,

The elements of the theory of the supply of index bonds are accordingly simple. The issue of bonds produces a tax advantage, but the more bonds are issued, the greater the possibility of bankruptcy. Thus, bonds will be issued to the point at which the tax benefit balances the expected bankruptcy costs. It should be noted that in the absence of differential tax treatment of interest and profit distribution, no bonds would be issued by the firm.[18]

This passage seems also to suggest that since the real debt service of a firm is maintained when indexed bond financing is used, whereas real debt service deteriorates when nominal bond financing is used owing to an unexpectedly high inflation rate, the tax liability of a firm will be smaller if it uses indexed bonds. The Brazilian case corresponds to this example. In general, over the period 1964–85, Brazilian law allowed firms to deduct nominal interest on both nominal ('pre-fixed indexed') and indexed bonds while dividends were not deductible.[19] The tax system explains in part the preference of Brazilian firms for debt financing as opposed to equity finance. It does not, however, explain private sector reluctance to contract index-linked liabilities. Brazilian private sector firms resisted the use of indexed bonds in spite of possible tax benefits. Hence, as claimed by Baer and Beckerman (1980), Levhari and Liviatan (1977), and Beckerman (1979), risk seems to inhibit rather than encourage a private supply of indexed bonds.

5.3 GOVERNMENT INDEXED BONDS AND THE INFLATION TAX

Should the government introduce indexed bonds when the private sector is reluctant to index their liabilities? The desirability of government indexed bonds remains a very controversial issue and arguments both for and against them have flourished. This section investigates arguments most relevant to the Brazilian case.

One conclusion from the analysis introduced in the preceding section is that the introduction of indexed government bonds would lower the risk premium and allow the government to reduce the cost of bond financing. The lowering of risk represents a welfare gain because a real credit expansion would be effected by government intermediation through the use of indexed bonds. Milton Friedman (1974) suggested that the government should index its debt in order to restore a portion of the real value of the bonds expropriated by the so-called inflation tax.[20] As argued below, the index linking of bonds protects only partially the real value of indexed bonds and may provide a way for the government to increase its 'inflation tax receipts' by maintaining a higher tax base, e.g. the monetary base, than would otherwise exist without indexation. Hence, the additional financial cost of using indexed bonds may be seen as a cost of inflation tax collection.

The main reason indexation can only partially compensate bond holders for inflationary erosion is that the bond price is only adjusted at discrete time intervals while inflation is a continuous process. It is easy to show that the average purchasing power of a bond will decrease with an anticipated acceleration of inflation if the adjustment interval does not change. Let a^* represent the average real purchasing power of a bond over one adjustment period, a_0 represent the real purchasing power of the beginning of the period, and Π be the (discrete time) one period inflation rate equal to $[P_1/P_0 - 1]$. The average real purchasing power of the bond over the period (assuming a constant rate of inflation) is:

$$a^* = \int_0^1 a_0(1+\Pi)^{-t}\, \mathrm{d}t = \int_0^1 a_0 e^{-t\,\ln(1+\Pi)}\, \mathrm{d}t \tag{5.1}$$

Solving yields

$$a^* = \frac{a_0\Pi}{(1+\Pi)\,\ln(1+\Pi)} \tag{5.2}$$

Differentiating (2) with respect to the inflation rate yields

$$\frac{\mathrm{d}a^*}{\mathrm{d}\Pi} = \frac{a_0[\ln(1+\Pi)-\Pi]}{[(1+\Pi)\,\ln(1+\Pi)]^2} \tag{5.3}$$

For positive inflation rates (i.e., $\Pi > 0$), $\mathrm{d}a^*/\mathrm{d}\Pi < 0$ as $\Pi > \ln(1+\Pi)$ for all real Π not equal to zero).[21] In other words, the average purchasing power of bonds decreases as inflation increases.

One might argue that this is irrelevant as individuals would wait until immediately after the adjustment date to sell their bonds. Individuals who try to maximise income from a risky portfolio, however, may need to liquidate portions of their assets if a shortfall in money balances arises. For an inter-adjustment period secondary market for indexed bonds, there would have to exist some sort of demand for these bonds. If inflation expectations or forecasts (as measured by the relevant index) were not homogeneous over individuals, a speculative demand for indexed bonds would arise. Trades would entail speculation on the outcome of that period's price index. This is what occurred in Brazil, especially during the period 1983–5. Day trading in indexed bonds became widespread, with maturities on repurchase agreements on indexed government bonds being as small as two hours.[22]

The main point of this discussion is to show that inflation risk exists even in indexed bond markets. Notice that the Central Bank could act similarly to the speculator above when conducting open-market operations. Whenever inflation (for the adjustment period) is higher than that expected in the market, the government gains from buying government bonds and increasing the monetary base.[23] Each time the government needs new financing or when indexed bonds mature, new indexed bonds are issued, which would be in part repurchased over the rest of the period. As long as individuals (mainly bank and non-bank intermediaries in the case of Brazil) are willing to hold indexed bonds, the government will 'collect' significant amounts in inflation tax 'revenues'. In the absence of indexed bonds, individuals would hold other types of constant purchasing power assets such as land and U.S. dollars from which the government could not extract seigniorage. Hence, one could argue that the reason a government creates indexed bonds is to allow them to maintain their ability to collect seigniorage even in high inflations.[24] Their existence, in this context, creates an incentive for the government to further inflate the economy. The cost to the government (ignoring the well-known social costs) of collecting additional amounts of the 'inflation tax' is just the added interest cost of indexed bonds.

To investigate this point further, consider the closed-economy continuous (instantaneous)-time government budget constraint at time s when all government debt is indexed:[25]

$$\dot{M}(s) + \dot{B}(s) = [G(s) - T(s)] + iB(s) \qquad (5.4)$$

where ( ) signifies an instantaneous change in the variable in question, B is the stock of indexed bonds, $(G - T)$ is the instantaneous public sector non-financial deficit, and i is the instantaneous interest rate (compounded continuously) paid on indexed bonds. Continuous time is used because inflation is roughly a continuous process.[26] Defining $m=M/P$, $b=B/P$, $g=G/P$, $\tau=T/P$, and dividing equation 5.4 by P, yields:

$$\frac{\dot{M}}{P} + \frac{\dot{B}}{P} = [g - \tau] + ib \tag{5.5}$$

The time index has been omitted for simplicity. Taking the time derivatives of m and b yields

$$\frac{\dot{M}}{P} = \dot{m} + \pi m \tag{5.6}$$

$$\frac{\dot{B}}{P} = \dot{b} + \pi b \tag{5.7}$$

where π is the instantaneous rate of inflation.

Substituting equations 5.6 and 5.7 into equation 5.5 yields

$$\dot{m} + \dot{b} = [g - \tau] + (i-\pi)b - \pi m \tag{5.8}$$

If we assume that bonds are linked to the actual inflation rate then $i=\rho+\pi$, and hence $\rho=i-\pi$, where ρ is the instantaneous real interest rate paid on indexed bonds. Equation 5.8 then may be written (with time indexes reintroduced) in the following way:

$$\dot{m}(s) + \dot{b}(s) = [g(s) - \tau(s)] + \rho(s)b - \pi(s)m(s) \tag{5.9}$$

The first two terms in equation 5.9 are the changes in real monetary base and in the real stock of indexed bonds over time. The first term on the right-hand side of 5.9 is the real government deficit, the second term is the real interest burden of the stock indexed bonds outstanding, and the final term represents the real value of the inflation tax collected. In order to get a one adjustment (discrete) period approximation to equation (5.9), we integrate (5.9) over one adjustment period ($t - 1$ to t). Since the period of adjustment of indexed bonds is only one month in Brazil it is safe to assume that the inflation rate is roughly constant over the interval. The approximation to equation 5.9 is thus[27]

$$\Delta m(t) + \Delta b(t) = \delta + \rho b(t-1) - \pi m(t-1) \tag{5.10}$$

where δ is the (constant) one period government deficit.

Finally, it should be noted that the instantaneous rate of change compounded continuously for a variable Z, γ, is related to its discrete (constant) rate of change, $\Gamma = [Z(t)/Z(t-1)] - 1$, in the following way:

$$\gamma = \ln(1+\Gamma) \tag{5.11}$$

where ln is the natural logarithm (base e).[28] Hence, equation 5.10 becomes

$$\Delta m(t) + \Delta b(t) = \delta + \ln(1+r)b(t-1) - \ln(1+\Pi)m(t-1) \tag{5.12}$$

where r and Π are the one period real interest rate on indexed bonds and inflation rate, respectively. Notice that this approximation captures the continuous compounding effect mentioned earlier owing to discrete inflation adjustments. This is due to the fact that $\ln(1 + r) < r$ for all non-zero r as mentioned above.[29] In other words, the actual real debt burden is less than the real one period interest rate paid on the bonds. Finally, the last term represents the amount of inflation tax 'revenue' on real cash balances received by the government.

Following Cagan (1956), the (constant) inflation rate which maximises inflation tax revenue can be derived in the following way.[30] Suppose the demand for monetary base has the following form:

$$\left(\frac{M}{P}\right)^D = e^{-\alpha\pi} = e^{-\alpha \ln(1+\Pi)} \tag{5.13}$$

Substituting equation 5.13 into the inflation tax term appearing in equation 5.12 yields the following expression for inflation tax revenue (IT):

$$IT = \ln(1+\Pi)e^{-\alpha \ln(1+\Pi)} \tag{5.14}$$

Maximising Π with respect to the yearly inflation rate, Π, yields the following estimate for the yearly inflation rate which maximises inflation tax revenue:

$$\Pi^* = e^{\frac{1}{\alpha}} - 1 \tag{5.15}$$

The semi-elasticity of real money base demand to inflation ($-\alpha$) has been estimated to fall between -0.6 and -0.9. Hence if α is constant, the (constant) inflation rate which maximises inflation tax revenue falls between 200% and 640% per year. As shown below, the assumption that α stays constant for all levels of inflation is probably not a good one and becomes larger in magnitude at higher levels of inflation. Hence, the inflation rate that maximises inflation tax revenue will, in all likelihood, be closer to 640% per year.

One should note that these values should be read with caution because they ignore the effect inflation has on real output, which has a positive effect on real money demand. If higher inflation causes higher real GDP in a 'Phillips curve' manner, then money demand would tend to be higher in the analysis above and the inflation rate that will maximise inflation taxes revenues will tend to be higher than these numbers. If inflation risk increases with the inflation rate, and thus higher inflation adversely affects real GDP, then the inflation rate that maximises inflation tax revenue will tend to be lower than those reported here. Given these qualifications, the reported range of inflation rates only indicate the inflation-tax-maximising inflation rates but by no means represent exact measurements.

Table 5.2 shows estimates of the inflation tax revenue collected by the Brazilian government from 1965 to 1985 in constant 1977 cruzeiros and as a percentage of GDP. The maximum revenue in constant 1977 cruzeiros was reached in 1980 at an inflation rate of 110.2%. The maximum inflation tax as a percentage of GDP was reached in 1983 with an inflation rate of 211%. These estimates, however, may not be indicative of the inflation tax achievable by the Brazilian government, as it could be argued that it did not fully exploit its ability to tax cash balances. The main message of Table 5.2, however, is that the inflation tax remained a large source of revenue for the Brazilian government (between 3% and 4% of GDP between 1979 and 1985) in spite of widespread financial indexation.

More difficult (and perhaps more important) is to determine whether or not the existence of financial indexation renders the inflation tax significantly smaller than it would have been without it. One could argue that in a chronic inflation individuals will hold a large proportion of their portfolio in the form of indexed assets and a minimal amount in money, thereby shrinking the inflation tax base. The above analysis suggests that this is not the case, because inflation tax revenues did not fall significantly as financial indexation progressed. In fact, inflation tax revenue increased as the Brazilian economy became more indexed. On the other hand, as argued earlier, the existence of indexed bonds inhibits individuals from

Table 5.2   Brazil: Inflation, the Real Monetary Base, and the
Inflation Tax

	Inflation $(\Pi)^{(a)}$	$m^{(b)}$	Inflation tax $=\ln(1 + \Pi)m(t - 1)^{(c)}$	As % of GDP
1964	91.9	0.6030		
1965	34.5	0.6712	0.1785	2.85
1966	38.8	0.6872	0.2201	3.31
1967	24.3	0.6830	0.1498	2.09
1968	25.4	0.7530	0.1544	1.99
1969	20.2	0.8420	0.1386	1.33
1970	19.2	0.8560	0.1482	1.41
1971	19.8	0.9060	0.1637	1.40
1972	15.5	0.9740	0.1404	1.07
1973	15.7	1.1360	0.1422	0.89
1974	34.5	1.2240	0.3374	1.85
1975	29.4	1.2900	0.3158	1.55
1976	46.3	1.3174	0.4902	2.05
1977	38.8	1.3885	0.4321	1.79
1978	40.8	1.4730	0.4749	1.72
1979	77.2	1.6100	0.8426	2.85
1980	110.2	1.3396	1.1962	3.89
1981	95.2	1.0520	0.8962	3.14
1982	99.7	0.9730	0.7280	2.51
1983	211.0	0.7390	1.1044	4.10
1984	223.8	0.6770	0.8683	3.21
1985	235.1	0.7270	0.8185	2.80

[a] Inflation as measured by the annual percentage increase in the average General Price Index (IGP-DI) of *Conjuntura Economica*.
[b] The average monetary base in constant 1977 billions of cruzeiros.
[c] The inflation tax in constant 1977 billions of cruzeiros.
Source: Banco Central do Brasil, *Boletim* and *Conjuntura Economica*.

holding other types of constant-purchasing-power assets that would escape seigniorage, such as the U.S. dollar, which has been the most important in recent Latin American experiences.[31] If indexed bonds diminish the flight to the dollar, the inflation tax base might not shrink as fast as in the absence of indexed bonds. It seems reasonable to postulate that both effects occur simultaneously. The difficulty lies in separating them.

One possible approach is to estimate a demand for base money function which has a more general form than equation (13). The one used here is the following:

$$m - p = \alpha_0 + \alpha_1 y = (\alpha_2 + \alpha_3 \pi)\pi + (\alpha_4 \pi + \alpha_5)\vartheta \qquad (5.16)$$

where m is the natural logarithm of the average yearly monetary base, p is the natural logarithm of the average yearly price level, π is the logarithmic inflation rate, y is the natural logarithm of real GDP, and ϑ is the growth in the average real stock of indexed bonds.

Notice that the equation attempts to separate the determinants of the semi-elasticity of real base money demand with respect to the inflation rate. The effects of indexed bonds are separated into two: (1) the direct effect or 'substitution' effect on real money balances as measured by α_5, and (2) the effect on the sensitivity of money demand to a larger real stock of indexed government bonds of inflation as measured by α_4. For the hypotheses outlined above to carry weight, α_4 and α_5 should be of opposite sign.

A second-order effect of the inflation rate on the sensitivity of real money demand is also included in equation 5.16 and is measured by $2\alpha_3$. If the sensitivity of real money demand to inflation increases with the inflation rate (i.e. α in equation 5.13 becomes larger in magnitude as inflation increases) then α_3 should be negative.

Equation 5.16 was estimated using yearly data from 1946 to 1985 for Brazil.[32] The results are as follows.

$$m - p = \begin{matrix} -0.64 \\ (3.80{***}) \end{matrix} + \begin{matrix} 0.60y \\ (13.248{***}) \end{matrix} + \begin{matrix} [0.246 \\ (0.937) \end{matrix} - \begin{matrix} 0.739\pi]\pi \\ (3.623{***}) \end{matrix}$$

$$+ \begin{matrix} (-0.359\pi \\ (1.222) \end{matrix} + \begin{matrix} 0.315)\vartheta. \\ (2.047){**} \end{matrix} \qquad (5.17)$$

$$F_{(5,32)} = 72.808{*} \qquad R^2 = 0.9169 \qquad \text{D.W.} = 1.625$$

The t statistics appear in parentheses below the parameter estimates corresponding to the null hypothesis that the parameter equals zero and *, **, and *** signify rejection of this hypothesis at significance levels of 10%, 5%, and 1%, respectively. One should note that significant pairwise multicolinearity existed, which may cause significant partial regression coefficients to appear not significantly different from zero. The coefficients that corresponded to the direct and interaction effects of inflation were jointly significantly different from zero.

The results in equations 5.14 separate the different effects of indexed bonds. The direct effects of increases in the stock of indexed bonds significantly increase the demand for monetary base. The interaction term between inflation and real indexed bonds does not significantly cause the demand for real monetary base to fall, although the sign is correct in the sense that it is opposite the direct effect of real growth in indexed bonds. The coefficient of the squared rate of inflation is significantly negative, while the coefficient for inflation is positive but not significantly different from zero. Hence the overall effect of inflation on the demand for real monetary base is negative, while growth in indexed bonds dampens the effect.

The average semi-elasticity of the demand for real money base with respect to inflation is $(-0.246 - 0.739(0.2) - 0.359(0.1)) = -0.43$, which is below the range of previously estimated values for α. If we follow Cagan's method of calculation (in spite of the fact it ignores the effect of inflation on output), the inflation rate which maximises inflation tax revenue according to these estimates is 925% per year.

These empirical results offer some support for the theory argued above. One should note, however, that the parameter estimates were sensitive to the inclusion or exclusion of certain variables and should be taken as only as indicative. The analysis might be improved by the use of monthly data and perhaps the estimation of a simultaneous system of equations which incorporates the real sector of the economy, a price equation, and a more extensive set of portfolio balance relationships. Further, money demand functions of this type suffer from errors in the variables problems, especially with monthly data, and one should use instrumental variables estimators in statistical analyses. Such an exercise is outside the scope of this chapter and is left to further research.

The main conclusion of this section is that the inflation tax provided the Brazilian government with substantial resources over the period 1964–85 in spite of the existence of indexed bonds. Clearly, the existence of indexed bonds did not render the inflation tax inoperative. However, the question of whether the existence of indexed bonds improved the Brazilian government's ability to maintain the inflation tax base by avoiding massive capital flight remains unresolved.

5.4 THE BRAZILIAN EXPERIENCE WITH FINANCIAL INDEXATION

In 1964, the Brazilian government introduced financial indexation on a large scale in Brazil with the creation of an indexed government bond called Adjustable Obligations of the National Treasury (ORTNs).[33] The 'Capital Markets Law' of 1965 extended the ORTN indexing rule to private debt instruments such as bills of exchange, corporate debentures, time deposits, and certificates of deposit.[34] After the creation of the Housing Finance System in 1964, indexation was extended to its passbook savings accounts (cadernetas de poupança) and to housing bonds in 1966.[35] The forced-savings funds described in Chapter 3, the Job Tenure Guarantee Fund (FGTS) of 1966, the Social Integration Fund (PIS) of 1970, and the Public Servants Patrimonial Program (PASEP) of 1971 were all indexed to the ORTN rate. Later, state governments exercised their ability to float their own adjustable obligations, specifically the states of Minas Gerais, São Paulo, Rio Grande do Sul, Rio de Janeiro and Santa Catarina.

Tables 5.3, 5.4, and 5.5 show the stocks of both indexed and non-indexed assets for the period 1965–85.[36] As noted above and shown in Table 5.1, indexed financial assets came to dominate as inflation increased over this period. The correlation coefficients of the stock of voluntary indexed assets (i.e. excluding forced-savings funds) and total indexed assets with the inflation rate for the period 1965–85 are 0.919 and 0.903, respectively, both significantly greater than zero at less than the 0.1% level. In other words, the degree of indexation increased as inflation increased.

The long-run objective of creating financial indexation was to increase savings.[37] Theoretical arguments as to why indexation (or interest rate liberalisation) will or will not increase savings were reviewed in Chapter 1. Other studies have shown that although financial savings increased after the introduction of indexation, private savings as a percentage of GDP were relatively insensitive to the introduction of indexation.[38] This conclusion agrees with Giovannini's (1985) evidence, which appears in Chapter 1.[39] Table 5.6 shows savings rates as a percentage of GDP by sector over the period 1965–84. The savings rate by the private sector was relatively constant at around 19% of GDP until 1979–80. The fall in the savings rate between 1980 and 1981 to around 15% of GDP can be explained by the fact that indexation was set at the beginning of 1980 at around 50%, while inflation reached around 100%.[40] The absence of a recovery of the savings rate after the preannounced indexation policy was abandoned in 1981 can be explained by the deep recession that Brazil experienced between 1981 and 1983. Hence, one might conclude that although indexation did not cause higher savings rates it kept savings rates from falling as inflation accelerated.[41] Many have argued that

Table 5.3   Brazil: Voluntary Indexed Financial Assets, 1965–85
(Cr$ Billions)

	Savings deposits	Housing bonds	ORTN[a]	Other[b]	Total
1965	—	0.009	0.430	0.033	0.472
1966	0.018	0.036	1.401	0.033	1.488
1967	0.086	0.290	2.482	0.038	2.896
1968	0.330	0.644	3.491	0.698	5.163
1969	1.980	1.195	5.881	0.911	9.967
1970	2.082	2.007	9.412	1.171	14.672
1971	3.771	3.128	11.564	1.490	19.953
1972	7.713	5.015	15.976	1.721	30.425
1973	14.122	6.517	20.944	3.232	44.815
1974	28.925	8.287	32.969	5.449	75.630
1975	55.234	8.937	60.112	13.870	138.153
1976	107.539	9.779	84.397	23.608	225.320
1977	177.280	10.809	119.380	31.226	338.695
1978	288.700	10.900	163.000	46.700	509.300
1979	523.500	12.949	251.200	84.300	871.949
1980	984.800	16.642	589.200	150.300	1,740.362
1981	2,484.900	26.563	1,986.600	413.100	4,911.163
1982	5,671.400	29.621	6,399.400	1,033.800	13,134.221
1983	18,153.500	79.000	20,722.900	2,674.900	41,630.300
1984	63,390.000	135.000	84,773.300	8,507.200	156,805.500
1985	215,234.000	127.000	341,129.700	34,110.000	590,600.700

[a] Includes state adjustable obligations ORTM, ORTP, ORTE-RS, ORTBA, ORTC, and ORTRJ.
[b] Outside the Central Bank.
Source: Banco Central do Brasil, *Boletim.*

the quality of savings and their allocation improved after the 1964 reforms.[42] Since that is the subject of the remaining chapters of this study, it will not be discussed here.

As described above, indexed bonds were not initially in large demand because individuals preferred investing in the legal and illegal bills of exchange market. The large default by the Mannesman group in 1967 led to (1) a movement into *ex post* indexed assets, and (2) stricter legislation regulating the bills of exchange market.[43] The latter development laid the foundation for the revitalisation of that market. The former represented the point when latent demand for indexed assets became an effective demand which, as noted earlier, grew throughout the period, especially as inflation accelerated after 1973.

Table 5.4   Brazil: Forced Savings Funds and Total Indexed Assets,
1965–85 (Cr$ Billions)

	FGTS	PIS	PASEP	Total forced savings funds	Total indexed assets[a]
1965	—	—	—	—	0.472
1966	—	—	—	—	1.488
1967	0.629	—	—	0.629	3.525
1968	1.902	—	—	1.902	7.065
1969	3.611	—	—	3.611	13.578
1970	6.040	—	—	6.040	20.712
1971	9.813	0.296	0.242	10.351	30.304
1972	14.788	1.628	1.354	17.770	48.195
1973	20.982	4.154	3.602	28.738	73.553
1974	32.897	10.192	7.242	50.331	124.961
1975	48.413	20.594	12.644	81.051	219.204
1976	79.011	38.886	20.812	138.709	364.029
1977	128.749	39.235	35.556	233.540	572.235
1978	206.172	116.813	57.372	380.357	889.657
1979	347.107	209.468	103.865	660.440	1,532.389
1980	631.156	406.573	182.010	1,220.143	2,960.503
1981	1,370.520	972.184	464.873	2,747.577	7,658.740
1982	3,057.848	2,068.561	975.520	6,101.929	19,236.150
1983	8,041.901	6,354.194	2,570.871	16,966.966	58,597.266
1984	25,875.692	20,600.965	9,308.395	55,785.052	212,590.552
1985	92,116.910	76,000.000[b]	32,073.876	200,140.791	790,741.491

[a] Both voluntary and forced.
[b] estimated.
Source: Banco Central do Brasil, *Boletim.*

The issue of *ex post* indexed liabilities by private sector institutions, however, was resisted throughout the period. *Ex post* indexed certificates of deposits only became common in the period 1982–3, when competition for domestic funds between the government and the private sector intensified with the curtailment of foreign credit in 1982. This competition manifested itself in heavy government borrowing in domestic financial markets in order to meet foreign debt service.[44]

There are various reasons for private sector resistance to issuing indexed liabilities. Baer and Beckerman (1980) argue that risk-averse firms would avoid creating liabilities in a constant-purchasing-power unit of account because their earnings are not perfectly linked to the inflation rate.[45] This argument is persuasive and generally correct.

Table 5.5   Brazil: Non-indexed Assets 1965–85 (Cr$ Billions)

	LTN	Time deposits	Bills of exchange	Demand deposits	Cash	Total
1965	—	0.257	0.695	7.365	1.730	10.047
1966	—	0.314	0.906	8.129	2.243	11.592
1967	—	0.704	2.105	12.448	2.944	18.201
1968	—	1.449	4.558	17.101	4.080	27.188
1969	—	2.103	6.172	22.601	5.384	36.265
1970	0.699	4.442	8.285	28.639	6.719	48.784
1971	3.880	9.487	15.177	37.710	8.555	74.809
1972	10.204	17.017	20.973	52.282	11.547	112.023
1973	17.400	25.881	34.820	77.408	16.427	171.936
1974	14.801	33.471	42.608	104.378	20.807	216.001
1975	37.400	54.568	55.809	148.314	31.631	327.122
1976	69.404	73.132	68.792	202.152	46.193	459.210
1977	121.001	133.711	85.633	277.065	65.205	682.615
1978	194.500	226.457	128.312	390.900	94.120	1,034.269
1979	266.500	406.660	186.912	670.900	167.300	1,701.272
1980	255.500	639.227	274.775	1,137.500	290.700	2,597.702
1981	1,101.900	687.753	493.607	1,979.000	523.200	4,785.460
1982	1,462.600	1,560.197	1,785.280	3,237.000	1,010.000	9,055.077
1983	4,712.200	9,647.000	4,697.000	6,784.500	1,881.000	27,721.700
1984	5,501.700	39,986.000	15,687.000	19,833.000	6,247.000	87,254.700
1985	61,600.000	147,877.000	47,828.000	82,890.000	23,741.000	363,936.000

Source: Banco Central do Brasil: *Boletim.*

One should not ignore the fact, however, that the usury law was not abolished when indexation was created. As long as financial institutions, especially commercial banks and 'financeiras', could count on a reliable source of funds, the usury law enabled them to extract monopolistic rent from intermediation. This was due to the fact that individual holders of deposits and bills of exchange had limited ability to receive more than the usury law allowed (deposit holders received luxury services and bills of exchange holders received the value of the discount). On the other hand, commercial banks and 'financeiras' avoided usury law interest ceilings on loans, as demonstrated in Chapter 2. Private sector financial institutions resisted indexation because the law allowed them to maintain a protected position in financial markets.[46]

Table 5.7 contains loan and deposit interest rates calculated by Christoffersen (1969) for the period 1952–66 and the implied spread.[47] It should be noted that the loan interest rates are understated, because the use of compensating balances and immediate interest payment will cause commercial bank balance sheets to over-

Table 5.6   Brazil: Investment and Savings by Sector 1965–84 (Percentage of GDP)

	Gross investment rate	Domestic savings		Foreign savings[a]
		Private	Government	
1965	22.0	21.3	1.9	–1.2
1966	22.1	17.0	5.0	0.1
1967	19.4	16.2	2.2	1.0
1968	21.5	15.3	4.9	1.3
1969	24.8	18.1	6.0	0.7
1970	25.5	18.8	5.4	1.3
1971	26.0	17.5	5.8	2.7
1972	26.1	17.7	5.8	2.6
1973	27.5	19.0	6.3	2.2
1974	30.5	19.2	4.5	6.8
1975	32.1	22.9	3.8	5.4
1976	27.4	19.1	4.3	4.0
1977	25.9	19.7	3.9	2.3
1978	25.2	19.5	2.3	3.4
1979	23.1	15.3	2.2	4.8
1980	23.3	16.1	1.3	5.4
1981	22.9	15.9	1.1	4.4
1982	21.0	15.2	0.3	5.7
1983	16.5	14.4	–0.8	3.3
1984	15.0	15.0	—	0.0
1985	17.4	17.3	—	0.1

[a] Includes factor income.
Sources: National Accounts, IBGE, Banco Central do Brasil, *Brazil Economic Program*, March 1989, and Celso L. Martone (1987): *Macroeconomic Policies, Debt Accumulation, and Adjustment in Brazil, 1965–1985*, World Bank Discussion Papers, No. 8.

state the value of loans.[48] The spread, although understated, increases with the inflation rate.[49]

Table 5.8 contains effective 'duplicata' discount and working capital loan interest rates and the interest rates on certificates of deposit for the period 1973–85. Again, as in the prior period, the spread increases with inflation. As the discussion in Chapter 2 indicated, the cost structure of commercial banks was organised around the maximisation of demand deposits. The creation of indexed liabilities would imply a complete restructuring of commercial banks' productive structure. It should therefore come as no surprise that indexation and the elimination of the usury law was resisted by the financial

142   *Capital Markets in the Development Process*

Table 5.7   Brazil: Average Nominal Interest Rates on Commercial Bank
Loans and Deposits, 1952–66

	Loan interest rate	Deposit interest rate	spread[a]	Inflation[b]
1952	14.1	4.1	9.61	10.3
1953	13.0	4.7	7.93	15.1
1954	13.0	4.9	7.72	30.3
1955	13.8	4.4	9.00	13.1
1956	14.5	4.2	9.89	19.2
1957	15.1	4.2	10.49	12.5
1958	16.0	4.7	10.79	12.2
1959	17.5	4.0	12.98	37.7
1960	18.6	4.0	14.04	30.9
1961	18.2	4.0	13.65	38.1
1962	21.0	3.8	16.57	53.2
1963	27.5	3.6	23.07	73.5
1964	33.2	3.6	28.57	91.6
1965	36.9	3.4	32.40	51.2
1966	32.7	2.0	30.10	36.0

[a] Calculated as $[(1 + i_L)/(1 + i_d)] - 1$ where i_L is the average loan interest rate and i_d is the average deposit interest rate.
[b] Percentage changes in the General Price Index (IGP-DI) of *Conjuntura Economica*.
Source: Leif E. Christoffersen (1969): 'Taxas de Juro e a Estrutura de um Sistema de Bancos em Condições Inflacionárias,' in *Revista Brasileira de Economia*, Vol.23, No.2, p.28.

sector. If Tables 5.7 and 5.8 are any indication, commercial and investment banks were able to maintain cost structures similar to those of the previous period.

The short-run objective of introducing indexed bonds was to create a viable market for government debt. This was accomplished. The medium-term objective of indexation was to bring down interest rates, because high real interest rates persisted even after the initial stabilisation shock of the period 1964–7. The government tried to get the private sector to index liabilities to the inflation rate, hoping to reduce the inflation risk premium component of interest rate. Additionally, the discussion above suggests that interest rates on nominal loans contained a monopoly rent component. What resulted was the peculiar 'pre-fixed indexation' system.[50]

Pre-fixed indexed assets and liabilities from private sector institutions would earn indexation equal to the (government's) expected inflation rate over the period in addition to interest. Baer and Beck-

Table 5.8 Brazil: Average Working Capital loans, Duplicata Discounts, and Certificate of Deposit Interest Rates, 1973–85 (% Per Year)

	Working capital loans[a]	Duplicata discounts[b]	Certificates of deposit[c]	Spread A[d]	Spread B[e]
1973	34.0	28.4	24.3	7.8	3.3
1974	38.5	32.9	31.8	5.1	0.8
1975	39.7	43.9	36.0	2.7	5.8
1976	52.9	57.7	40.0	9.2	12.6
1977	59.7	63.7	48.0	7.9	10.6
1978	70.4	69.7	50.3	13.4	12.9
1979	83.5	87.6	57.5	16.5	19.1
1980	88.0	110.0	64.1	14.6	28.0
1981	141.7	160.1	106.8	16.9	25.8
1982	160.3	223.9	116.4	23.0	49.7
1983	266.8	278.9	160.8	40.6	75.5
1984	348.6	379.0	240.8	31.6	40.6
1985	314.2	496.4	285.4	7.5	54.8

[a] Effective (including taxes compensating balances, commissions, etc.) average monthly interest rates on 180-day working capital loans extended by investment banks.
[b] Effective average monthly interest rates on 90-day duplicata discounts.
[c] Average monthly interest rates on 180-day certificates of deposit.
[d] Interest rate spread of working capital loans over certificates of deposit.
[e] Interest rate spread of duplicata discounts over certificates of deposit.
Source: *Análise Financeira.*

erman (1980) argue that the private sector preferred 'pre-fixed' indexation over 'post-fixed' indexation owing to inflation risk considerations. If a firm has *ex post* indexed liabilities, it will not know in advance what the nominal payment of interest and monetarily corrected principal will be, as they depend upon the realised inflation over the period *ex post*. Since a firm's receipts are not perfectly indexed to the inflation rate, this would expose the firm to balance sheet risk.[51]

There is, however, another good reason why financial intermediaries would choose pre-fixed indexation over post-fixed indexation. Commercial banks and 'financeiras' were able to earn monopoly rents disguised as risk premia on loans by requiring compensating balances and charging interest on the date the loan was granted. With pre-fixed indexation this practice is still possible, because the nominal interest payment (and rate) is known at the time the loan is granted. If post-fixed indexation were used, on the other hand, then compensating balances would be difficult to justify (and would have to be post-fixed indexed) and interest charges could be made only when interest (and principal) were paid.[52] Hence, the pre-fixed indexation scheme allowed private financial intermediaries to maintain (and increase) profits without significantly changing their cost structures.[53]

In January 1970, the Brazilian government created National Treasury Bills (LTNs), which carried pre-fixed indexation and were of short maturity (90 and 180 days) in order to conduct open-market operations. Until then, monetary policy had been conducted mainly through changes in the required reserve ratio. LTNs initially allowed short-term liquidity control because they compete directly with bills of exchange, certificates of deposit, and other pre-fixed indexed assets. The LTN proved to be popular with commercial banks in the first couple of years after their creation because they could hold free reserves in the form of an interest-bearing, highly liquid asset.[54] As will be shown, commercial banks eventually came to prefer holding free reserves in repurchase agreements using ORTNs.

The persistence of high real (loan) interest rates after three years (1964–7) of sluggish growth and (slowly) falling inflation rates led the government to impose direct interest rate ceilings on loans.[55] As in the past, these ceilings were easily avoided by financial intermediaries. Beginning in 1972, interest rate ceilings were then extended to the liabilities of financial institutions. Table 5.9 summarises the values of interest rate ceilings on prefixed indexed liabilities of financial institutions.

As long as inflation declined, as it did through 1973 (see Table 5.2), the Brazilian financial system of pre-fixed and post-fixed indexed assets, inflows of foreign funds through resolution 63 loans, and an effective apparatus for open market operations fostered an orderly and strong economic expansion from 1967 to 1973. Interest rates on pre-fixed indexed assets were in general market-determined, as was the spread between pre-fixed and post-fixed indexed assets until 1973. With the OPEC oil embargo of 1973, inflation accelerated from 15.7% in 1973 to 35% in 1974 and interest rate ceilings on pre-fixed indexed assets became binding. The resultant increase in the spread between pre-fixed indexed and post-fixed indexed assets from around 6% for 1970 through 1972 to 12.5% in 1973 and 22.9% in 1975 (see Table 5.10), compounded by expectations of accelerating inflation and increased 'uncertainty' about inflation, led to a large portfolio shift from pre-fixed indexed assets into post-fixed indexed assets. This is shown in Table 5.1 by an increase in the voluntary indexed-

Table 5.9   Brazil: Interest Rate Ceilings on Pre-fixed Indexed Assets, 1969–79 (% Per Year)

Time period	Deposits[a]	Bills of Exchange[b]
1 June 1969–1 March 1970	30%	Free
1 March 1970–5 January 1972	Free	Free
16 January 1972–15 January 1973	24%	25.5%
16 January 1973–5 May 1974	21%	23%
6 May 1974–22 July 1974	24.5%	25.5%
23 July 1974–5 February 1975	27.5%	28%
8 March 1975–1979	Free	Free

[a] Commercial bank and investment bank time deposits.
[b] Financeira and investment bank bills of exchange.
Source: Walter L. Ness, Jr. (1977): *A Inflûencia da Correção Monetária no Sistema Financeiro* (Rio de Janeiro: IBMEC), p. 73.

Table 5.10   Brazil: Average Effective Interest Rates on 6-Month Bills of Exchange and 6–12-month ORTNs (% Per Year)

	Bills of Exchange	ORTN	Spread
1966	29.1	55.5	20.5
1967	33.8	36.5	2.1
1968	31.7	39.8	6.8
1969	30.4	35.5	3.9
1970	30.7	37.6	5.3
1971	28.1	36.1	6.3
1972	25.3	32.5	5.7
1973	22.3	37.6	12.5
1974	25.1	53.8	22.9
1975	26.7	40.0	10.6

Source: Walter L. Ness, Jr. (1977); *A Influência da Correção Monetária no Sistema Financeiro* (Rio de Janeiro: IBMEC), pp. 173–8.

to-non-indexed asset ratio from 0.261 in 1973 to 0.491 in 1976.

This portfolio shift caused a financial crisis because private sector institutions which issue pre-fixed indexed liabilities found themselves illiquid while institutions which issued post-fixed indexed liabilities (e.g. state banks, Caixas Economicas and other SFH institutions) saw their liabilities increase faster then they could create new assets. Monetary policy, which had been tight in the beginning of 1974 in order to contain inflation, became very loose as the monetary authorities acted as the lender of last resort by injecting resources into the system with open-market operations and lowering the required reserve ratio. Additionally, the Central Bank extended loans to troubled institutions at a highly subsidised nominal interest rate of 6% per year, which came under the heading of 'compensatory refinancing' in 1975.[56] The failure of the Halles group in 1974 compounded the flight to post-fixed indexed assets.

Interest rates could not achieve equilibrium in the existing institutional setting. With binding interest rate ceilings on pre-fixed indexed assets, the burden of interest rate adjustment fell on the nominal interest rates of post-fixed indexed assets. Adjustment, however, was impossible as the nominal interest rate on these assets depended upon the *ex post* realised inflation rate and therefore could not adjust downward *ex ante* to stem or at least smooth the portfolio shift. Small adjustments upward in the interest rate ceilings (see Table 5.6) proved insufficient. In August 1975, the government introduced a 'purged' ORTN index, which eliminated random or temporary price increases due to 'supply shocks' from the index. Although this lowered the indexation component on the nominal interest rate on ORTNs, they started selling at a discount to make up for this 'index tampering'.[57] This measure also proved insufficient to realign interest rates.

When prices are rigid quantities must adjust. The Brazilian government introduced a stepped-up policy of 're-lending' (repasses) from public institutions such as the BNDE, the BNH, FINAM, the Caixas Economicas, and the Central Bank that had post-fixed indexed liabilities to private sector institutions in difficulty.[58] To further promote this reallocation of resources from public sector to the private sector, indexation on BNDE loans was limited to 20% per year in November 1974 and the BNDE subsidiaries EMBRAMEC, IBRASA, and FIBASE were created in 1975 to underwrite preferred stock.[59] This re-lending scheme allowed public sector institutions to increase their assets while it eased the liquidity problems of the private sector. Unfortunately, a good portion of this credit expansion was ultimately financed through money creation. The financial crisis forced the monetary authorities to abandon a tight monetary stance for an expansionary one. The feeling that a tight monetary policy to fight inflation could only be implemented with market-determined interest rates led to interest rate liberalisation in 1976.

It would be extremely shortsighted to argue that the only cause of the problems experienced by financial markets was faulty interest rate policy, although it did exacerbate financial market instability.

Direct interest rate controls were imposed because real interest rates on loans did not decline, as predicted by the McKinnon–Shaw argument. The main failure of interest rate policy in this context is that it was not able to do what it was intended to do, which was reduce the loan rates extended to the private sector. Secondly, the portfolio shift continued even in the context of relatively free interest rates, as Table 5.1 shows. Clearly, risk and uncertainty, especially inflationary uncertainty, were just as important, as rates of return, if not more so.

During the financial crisis of 1974–6 the use of repurchase agreements with ORTNS first became popular. This allowed financial intermediaries to tailor (shorten) the effective maturity of indexed assets to individuals' tastes. This came to be known as the overnight market. Banks were able to finance their positions in indexed bonds and to charge a fixed rate of markup with these operations. Starting in the period 1974–6, maturities on these repurchase agreements started to shrink.[60] This facilitated the portfolio shift from pre-fixed to post-fixed indexed assets because their liquidity was essentially the same in spite of the fact that ORTNs are of two and five years' maturity. By 1984–5, a good portion of the maturities of these repurchase agreements was close to 24 hours. Hence, those who had access to the overnight market could hold an indexed asset whose liquidity was that of a demand deposit, as the only penalty for early withdrawal was the nominal interest foregone.

Baer and Beckerman (1980) identify the indexation system used in Brazil as the root of the problem. In their view, inflationary uncertainty increases as inflation increases, causing individuals to shift to a constant-purchasing-power asset (or unit of account). Although the relationship between inflation and inflation risk was an assumption on their part, the next section presents evidence confirming such a relationship. Institutions that are willing to index their liabilities will experience an increase in their exposure to inflation uncertainty, while institutions with nominal liabilities will have a lower exposure to inflation risk at the cost of a higher probability of bankruptcy due to illiquidity. Attempts by the government and Central Bank to rescue failing financial institutions usually involve inflationary finance. In other words, indexation renders the money supply endogenous.

A more flexible interest rate policy would have dampened the size and the necessity for the re-lending programmes used during 1974–6. Developments caused by the continuing flight to indexed assets in the context of relatively free interest rates from 1976 to 1985,[61] however, strengthened inflation feedback mechanisms in financial markets. A major catalyst to this process, other than increasing inflation risk (and uncertainty), was the collapse of foreign lending to Brazil in 1982 after the Mexican moratorium on interest payments on foreign debt. With no inflows of foreign saving, Brazil had to transfer resources to foreign lenders to meet debt service on the order of 5% of GDP. Because about 80% of Brazil's foreign debt outstanding falls under the responsibility of the public sector, the service of foreign debt necessitated a continuous transfer from the private to the public sector and then abroad. This process consequently led to large increases in public sector debt, which was comprised mainly of indexed bonds floated in the overnight market.[62]

As of 1978, the placing of ORTNs and LTNs by the Central Bank was achieved by the process termed the 'go round' auction.[63] The Central Bank through its dealers would communicate the desire to sell government bonds to financial institutions and then collect offers. It would then decide on a trading discount rate. This became a strong source of leverage for the commercial banks on the Central Bank between 1982 and 1985, as they could refuse to buy government bonds if conditions in the market were not to their liking. Most government bond debt by this time was financed in the overnight market. In other words, financial institutions were the main holders of government debt, financing their positions in indexed government bonds with repurchase agreements with the general public of very short maturity. Also, the development of a true interbank market for indexed government bonds (and funds) was pre-empted by a Central Bank resolution that forced financial institutions to clear repurchase agreements in government bonds only with bank reserves. Banks could not borrow and lend to each other using repurchase agreements to carry over their positions in government bonds until the next day. The situation forced the Central Bank to enter the market at the end of the day to buy on a twenty-four-hour basis any government bonds left unfinanced, thus directly expanding the monetary base.[64] Together, these institutional arrangements rendered a contractionary monetary policy unsustainable in the medium term in the context of the transfer of resources from the private to the public sector outlined above. If the Central Bank used open-market operations to tighten credit, interest rates in the overnight market rose. If the overnight interest rates rose higher than the average interest rate on the bonds outstanding held by financial institutions then they would begin to lose money on such operations. They would then refuse to purchase government bonds in the subsequent go round auction, forcing the Central Bank to ease credit because the government would not be able to finance itself. Such confrontations occurred at different times during the period 1982–5, the most severe of them leading to the fall of Minister of Finance Dornelles in August 1985.

Another way in which the continuing portfolio shift increased inflation feedback mechanisms was that it rendered open market operations in the pre-fixed indexed asset LTN impossible. As inflation accelerated and the system of repurchase agreements became more entrenched, the willingness of institutions to hold LTNs disappeared. Open market operations in LTNs could no longer be used while the system of repurchase agreements left open market operations in ORTNs unwieldy at best. This development precipitated the change in the ORTN indexation rule in March 1985. The indexation rate on post-fixed indexed assets in the current month would be determined by a three-month moving average of the previous three months.[65] Hence, one could know in advance the particular month's indexation rate on post-fixed indexed assets. This enabled the pre-fixed indexation rate to be the same as that on post-fixed indexed assets. Open-market operations again became a viable policy tool as long as inflation was constant or decreasing. From March to August 1985 a contractionary monetary policy was put into place through open-market sales of LTNs. This policy was reversed, for reasons outlined above, and the fact that as inflation accelerated over the period the indexation rate became considerably lower than the inflation rate.[66] Consequently, the indexation rule was discarded in August 1985 with the resignation of Minister Dornelles and the market for LTNs disappeared.

At the heart of these problems was the flight to indexed assets. Partial remedies, such as preannouncing indexation rates (1980) and changes in the indexation rule (1985), failed to change the trend. As inflation accelerated the shift to indexed assets continued, even in the context of relatively free interest rates. This was suggested by Baer and Beckerman (1980) as evidence supporting their assertion that inflation risk (and uncertainty) increases as inflation increases. We may now turn to determining whether such a relationship exists in the Brazilian case.

5.5 THE INFLATION RATE, INFLATION VARIANCE, AND UNCERTAINTY

Central to the above discussion of the usefulness of indexed bonds is the supposition that inflation uncertainty increases with the inflation rate. Milton Friedman (1977) maintains that it does, and that this is the predominant danger of inflation. Such a relationship would explain the shift into indexed assets discussed above. The problem is gauging whether one exists or not.

Many studies attempted to develop appropriate methodologies for testing whether positive relationships exist between inflation uncertainty and inflation rates. Most of these studies use some measure of the variance as a proxy for inflation uncertainty, in other words they reduce the question to one of inflation risk. A full discussion of these methodologies goes beyond the scope of this chapter.

Recent work by Engle (1983) shows that a positive relationship between the inflation rate and the variance of inflation suggested by Friedman (1977) does not exist in the United States. Inflation rates in the U.S., however, have historically been low (even in the 1970s) compared with those of Brazil. A relationship may exist at high levels of inflation. Kadota and Moura da Silva (1982) looked carefully at the Brazilian case and concluded that there was a significant inflation-level–inflation-variance trade-off.[67] The problem with this work is that inflation variance and levels are calculated using moving averages. Arguably, individuals form their inflation forecasts and variance estimates in a forward-looking way. Welch (1989) follows Engle (1982) in allowing the variance of inflation to be calculated around a 'rational' forecast of inflation and shows that a significant positive association between the variance of inflation and the inflation rate exists in Brazil.[68]

5.6 SUMMARY AND CONCLUSIONS

This chapter has explored some of the main arguments for and against financial indexation and has looked at the Brazilian case in detail. The main conclusions are the following. Governments have an interest in using indexed bonds as liabilities, especially in an inflationary context, because it keeps individuals from creating informal techniques of indexation which decrease the government's ability to collect seigniorage such as currency substitution. As there are difficulties and time lags in data collection and calculation of indexes, currency substitution may occur in spite of indexation if inflation reaches high enough levels. The cost of using indexation, however, is increased inflation feedback mechanisms and a decreased ability to reduce inflation rates. In the face of inability to reduce inflation rates, the inflation rate can either remain constant or increase. Hence, indexation allows the economy to 'live' with higher rates of inflation but does not make hyperinflations inevitable.

Secondly, inflation risk and uncertainty still exist in indexed economies, especially the Brazilian one. Recent studies show that inflation risk increases with the inflation rate in Brazil. Hence, as inflation accelerates individuals hold more and more indexed assets of one form or another. This occurred in Brazil throughout the period because there was a steady movement into indexed assets. Although the demand for indexed assets increased, the private sector refused to index their liabilities to the inflation rate even in the face of severe liquidity constraints and government pressure to do so. This can be explained as due to firms not wanting to be exposed to balance sheet risk and also as due to financial institutions standing to lose significantly in underwriting indexed liabilities or in offering their own indexed liabilities. Only as inflation accelerated and the Brazilian government started borrowing very heavily between 1982 and 1985 did private issues of indexed liabilities appear to any degree.

The fundamental problems of the Brazilian financial system were not solved by financial indexation, although it allowed the financial system to grow significantly. Those problems are: (1) the high cost of credit to the private sector from private sector institutions and (2) inflation. The former led to the use of direct interest rate controls, which exacerbated financial market instability as inflation accelerated after 1974. Although indexation allowed the system to 'live' with inflation it helped higher inflation become a fact of life.

The perception that the system of indexation made stabilisation an arduous task led to a few futile attempts at partial de-indexation in 1975 and 1980. The failure of these programmes led many to believe that full de-indexation was necessary, culminating in the monetary reform of February 1986, which was coined the Plano Cruzado.[69] Unfortunately, any such programme reintroduces the possibility of capital flight, currency substitution, and increased financial market instability.[70]

6 Commercial Banks, Investment Banks, Conglomeration, and the Financial Structure of Firms

6.1 INTRODUCTION

Commercial banks historically have been the key institutions in the Brazilian financial system. They were affected directly by the following developments in different degrees over the last twenty years: (1) the institution of formal financial indexation to the inflation rate and the subsequent strengthening of the secondary market for 'pre-fixed indexed' assets – LTNs, certificates of deposits, bills of exchange, etc. – and 'post-fixed indexed' assets – mainly ORTNs – in the so-called 'open market'; (2) competition from non-bank intermediaries; (3) the ability to contract foreign loans through Central Bank Resolution 63; and (4) the explicit promotion by the Brazilian government of financial conglomeration. It should be noted that the importance of non-bank competition *vis-à-vis* commercial banks was dampened by the process of conglomeration because commercial banks are usually the central institution in a financial conglomerate. The typical financial conglomerate in Brazil is centred on a commercial bank; other members are an investment bank, a 'financeira', a broker and dealer.[1]

Table 6.1 shows the number of financial institutions in existence in Brazil during different years. Clearly, the number of commercial banks has declined while that of non-bank institutions has been on the rise. These figures are interesting in light of the data shown in Chapter 3 in that private commercial banks were able to maintain their share of loans to the private sector in spite of the drastic reduction in the share of the whole monetary system in such credit. Hence, there seems to have been an increased amount of concentration in the commercial banking sector in credit to the private

Table 6.1   Brazil: Number of Financial Institutions (Publicly and Privately Owned)

	1950	1960	1970	1980
Commercial banks	413	338	172	118
Development banks	—	—	10	14
Real estate credit societies	—	—	44	58
Savings and loan associations	—	—	32	35
Investment banks	—	—	30	39
Federal caixas economicas	21	22	1	1
State caixas economicas	2	3	5	4
Distributor societies	—	—	575	453
Brokerage societies	—	—	404	270
Insurance companies	—	—	284	97
Credit, finance, and investment societies or 'financeiras'	—	—	214	120

Source: Banco Central do Brasil, *Boletim*; IBGE, *Anúario Estatistico*; Luiz A. Perdigão (1983): *Conglomerados Financeiros: Análise do Seu Desempenho no Brasil* (Rio de Janeiro: IBMEC), p. 35

sector. Further, the fact that most of the non-monetary financial institutions shown in Table 6.1 are affiliated with a commercial bank in a financial conglomerate underscores the importance of financial conglomerates in Brazil's current financial system.

This chapter examines the implications of the policies that led to these developments for the structure of the Brazilian financial system, the cost of credit, and monetary stability. Finally, a few conclusions will be drawn concerning the problems with the current financial structure.

6.2   THE STRUCTURE OF COMMERCIAL BANKS, 1964–85

The asset and liability structures of commercial banks underwent drastic changes over the period. Table 6.2 shows the shares of the main liability categories in total liabilities.[2] Total deposits declined from 77.6% of total liabilities in 1963 to 25.2% in 1985. This was due to the dramatic fall in demand deposits from 73.7% of total liabilities in 1963 to 9.8% in 1985. Time deposits generally rose over the period from around 4% of total liabilities in 1963 to 13% in 1985. Loans from the monetary authorities oscillated between 3% and 10% in no

Table 6.2 Brazil: Commercial Bank Liability Structure, 1963–84[a] (Percentage of Total Assets)

	Deposits				Monetary authority loans	Loans from other government financial institutions (BNH, FINAM, BNDES, CEF and State Banks)	Tax float	Foreign exchange operations	Capital account	Other liabilities
	Demand	Time	Other	Total						
1963	73.7	3.9	—	77.6	4.1	—	—	—	8.4	9.9
1964	69.6	3.4	—	72.9	4.3	—	—	—	13.2	9.6
1965	72.0	3.0	—	75.0	2.9	—	—	—	12.3	9.8
1966	60.6	2.7	6.8	70.1	4.1	—	—	—	14.1	11.7
1967	59.3	3.2	7.1	69.6	3.9	0.0	—	—	13.2	13.3
1968	57.7	4.0	7.8	69.5	6.4	1.9	2.4	6.7	13.1	
1969	54.7	2.7	7.6	65.1	7.1	2.0	2.7	9.4	13.7	
1970	52.8	3.5	7.2	63.5	6.6	2.7	2.4	11.0	13.8	
1971	48.6	5.6	4.4	58.6	5.6	4.8	5.0	12.0	13.9	
1972	46.9	7.0	3.5	57.4	5.0	5.3	5.5	14.4	12.4	
1973	48.7	5.2	3.6	58.0	5.4	5.8	4.6	14.0	12.2	
1974	45.4	4.4	4.0	53.8	7.4	7.3	5.4	14.7	11.3	
1975	45.3	4.4	3.2	53.0	9.6	9.7	5.3	11.0	10.8	
1976	39.1	4.7	2.7	46.6	8.3	11.8	5.4	16.6	11.3	
1977	35.1	7.0	2.6	44.7	7.6	13.1	5.5	17.4	11.8	
1978	29.9	9.1	2.8	41.8	5.8	13.6	4.5	21.8	12.5	

1979	28.9	8.5	3.7	41.2	5.0	12.8	3.8	27.8	9.8
1980	28.1	5.7	3.4	37.2	5.1	13.4	4.4	30.4	9.5
1981	23.8	5.7	2.9	32.3	5.0	13.6	4.2	34.1	10.8
1982	18.1	7.6	3.1	28.8	4.5	15.4	4.2	35.0	12.0
1983	11.5	8.7	2.2	22.4	3.3	13.0	2.0	47.4	12.1
1984	9.8	13.0	2.3	25.2	3.2	12.1	3.0	44.3	12.3

(a) Excludes the Bank of Brazil. Because of a change in accounting standards in 1967, the years before 1967 are not strictly comparable with those after and including 1967. Essentially those items listed as 'other liabilities' were incorporated in specific accounts as of 1967.

Source: Banco Central do Brasil, *Boletim*.

real discernable pattern, while loans from other government-owned financial institutions grew from 0% in 1967 to a peak of 15.4% in 1982, then fell slightly to 12.1% in 1985. This was due to the adjustment mechanism outlined in Chapter 5, when a large portfolio shift from pre-fixed indexed into post-fixed indexed assets occurred. Commercial bank capital remained fairly high, oscillating between 8% and 14% of total liabilities. Foreign exchange operations dramatically increased over the period, from 6.7% of total liabilities in 1967 to 44.3% in 1984.

As mentioned in previous chapters, the commercial banking system extended the services it offered, even becoming the main vehicle for tax collection in Brazil. Banks could hold the funds collected in taxes for as long as 15 days before remitting the receipts to federal, state, and local governments.[3] Hence, 'tax float' was an extremely cheap source of funds for banks because there are no associated financial costs as in the case of demand deposits. The data in Table 6.2 show that tax float grew from 2.4% of total liabilities in 1968 to a peak of 5.5% in 1977 then fell to 3% by 1985.

In sum, demand deposits fell as a source of funds for commercial banks, while time deposits, loans from public sector institutions, and foreign exchange operations through Central Bank resolution 63 (as discussed in the Introduction) increased in their importance as liabilities. Further, commercial banks remained fairly well capitalised in spite of these changes.

The asset structure of commercial banks over the period 1964–84 appears in Table 6.3. Total reserves fell from 27.5% of total assets in 1963 to 5.9% in 1984, owing mainly to the fall in demand deposits. Both required reserves and voluntary reserves declined, although the more accentuated fall occurred in voluntary reserves. This stems from the fact that the Brazilian monetary authorities actively used reserve requirements in conducting monetary policy in spite of the development of an open market. It should also be noted that required reserves could be held in the form of government bonds in varying proportions set by the Central Bank. The proportion of total required reserves which were held in the form of government bonds grew from 4% in 1964 to a peak of 69% in 1974, then fell gradually to 8% in 1983 before jumping back to 45% in 1984.[4] To the extent that required reserves could be held in the form of government bonds, required reserves were earning assets.

Credit operations maintained a relatively stable proportion of commercial bank assets, rising gradually from 53% in 1963 to a peak

Table 6.3 Brazil: Commercial Bank Asset Structure, 1963–84[a] (Percentage of Total Assets)

	Voluntary reserves				Required reserves			Total reserves	Credit operations	Foreign exchange operations	Equities	Bonds and securities	Permanent assets	'432 accounts'	Other accounts
	Vault cash	Deposits at Bank of Brazil	LTNs	Total	Coin	Government bonds	Total								
1963	6.0	9.8	—	15.8	10.3	1.8	12.1	27.9	53.9	2.1	—	1.6	4.4	—	10.1
1964	5.3	8.7	—	14.0	10.3	0.4	10.7	24.7	51.8	2.1	—	1.0	9.4	—	11.0
1965	4.3	8.9	—	13.2	13.8	0.5	14.3	27.5	49.4	1.1	—	0.9	8.2	—	12.9
1966	4.0	8.3	1.1	13.4	10.0	1.8	11.8	25.2	52.2	1.4	—	2.2	8.3	—	10.7
1967	3.4	5.5	0.8	9.7	9.6	2.6	12.2	21.9	54.9	1.0	—	3.4	7.5	—	11.3
1968	4.0	4.6	0.0	8.6	8.8	4.3	13.1	21.7	62.4	3.6	1.0	2.2	7.2	—	2.9
1969	2.7	4.2	0.2	7.1	6.4	5.2	11.6	18.7	63.4	2.8	1.1	2.4	6.8	—	5.9
1970	2.3	3.4	0.2	5.9	4.5	6.5	11.0	16.9	64.4	3.2	1.4	2.4	6.5	—	6.6
1971	1.6	3.7	1.5	6.8	4.2	6.0	10.2	17.0	65.0	4.2	1.8	2.9	5.4	—	5.5
1972	1.4	2.7	3.3	7.3	3.8	5.2	9.0	16.4	63.7	5.0	1.8	3.0	4.8	—	7.1
1973	1.6	2.6	3.1	7.3	4.3	5.8	10.1	17.4	64.6	5.3	1.9	2.8	4.1	—	5.8
1974	1.4	2.5	3.4	7.3	2.4	5.3	7.7	15.0	65.7	5.9	1.7	3.6	3.9	0.1	5.9
1975	1.2	1.8	2.8	5.8	1.5	5.3	6.8	12.6	69.1	4.2	1.6	5.1	3.9	0.1	5.1
1976	1.0	1.4	3.9	6.3	4.2	5.1	9.3	15.6	67.5	4.3	1.5	5.3	3.5	0.1	3.8
1977	0.8	1.1	3.3	5.2	6.4	4.6	11.0	16.2	65.8	6.1	1.5	4.2	3.8	0.6	3.9
1978	0.7	0.5	3.3	4.5	6.3	3.1	9.4	13.9	62.1	9.7	0.6	3.6	6.4	1.6	4.3
1979	0.9	0.8	1.9	3.6	6.0	2.0	8.0	11.6	60.7	12.9	0.0	2.9	7.1	2.1	4.8
1980	0.9	0.3	1.6	2.8	6.0	1.4	7.4	10.2	59.1	12.5	0.0	6.4	7.2	1.4	4.6
1981	0.7	0.2	2.6	4.0	4.0	1.0	5.0	8.5	55.9	12.6	0.0	8.9	8.1	2.5	3.4
1982	0.6	0.3	1.0	1.9	4.2	0.9	5.1	7.0	56.7	11.2	0.0	10.8	9.8	2.3	2.3
1983	0.3	0.1	0.0	0.4	3.0	0.3	3.3	3.7	51.0	18.0	0.0	7.2	9.3	7.4	3.4
1984	0.4	0.1	0.1	0.6	2.9	2.4	5.3	5.9	50.3	17.1	0.0	5.9	9.6	5.7	5.8

(a) Excluding the Bank of Brazil. Because accounting standards were changed in 1967, the data for years prior to 1967 are not strictly comparable with those in the years following and including 1967.

Source: Banco Central do Brasil, *Boletim*.

157

of 69.1% in 1975 then slowly falling to 50.3% in 1984. Bank holdings of bonds increased from 1.6% in 1963 to a peak of 10.82% in 1982, then fell back to 5.9% in 1984. Commercial bank holdings of equities were small as of 1969 and disappeared by 1978. Foreign exchange operations grew significantly throughout the period, from 2.1% of total assets in 1963 to a peak of 18% in 1983, then fell slightly to 17% in 1984. Similarly, '432 accounts' grew from 0.1% of total assets in 1974 to a peak of 7.4% in 1983, then fell slightly to 5.7% in 1984.[5]

In sum, commercial banks' asset structure, like the evolution of their liability structure, became increasingly linked to dollar-denominated instruments, although credit operations were not significantly affected. This was a natural consequence of the increase in commercial bank dollar-denominated liabilities through the matching of assets to liabilities implied by Central Bank resolution 63 'relending'.

Table 6.4 presents a profile of commercial bank loans by recipient sector from 1978 to 1984. Loans to industry fell from 40.2% of total loans in 1978 to 32.1% in 1984. Similarly, loans to firms dealing in commerce fell from 13.9% of all loans in 1978 to 7.8% in 1984. Loans to other business firms, which includes the service sector, however, increased from 7.3% in 1978 to a peak of 14.6% in 1983, then fell slightly to 13.5% in 1984. Loans to agriculture stayed relatively constant, oscillating between 8.6% and 10.3% until 1983, when subsidised credit programmes to agriculture were dismantled, falling drastically to 6.7% in 1984.

6.3   THE STRUCTURE OF INVESTMENT BANKS

Investment banks, which were created by the 'Capital Markets Law' of 1965, experienced changes in their asset and liability structures similar to those of commercial banks.[6] Table 6.5 presents the shares of the main liability items in total liabilities over the period 1975 to 1984. Investment banks stayed reasonably well capitalised, with a net increase in capital from 10.81% of total liabilities in 1975 to 15.03% in 1984. Foreign loan liabilities (Central Bank resolution 63) increased significantly from 15.73% of total liabilities in 1975 to a peak of 28.91% in 1983, then fell slightly to 25.72% in 1983. Loans from government-owned financial institutions first increased from 9.75% of total liabilities to 12.82% in 1978 owing to the adjustment mechanism outlined in Chapter 5, then fell after interest rate controls were lifted, especially as of 1981, to 7.01% in 1984. Time deposits showed

Table 6.4 Brazil: Profile of Private Commercial Bank Loans by Recipient Sector (Percentage of Total Loans)

	Industry[a]	Commerce[a]	Other business firms[a]	Agriculture and livestock[a]
1978	40.2	13.9	7.3	9.7
1979	39.8	13.4	9.3	9.4
1980	38.5	11.2	11.1	8.6
1981	36.7	9.2	12.4	9.6
1982	35.3	8.7	13.1	10.2
1983	31.4	7.1	14.6	10.3
1984	32.1	7.8	13.5	6.7

[a] Direct and indirect (through credit cooperatives) credit to each sector.
Source: Banco Central do Brasil, *Boletim*.

Table 6.5 Brazil: Investment Bank Liability Structure, 1975–84 (Percentage of Total Liabilities)

	Capital	Loans for 're-lending'			Time deposits	Other deposits
		Domestic	Foreign	Total		
1975	10.81	9.75	15.73	25.48	48.92	14.79
1976	11.03	10.29	15.08	25.37	46.35	17.25
1977	11.68	13.98	12.96	26.94	48.82	12.54
1978	8.73	12.82	16.58	29.40	50.78	3.65
1979	8.01	10.66	18.67	29.33	52.47	4.66
1980	9.32	10.52	19.76	30.28	51.96	4.84
1981	10.60	8.97	21.71	30.68	48.31	5.20
1982	13.31	6.97	22.89	29.86	45.91	6.73
1983	14.31	5.37	28.91	34.28	44.08	4.74
1984	15.03	7.01	25.72	32.73	47.36	3.65

Source: ANBID, *Boletim*; Ney R. O. de Brito and Fernando A. Paiva (1987): 'Bancos de Investimento: Evolução e Estrutura Financeira,' in *Revista Brasileira de Mercado de Capitais*, Vol. 13, No. 38, p. 41.

relative stability over the period, hovering between 52.47% of total liabilities to 44.08%. Finally, other accounts fell from 14.79% of total liabilities in 1975 to 3.65% in 1984.

In sum, as with the commercial bank liability structure, dollar-denominated liabilities of investment banks increased substantially throughout the period. In spite of this, time deposits, which had recovered after the 1964–5 reforms, maintained an important share of investment bank liabilities.

Table 6.6 shows the shares of the main asset categories in total assets for investment banks over the period 1975 to 1984. Unlike commercial banks, credit operations generally declined over the period from 53.09% of total assets in 1975 to 37.60% in 1984. 'Re-lending' of funds increased significantly from 15.92% of total assets in 1975 to 21.49% in 1984. 'Re-lending' of domestic funds (from publicly owned financial intermediaries) at first increased from 9.76% of total assets in 1975 to 14.24% in 1977, but then fell to 6.66% in 1984, significantly below the 1975 level. 'Re-lending' from foreign sources increased continuously over the period from 15.92% of total assets in 1975 to a peak of 23.90% in 1983, then fell slightly to 23.49% in 1984.

The striking similarity in the experiences of commercial and investment banks over the period is the increasing reliance on foreign funds through Central Bank Resolution 63. Further, the amount of resources received were usually larger than the amount 're-loaned' in this type of operation. It seems that commercial and investment banks used foreign funds for purposes other than for purely 're-lending' at similar interest rates and maturity, such as financing reserves or positions in bonds, etc.

6.4   CONGLOMERATION

The banking system is 'special' in the sense that bankruptcies generate large, undesirable externalities in the form of bank runs and further bankruptcies. The goal of developing a 'solid' banking system is usually one of the main priorities of monetary authorities. The Brazilian case is no exception. The Brazilian experience with conglomeration in the 1960s and 1970s can be dated to concerns generated in the 1940s and 1950s. SUMOC constantly acted to stem the over-proliferation of banks and bank agencies and liquidated the many bankruptcies which occurred during the 1950s.[7] This concern carried over into the following decades and became an important argument in favour of policies for solidifying the financial system through conglomeration.

As mentioned in previous chapters, the objectives of the Brazilian government in promoting conglomeration, however, were not solely directed at 'solidifying' the Brazilian financial system. Authorities felt that conglomeration would allow financial firms to exploit supposed

Table 6.6 Brazil: Investment Bank Asset Structure, 1975–84 (Percentage of Total Assets)

	Cash	loans	Re-lending			Bonds	Investments (equities)	Permanent assets	Other loans
			Domestic sources	Foreign sources	Total				
1975	2.10	53.09	9.76	15.92	25.68	5.61	N.A.	N.A.	N.A.
1976	1.80	52.03	10.55	15.22	25.77	4.82	N.A.	N.A.	N.A.
1977	2.43	55.34	14.24	12.56	26.80	3.74	N.A.	N.A.	N.A.
1978	1.47	56.29	12.38	14.14	26.52	1.74	3.10	1.15	7.77
1979	1.22	59.64	10.35	15.27	25.62	1.52	2.96	1.00	6.58
1980	2.07	53.33	9.78	18.75	28.53	4.31	3.74	1.13	5.85
1981	2.09	48.74	7.36	18.78	26.14	10.49	3.85	1.11	7.28
1982	0.97	42.35	5.77	21.22	26.99	14.39	5.25	1.27	8.37
1983	0.77	39.24	4.88	23.90	28.78	8.74	6.04	1.13	15.02
1984	0.79	37.60	6.66	21.49	28.15	6.40	6.74	1.13	18.95

Source: ANBID, *Boletim*; and Ney R. O. de Brito and Fernando A. Paiva (1987), op. cit., p. 35.

economies of scale, thus decreasing operating costs. They felt that the downward rigidity of real interest rates in the recession of 1964–7 was due mainly to the inefficient financial production structure developed in the previous inflationary period.[8] Hence, conglomeration was seen as a way to bring down the cost of capital in the medium to long term.

There are weaknesses in this rationalisation of conglomeration. Firstly, the studies which showed that economies of scale exist in the production of financial services in Brazil suffered from a fatal flaw: they had no criterion for determining what represents an input or what represents an output to the financial firm.[9] Only recently has a method of determining inputs and outputs to and from financial firms been developed.[10] Secondly, the expectation of economies of scale from conglomeration might be erroneous in that it does not seem, *a priori*, a necessary result because financial conglomeration represents diversification into the production of different financial services and not an increase in the output of some homogeneous good.[11] Even ignoring the flaws in existing studies, no clear-cut support for the existence of economies of scale can be found. In fact, some studies even found negative returns to scale in the commercial banks.[12]

Thirdly, even if conglomeration did lead to the exploitation of economies of scale, there is no reason to believe that this would be translated into lower loan interest rates, especially in light of the increased concentration of market power inherent in a process of conglomeration. Another argument for conglomeration states that conglomerates will be better able to diversify both their assets and liabilities and so decrease the risk of their portfolio, which might manifest itself in lower risk premia. The lowering of risk depends upon whether the conglomerate can diversify into assets which are negatively correlated with each other, i.e. hedge. This argument does not hold much weight in terms of the form conglomerates took in Brazil, because the returns on credit operations, although different, are usually positively correlated.[13]

The most important instrument used to slow the appearance of commercial banks and other financial institutions in Brazil was the fixing of the number of bank charters or 'cartas patentes'. This policy-induced barrier to entry was responsible for most of the increased concentration after 1967. Further, a secondary market for 'cartas patentes' evolved and was promoted by the authorities. Once the new issues of charters had been suspended in the early 1970s, this market flourished.[14] The existence of such a market created two contradictory incentives for existing banks. Firstly, this system allowed less efficient banks (or even more efficient ones that had reached a level of activity larger than their administrative infrastructure could handle) to be absorbed by stronger financial institutions. The problem with the flourishing of the secondary 'carta patente' market was that it became a source of profit for inefficient banks. It created a quasi-moral hazard problem in that it was profitable to become over-extended, file for bankruptcy, and then auction the bank's charter in the market.[15] This was exacerbated by the fact that when banks (especially large ones) filed for bankruptcy ('concordata'), the Central Bank intervened by performing a so-called 'extrajudicial' liquidation or reorganisation ('liquidação extrajudicial'), freezing assets and liabilities in such a way as to allow indexation of assets but not of liabilities.[16] With inflation rates at levels between 100% and 200% per year, it was only a short period of time before the bank was solvent again at the cost of the depositors. The 'carta patente' could be then auctioned at a hefty profit.[17] Additionally, the Central Bank extended loans to the buyers of the institution in order to finance the acquisition.[18]

The interest rate ceilings and subsidies given banks who met these interest rate controls[19] imposed during the 1967–74 period also promoted conglomeration. Such interest rate controls forced less efficient banks into bankruptcy, even in cases where banks used compensating balances and the other devices outlined in previous chapters.[20] Other policies used to promote conglomeration included increasing capital and permanent asset requirements, allowing interstate banking, controlling the number of agencies in different banking districts, and allowing successive interlocking directorates between commercial banks and investment banks, especially as of 1971.[21]

The increase in concentration of market power due to conglomeration is documented in Tables 6.7–6.11. Table 6.7 shows the number of commercial bank headquarters and agencies. The number of headquarters of privately owned commercial banks declined steadily after 1959 while the number of agencies increased. Consequently, the number of agencies per private commercial bank increased from 10 in 1959 to 100 in 1981. The data in Table 6.8 underscore this trend. Private commercial banks saw an increase in the concentration of agencies. The largest commercial bank owned 7.3% of the total private commercial bank agencies in 1968. By 1981, the largest bank owned 17.3% of all such agencies. In 1968, the four largest commercial

Table 6.7   Brazil: Commercial Bank and Bank of Brazil Agencies

	Commercial banks		Banco do Brasil	Total	Average dependent/ commercial bank[c]
	Headquarters[a]	Agencies[b]	Total			
1956	403	3,714	4,117	362	4,479	10
1967	262	7,060	7,322	697	8,019	28
1973	114	7,139	7,253	793	8,046	64
1981	110	10,926	11,036	1,271	12,307	100

[a] Includes the headquarters of foreign banks.
[b] Includes foreign subsidiaries.
[c] Excludes the Bank of Brazil and is calculated by dividing column 3 by column 1.
Source: Banco Central do Brasil, *Boletim*; *Conjuntura Economica*; Banco do Brasil, *Relatório*; and Martus A. R. Tavares and Nelson Carvalheiro (1985): *O Setor Bancário Brasileiro: Alguns Aspectos do Crescimento e da Concentração* (São Paulo: IPE/University of São Paulo Press), p. 56, Table 6.1.

banks owned 21% of all private commercial bank agencies. By 1981, they owned 41.1% of all the agencies. Finally, the seven largest commercial banks increased their ownership from 32.6% of all private commercial bank agencies in 1968 to 60.6% in 1981. It should be noted that all three strata of commercial banks had reached a maximum share of private commercial bank deposits between 1978 and 1979, which shows that by 1979 the process of market concentration in terms of agencies had run its course.

The share of the largest, four largest, and seven largest (including those publicly owned) commercial banks in the total of commercial banks showed similar trends. The fact that the level of agency concentration of all commercial banks is lower than for private commercial banks implies that publicly owned commercial banks did not expand by increasing the number of agencies as did privately owned commercial banks. To the extent that the overabundance of agencies contributes to the high cost of intermediation in Brazil, publicly owned banks acted in a socially optimal way compared with private banks. This stems from the fact that the private return to investing in agencies is higher than the social return due to inflation.

Table 6.9 reports the real level of deposits and loans along with the average level of loans and deposits per bank and per dependent (which include headquarters and agencies). Real deposits and real loans generally grew from 1963 to 1979, but contracted in 1980 and

Table 6.8   Brazil: Size Distribution of Commercial Bank Agencies[a]
(Percentage of Total)[b]

	1965		1968		1971	
	Private	Total	Private	Total	Private	Total
Largest bank	N.A.	4.4	7.3	2.5	7.5	2.7
4 Largest banks	N.A.	12.9	21.0	14.0	23.9	14.2
7 Largest banks	N.A.	19.7	32.6	20.9	33.6	24.5

	1972		1973		1976	
	Private	Total	Private	Total	Private	Total
Largest bank	8.0	3.4	12.8	4.3	13.6	10.0
4 Largest banks	25.2	17.5	35.1	26.6	42.9	29.5
7 Largest banks	39.3	31.4	47.7	38.3	62.6	44.3

	1979		1980		1981	
	Private	Total	Private	Total	Private	Total
Largest bank	17.4	12.7	16.6	12.1	17.3	12.4
4 Largest banks	42.6	32.0	42.7	32.2	41.1	28.8
7 Largest banks	63.5	49.0	60.9	43.9	60.6	43.2

[a]   Classified by deposits.
[b]   The private share corresponds to private total only.
Source: *Revista Bancária Brasileira*; and Martus A. R. Tavares and Nelson
Carvalheiro (1985): *O Setor Bancário Brasileiro: Alguns Aspectos do Crescimento e da Concentração* (São Paulo: IPE/University of São Paulo Press),
p. 65, Table 6.6.

1981, in line with data presented in previous chapters. Real loans and
deposits per bank and per dependent emulated the behaviour of total
loans and deposits. These data imply that the average size of commercial banks in terms of loans and deposits grew over the period in
question. As in the case of commercial bank agency concentration,
these data point to 1979 as the year ending the process of market
concentration.

Not only did the average size of loans and deposits increase but
their concentration in the largest commercial banks did as well. Table
6.10 shows that between 1970 and 1980 the proportion of total
commercial bank deposits held by the five largest commercial banks
increased from 29.7% to 37.2%. The ten largest banks increased
their combined share of deposits from 43% in 1970 to 54.4% in 1980.

Table 6.9   Brazil: Real Deposits, Real Loans per Commercial Bank, and per Dependent (Includes Headquarters and Agencies), 1963–81 (1977 Cr$ millions)

	Deposits	Loans	Loans per:		Deposits per:	
			Bank	Dependent	Bank	Dependent
1963	89,650	62,250	267.6	14.9	185.8	10.3
1964	86,973	61,757	258.8	13.9	183.8	9.9
1965	104,172	68,724	314.7	15.6	207.6	10.3
1966	86,086	64,160	275.0	12.5	205.0	9.3
1967	105,077	82,846	401.1	14.4	316.2	11.3
1968	119,884	107,535	537.6	16.2	482.2	14.5
1969	129,028	125,703	648.4	17.6	631.7	17.2
1970	138,855	140,833	784.5	19.0	795.7	19.3
1971	152,129	168,580	987.9	20.9	1094.7	23.2
1972	188,840	209,557	1486.9	29.0	1650.1	28.9
1973	234,500	260,818	2057.0	32.3	2287.9	36.0
1974	242,211	295,613	2242.7	32.1	2737.2	39.1
1975	268,492	349,903	2557.1	34.8	3332.4	45.3
1976	260,301	376,608	2479.1	32.6	3586.7	47.1
1977	273,619	402,764	2581.3	32.2	3799.7	47.4
1978	308,709	458,280	2912.3	34.0	4323.4	50.4
1979	348,170	513,600	3253.9	36.1	4800.0	53.2
1980	280,914	446,048	2553.8	27.5	4055.0	43.6
1981	218,831	427,643	1989.4	19.8	3887.7	38.7

Source: Banco Central do Brasil, *Boletim*; and Martus A. R. Tavares and Nelson Carvalheiro (1985): *O Setor Bancário Brasileiro: Alguns Aspectos do Crescimento e da Concentração* (São Paulo: IPE/University of São Paulo Press), p. 57, Table 6.2.

The remaining (cumulative) strata increased their share of total deposits by between 15 and 20 percentage points. Table 6.11 presents the same type of pattern not only for deposits but also for capital and loans as well. In sum, according to all measures, market power in the commercial banking sector became significantly more concentrated during the post-reform period.

The process of concentration of market power of commercial banks was not a balanced one. A recent study by Tavares and Carvalheiro (1985) shows that what they call 'relative concentration' decreased. In other words, the relative size of commercial banks tended to converge over the period 1964 to 1981, because banks that were small in 1964 displayed larger growth rates than large banks, becoming themselves medium-sized or large banks by 1981.[22] One incentive for this was that good financial performance increased the

Table 6.10   Brazil: Size Distribution of Commercial Bank Deposits[a]
(Percentage of Total Deposits Held)

Banks by size	1970	1980
5 largest banks	29.7	37.2
10 largest banks	43.0	54.4
15 largest banks	50.3	65.0
20 largest banks	57.8	73.4
25 largest banks	63.2	81.4

[a] Excludes the Bank of Brazil and the Bank of the Northeast.
Source: Banco Central do Brasil, *Boletim*, and Luiz A. Perdigão (1983): *Conglomerados Financeiros: Análise do Seu Desempenho no Brasil* (Rio de Janeiro: IBMEC), p. 35, Table 8.

Table 6.11   Brazil: Size Distribution of Commercial Bank Deposits, Loans, and Capital 1968–81 (Percentage of Total)

	1968			1971			1973		
	Deposits	Loans	Capital	Deposits	Loans	Capital	Deposits	Loans	Capital
Largest bank	9	8	8	9	8	9	13	11	11
4 largest banks	25	21	18	30	24	21	31	28	24
7 largest banks	36	31	28	41	34	31	46	40	36

	1975			1980			1981 (Nov)		
	Deposits	Loans	Capital	Deposits	Loans	Capital	Deposits	Loans	Capital
Largest bank	16	15	13	17	8	13	19	9	16
4 largest banks	41	37	30	41	21	24	48	23	28
7 largest banks	56	52	43	55	30	32	65	33	39

Source: Banco Central do Brasil, *Boletim*; *Revista Bancária Brasileira*; and Martus A. R. Tavares and Nelson Carvalheiro (1985): *O Setor Bancário Brasileiro: Alguns Aspectos do Crescimento e da Concentração* (São Paulo: IPE/University of São Paulo Press), p. 60, Table 6.4.

likelihood of merger with a financial conglomerate. Further, the slower growth of larger commercial banks can be explained by their greater ability to diversify into other sectors of the financial market by forming conglomerates and by the fact that a commercial bank cannot be expected to grow at high rates forever.[23]

What was the net effect of the process of conglomeration and concentration on the cost of financial capital? Table 6.12 shows effective nominal and real interest rates on working capital loans (from investment banks), 'duplicata discount' loans (from commercial banks and 'financeiras'), and resolution 63 loans (from commercial and investment banks). All displayed high positive real interest

Table 6.12   Brazil: Effective Nominal and Real Loan Interest Rates
1973–85[a] (Percentage Per Year)

	Working capital[b]		'Duplicata discount'[c]		Resolution 63[d]	
	Nominal	Real	Nominal	Real	Nominal	Real
1973	34.0	10.6	28.4	9.8	34.6	5.9
1974	38.5	7.0	32.9	0.0	49.9	16.9
1975	39.7	4.1	43.9	10.0	57.0	12.7
1976	52.9	4.4	57.7	8.0	56.8	9.2
1977	59.7	16.8	63.7	19.1	49.4	8.0
1978	70.4	18.4	69.7	19.8	68.5	12.3
1979	83.5	0.1	87.6	4.6	187.1	47.9
1980	88.0	−13.4	110.0	−1.8	105.9	−5.2
1981	141.7	25.7	160.1	34.5	162.4	36.4
1982	160.3	24.6	223.9	60.7	248.9	64.3
1983	266.8	13.4	279.7	20.9	333.2	34.7
1984	348.6	36.4	379.8	45.4	303.7	22.9
1985	314.2	32.1	496.4	86.5	310.4	22.2

[a] The effective rate includes commissions, compensating balances and the tax on financial operations (IOF).
[b] Loans extended by investment banks.
[c] Working capital loans extended by commercial banks by discounting accounts receivable.
[d] 'Relending' of foreign loans by commercial and investment banks by Central Bank resolution 63 (see the introduction).
Source: *Análise Financeira*.

rates throughout the period except for the outlier year 1980.[24] Real interest rates after 1980, when the process of conglomeration had ended, were extremely high, ranging from 15% per year to almost 90% per year.[25] The real cost of capital clearly did not decline, but seems to have increased with conglomeration.

It is difficult, however, to attribute the high levels of real interest rates on these loans to conglomeration *per se*, because they are as much a function of monetary policy, the ability of the government to service its substantial domestic and foreign debt, and market fragmentation. The results of a recent study of Brazilian financial conglomerates by Perdigão (1983), however, may allow some inferences along this line.[26] He calculates a proxy for a global spread between rates of return on assets and liabilities of the ten largest financial conglomerates from 1978 to 1981 using weighted averages of returns and financial costs. Although his analysis suffers because he aggregates financial goods which are heterogeneous, his results are none the less suggestive. Firstly, the correlation between the spread and a conglomeration index is significantly positive, which could reflect either economies of scale and/or monopoly rents due to higher market power. Secondly, he showed that the main determinant of the increase in profit margins from 5.18% in 1979–80 to 43.11% in 1980–1 can be attributed only to higher interest rates. This suggests that conglomerates were able to increase the rate of interest on their assets more than they needed to on liabilities. The fact that real interest rates were high on loans and spreads increased leads to the conclusion that, at best, any realised economies of scale were not translated into lower borrowing costs and, at worst, no economies of scale were realised and the increase in the spread was due exclusively to the increase in market concentration.

6.5 INTERNATIONAL EVIDENCE ON THE EFFICIENCY OF BRAZILIAN FINANCIAL INTERMEDIARIES

Comparing the Brazilian banking system with those of other Latin American countries will prove instructive in trying to gauge its efficiency. Firstly, the size of the banking systems scaled by gross domestic product (GDP) differs widely among Latin American countries. Table 6.13 shows value added of the financial sector as a percentage of GDP while Table 6.14 shows the average ratio of M_2 and total credit to GDP. The countries that show the largest value added share of GDP of the financial sector are Colombia, Brazil, Bolivia, Chile, and Venezuela while the countries which show the smallest shares are Uruguay and Argentina. Clearly, Brazilian banks are extremely profitable compared with their Latin American counterparts.

Large value added does not necessarily imply large financial sector 'output'. The countries that 'produced' more M_2 as a percentage of GDP were Uruguay and Venezuela, while the countries that produced the smallest M_2-to-GDP ratio were Brazil and Argentina, as presented in Table 6.14. A better indicator of financial sector 'production', however, is the ratio of total credit to GDP, because there was significant financial innovation in many countries especially Brazil. The countries whose financial sector produced the largest amount of credit to GDP were Uruguay, Colombia, and Argentina, while the smallest credit-to-GDP ratios were produced by Bolivia, Peru, Brazil, and Ecuador.

Table 6.13   Latin America: Value Added by Financial Services as a
Percentage of GDP

	1960	1970	1980	1984	1985	1986	1987
Argentina	7.4	6.7	7.9	6.7	6.9	7.0	7.1
Bolivia	11.3	12.2	15.1	13.0	13.3	14.0	14.2
Brazil	16.4	18.8	14.2	16.5	16.6	16.3	16.3
Chile	12.4	14.5	16.6	16.3	15.6	15.6	15.4
Colombia	5.5	14.8	14.6	24.9	24.9	24.8	24.7
Ecuador	16.0	10.0	8.6	8.4	8.3	8.2	8.7
Mexico	8.8	9.0	7.5	8.5	8.6	9.3	9.5
Peru	8.9	8.3	8.2	8.4	8.6	8.6	8.3
Uruguay	13.2	6.7	5.3	6.3	6.4	6.0	5.8
Venezuela	10.0	14.0	14.0	16.2	15.3	15.0	15.3

Source: Inter-American Development Bank (1988): *Economic Development and Social Progress in Latin America.*

Table 6.14   Latin America: Average Financial Market Size, 1981–6

	M_2/GDP	Credit/GDP
Argentina	15.1	56.7
Bolivia	18.2	21.0
Brazil	11.8	28.9
Chile	28.0	66.5
Colombia	21.2	22.0
Ecuador	21.2	28.0
Mexico	29.5	39.6
Peru	26.8	25.5
Uruguay	47.0	72.9
Venezuela	41.1	28.5

Source: International Monetary Fund (1989): *International Financial Statistics.*

In an effort to gauge the efficiency of each country's financial sector, the author constructed two 'efficiency' indices, which appear in Tables 6.15 and 6.16 respectively. The first is the ratio of M_2 to financial sector value added and the second is the ratio of total credit extended to value added of the financial sector. Admittedly, these are very rough measures of the productivity of the financial sector and the following interpretations should be taken as mildly indicative rather than precise. If we use either index, Uruguay stands out as having by far the most efficient financial sector. According to the

Table 6.15   Latin America: Financial Efficiency Index (M_2/Value Added in Financial Services Sector)

	1984	1985	1986	1987	Average
Argentina	1.64	1.59	2.36		1.86
Bolivia	1.21	0.21	0.34		0.59
Brazil	0.71	0.86			0.79
Chile	1.80				1.80
Colombia	0.84	0.80			0.82
Ecuador	2.48	2.41	2.43	2.56	2.47
Mexico	3.41	3.05	2.95		3.14
Peru	3.38	3.22			3.30
Uruguay	7.16	7.69	8.20	7.12	7.54
Venezuela	2.46	2.56	2.94	2.31	2.64

Sources: International Monetary Fund (1989): *International Financial Statistics*; Inter-American Development Bank (1988): *Economic Development and Social Progress in Latin America*.

Table 6.16   Latin America: Financial Efficiency Index (Total Credit/Value Added in Financial Services Sector)

	1984	1985	1986	1987	Average
Argentina	8.19	6.14	5.60		6.61
Bolivia	1.77	0.38	0.29		0.81
Brazil	1.67	1.84			1.75
Chile	4.82				4.82
Colombia	1.04	0.98			1.01
Ecuador	3.81	3.61	3.53		3.65
Mexico	4.13	4.36	4.75		4.41
Peru	3.34	2.28			2.81
Uruguay	13.08	11.66	10.55		11.76
Venezuela	1.72	1.48	1.92	1.67	1.70

Sources: International Monetary Fund (1989): *International Financial Statistics*; Inter-American Development Bank (1988): *Economic Development and Social Progress in Latin America*.

credit efficiency index, Argentina, Chile, Mexico, and Ecuador appear to be moderately efficient while Bolivia, Venezuela, and Brazil lie on the low end of the efficiency spectrum.

Another measure of efficiency is labour costs as a percentage of loans (although this does not measure the opportunity cost of intermediation to society). Tables 6.17 and 6.18 show labour costs as a percentage of total loans for Brazil, Argentina, Chile, and the United

Table 6.17   Brazil: Administrative Costs of Commercial Banks as a
Percentage of Total Loans

	Including Bank of Brazil	Excluding Bank of Brazil
1983–1	5.82	6.69
1983–2	5.19	6.11
1984–1	5.12	5.91
1984–2	6.12	6.30
1985–1	5.44	6.48

Source: FEBRABAN.

Table 6.18   Argentina: Administrative Costs as a Percentage of Loans

	1981	1982
Official national banks[a]	2.8	4.0
Official state and municipal banks	12.8	13.3
Domestic private banks	7.7	9.9
Foreign private banks	9.2	9.6
Chile	5.0	4.7
U.S.A.	3.3[b]	3.2[b]

[a] December 1981 and 1982 figures.
[b] 1980 and 1981 figures, respectively.

States. Brazil's costs are significantly higher than those of the U.S. and Chile, although lower than Argentina's.

Clearly, Brazil has one of the most profitable and dynamic banking systems in Latin America, especially when compared with the Southern Cone countries of Argentina and Uruguay. Further, it has not suffered the instability that the financial sectors of other Latin American countries have endured, partially as a function of the system of indexation and the intervention by the authorities, viz. the 'extrajudicial intervention'. It is, however, an expensive intermediation system, as is shown by the large amount of surplus captured by the financial sector as compared with the stock of loans outstanding.

6.6   FIRM FINANCIAL STRUCTURE AFTER 1964

Between 1967 and 1982, the Brazilian economy expanded along with financial markets. With the Mexican moratorium and the subsequent collapse of international financial markets, the restrictive monetary and fiscal policies in stabilising the balance of payments necessitated a debt deflation on the part of Brazilian firms after 1982. During the expansion period (1967–82), the main sources of financing of firms still remained retained earnings and loans in spite of the extensive measures described earlier to create a vigorous new issues market for equities. During the contraction, firms that were able to keep from failing decreased their level of indebtedness relative to capital when faced with the extraordinary high interest rates of the period 1982 to 1984. The financial structure of firms reflects these facts. Tables 6.19 and 6.20 show the financial structures of two different samples of Brazilian firms for the years 1969 to 1977 and 1980 to 1985, respectively.[27] Tables 6.21–6.24 present debt-to-equity ratios of two different samples for different periods, in addition to a third sample which overlaps the two other periods. During the 1969 to 1977 period, the debt-to-equity ratios of all firms rose. On average, the debt-to-equity ratio increased from 0.88 in 1969 to 1.32 by 1977. Of the types of firms involved, firms owned by private nationals showed the largest debt-to-equity ratio during this period. Clearly, the vulnerability of Brazilian firms to financial or macroeconomic shock grew over the 1969 to 1977 period.

The financial vulnerability of firms reached a peak during the period 1977–82. As can be seen from the marginal debt-to-equity ratios in Table 6.23, the extra borrowing was between three and twelve times as large as the increase in equity. The increase in U.S. interest rates in 1979 due to restrictive monetary policy caused firms to increase their borrowing both domestically and abroad. Again, as in 1964, this increasing leverage caused firms to be very susceptible to any type of price or interest rate shock.

Debt deflation was the order of the day over the period 1981 to 1985, in which debt-to-equity ratios declined for all firms except state enterprises, which showed an increase over this period. On average, the debt-to-equity ratio of firms declined from 1.16 in 1980 to 1.01 in 1985. If one looks at the decline in the debt-to-equity ratios of private national corporations and foreign-owned corporations, the fall is much more dramatic: from 0.95 in 1980 to 0.40 in 1985 for private nationals and from 1.40 in 1980 to 0.89 for foreign owned corporations. Although the three sets of data are not perfectly comparable, they clearly illustrate the fact that Brazilian firms showed an increase in financial vulnerability during the debt-led expansion phase and the large contraction undertaken by the private sector after 1981. This underscores the severity of the depression experienced by the

Capital Markets in the Development Process

Table 6.19   Brazil: Financial Structure of Firms, 1967–77 (Percentage of Total Assets)

	1969	1972	1975	1977
All firms (3,790)				
Assets				
Fixed (net)	44.05	44.08	39.60	42.92
Liquid	42.26	47.58	52.15	48.08
Non-operating	6.73	8.36	8.24	9.00
	1969	1972	1975	1977
Liabilities				
Capital	53.29	50.04	44.41	43.10
Financial	22.43 |	26.38 |	31.80 |	33.95 |
Other	24.28 | 46.71	23.58 | 49.46	23.79 | 55.59	22.95 | 56.90
Private national (3,326)				
Assets	35.63	33.67	30.88	30.58
Fixed (net)	55.79	53.28	59.35	53.26
Liquid				
Non-operating	8.59	10.05	9.77	11.16
	1969	1972	1975	1977
Liabilities				
Capital	49.88	46.01	40.88	41.14
Financial	20.85 |	25.79 |	30.39 |	30.70 |
Other	29.17 | 50.02	28.20 | 53.99	28.79 | 59.12	28.16 | 58.86
Foreign firms (428)				
Assets				
Fixed (net)	38.45	36.58	31.26	35.53
Liquid	54.57	54.09	60.52	56.91
Non-operating	6.97	9.33	8.52	9.57
	1969	1972	1975	1977
Liabilities				
Capital	54.88 |	53.87 |	44.45 |	43.80 |
Financial	21.69 | 45.12	22.62 | 46.13	28.44 | 55.55	30.05 | 56.20
State enterprises (36)				
Assets				
Fixed (net)	80.08	78.85	68.55	77.75
Liquid	17.85	18.14	26.65	18.27
Non-operating	2.07	3.01	4.80	3.99
	1969	1972	1975	1977
Liabilities				
Capital	58.96	55.41	52.33	46.36
Financial	14.01 |	32.37 |	38.69 |	44.59 |
Other	22.03 | 41.04	12.22 | 45.59	8.98 | 47.67	9.05 | 53.64

Source: Alvaro A. Zini, Jr. (1984): 'Evolução da Estrutura Financeira das Empresas no Brasil 1969–1977,' in *Estudos Economicos*, Vol. 14, No. 1, Jan.–April, p. 87.

Table 6.20   Brazil: Financial Structure of Firms, 1980–5 (Percentage of Total Assets)

	1980	1981	1982	1983	1984	1985
All firms						
(1,000)						
Assets						
Fixed	65.0	66.0	69.0	71.0	72.0	71.0
Long term	8.0	10.0	10.0	10.0	9.0	10.0
Liquid	27.0	24.0	21.0	19.0	19.0	19.0
Liabilities						
Capital	46.0	47.0	49.0	47.0	50.0	50.0
Short term	25.0 |	23.0 |	20.0 |	20.0 |	19.0 |	20.0 |
Long term	29.0 | 54.0	30.0 | 53.0	32.0 | 52.0	33.0 | 53.0	31.0 | 50.0	30.0 | 50.0
Private						
national (800)						
Assets						
Fixed	51.0	54.0	57.0	60.0	61.0	67.0
Long term	4.0	4.0	4.0	4.0	3.0	2.0
Liquid	45.0	42.0	39.0	36.0	35.0	29.0
Liabilities						
Capital	51.0	54.0	58.0	59.0	65.0	71.0
Short term	33.0 |	31.0 |	27.0 |	25.0 |	23.0 |	19.0 |
Long term	16.0 | 49.0	15.0 | 46.0	15.0 | 42.0	16.0 | 41.0	13.0 | 46.0	10.0 | 29.0
Foreign (92)						
Assets						
Fixed	39.0	43.0	48.0	49.0	52.0	51.0
Long term	4.0	5.0	4.0	6.0	4.0	4.0
Liquid	56.0	52.0	48.0	44.0	44.0	45.0
Liabilities						
Capital	42.0	45.0	49.0	46.0	52.0	53.0
Short term	46.0 |	41.0 |	38.0 |	34.0 |	33.0 |	33.0 |
Long term	12.0 | 58.0	14.0 | 55.0	13.0 | 51.0	20.0 | 54.0	15.0 | 48.0	14.0 | 47.0
State						
enterprises						
(108)						
Assets						
Fixed	75.0	74.0	77.0	77.0	77.0	74.0
Long term	10.0	12.0	12.0	12.0	12.0	14.0
Liquid	15.0	14.0	11.0	11.0	11.0	11.0
Liabilities						
Capital	45.0	44.0	45.0	43.0	45.0	39.0
Short term	18.0 |	18.0 |	15.0 |	17.0 |	16.0 |	19.0 |
Long term	37.0 | 55.0	38.0 | 56.0	40.0 | 55.0	40.0 | 57.0	40.0 | 55.0	42.0 | 61.0

Source: 'Balanço de Mil Sociedades por Ações,' in *Conjuntura Economica*, December 1988, pp. 55–117.

Table 6.21   Brazil: Debt–Equity Ratios, 1969–77

	1969	1972	1975	1977
All firms (3,790)	0.88	1.00	1.25	1.32
Private nationals				
(3,326)	1.00	1.17	1.45	1.43
Foreign firms (428)	0.82	0.86	1.25	1.28
State enterprises (36)	0.70	0.82	0.91	1.15

Source: Calculated from Table 6.19.

Table 6.22   Brazil: Debt Equity Ratios of Non-financial Firms, 1975–82

	Private domestic	State owned	Foreign owned	All firms
1975	1.26	0.72	0.97	0.82
1976	1.23	1.00	1.07	1.04
1977	1.19	0.86	1.11	0.93
1978	0.80	0.79	0.87	0.80
1979	0.86	1.07	1.04	1.02
1980	1.07	1.29	1.10	1.23
1981	0.90	1.20	1.06	1.13
1982	0.85	1.28	0.88	1.15

Source: Calculated from Domingo G. Rodrigues (1984a): 'A Evolução das Empresas Não-Financeiras no Brasil no Periódo 1975–82,' in *Revista Brasileira de Mercado de Capitais*, Vol. 10, No. 30, April–June, pp. 142–3.

Brazilian economy in the period 1981 to 1984.

Another indicator of financial vulnerability is the weight of financial costs imposed upon firms. Tables 6.25 and 6.26 show financial costs as a percentage of net operating profits for the periods 1969 to 1977 and 1980 to 1985, respectively, while 6.27 shows financial costs as a percentage of total sales for the period 1975 to 1982. Financial costs increased for all types of firms from an average of 3.44% of net operating income in 1969 to 6.9% in 1977. By 1981, they had reached on average of 21% of net operating income. Financial costs for all firms increased from 1980 to 1983 in spite of the fact that debt was reduced. This reflects the significantly higher interest rates over this period. Private national and foreign-owned firms saw only a small decline in financial costs in 1984 and 1985 while state enterprises were able to decrease their financial costs substantially.

The fact that Brazilian firms relied mainly on debt financing after

Table 6.23   Brazil: Marginal Debt–Equity Ratios of Non-financial Firms, 1978–82[a]

	Private domestic	State owned	Foreign owned
1978	1.53	3.04	1.71
1979	2.32	5.55	1.58
1980	2.94	4.57	0.48
1981	7.95	3.41	0.58
1982	2.32	3.88	12.30

[a]. Equity includes direct and indirect stock issues. It does not include internal sources of financing such as retained earnings, depreciation, indexation, etc.

Source: Calculated from Domingo G. Rodrigues (1984b): 'Evolução de Financiamento e Investimento das Empresas Não Financeiras no Brasil: 1978–1982,' in *Revista Brasileira de Mercado de Capitais*, Vol. 10, No. 31, July–Sept., pp. 266–73.

Table 6.24   Brazil: Debt–Equity Ratios, 1980–5

	1980	1981	1982	1983	1984	1985
All firms (1,000)	1.16	1.14	1.06	1.15	0.99	1.01
Private nationals (800)	0.95	0.86	0.73	0.70	0.54	0.40
Foreign firms (92)	1.40	1.24	1.05	1.17	0.93	0.89
State enterprises (108)	1.23	1.27	1.22	1.35	1.24	1.54

Source: 'Balanço de Mil Sociedades por Ações,' in *Conjuntura Economica*, December 1988, pp. 55–117.

Table 6.25   Brazil: Financial Costs as a Percentage of Net Operating Income, 1969–77

	1969	1972	1975	1977
All firms (3,790)	3.44	3.54	5.33	6.90
Private nationals (3,326)	3.30	3.28	4.97	5.59
Foreign firms (428)	3.57	3.43	5.10	6.78
State enterprises (36)	4.22	7.32	10.75	18.16

Source: Zini (1984), op. cit., p. 94.

Table 6.26   Brazil: Financial Costs as a Percentage of Net Operating
Income, 1980–5

	1980	1981	1982	1983	1984	1985
All firms (1000)	14.0	21.0	18.0	34.0	20.0	13.0
Private nationals (800)	7.0	10.0	9.0	13.0	12.0	10.0
Foreign firms (92)	6.0	8.0	7.0	12.0	10.0	10.0
State enterprises (108)	27.0	42.0	35.0	70.0	35.0	18.0

Source: 'Balanço de Mil Sociedades por Ações,' in *Conjuntura Economica*,
December 1988, pp. 55–117.

Table 6.27   Brazil: Financial Costs as a Percentage of Sales, 1975–82

	1975	1976	1977	1978	1979	1980	1981	1982
All firms (90)	4.4	4.5	5.9	7.1	19.9	45.1	20.6	26.7
Private nationals (62)	4.6	5.3	5.1	5.3	7.6	7.5	9.6	10.0
Foreign firms (16)	3.6	4.3	4.1	4.5	7.8	5.5	10.2	10.6
State enterprises (12)	4.5	4.0	6.8	9.2	29.9	20.9	27.6	37.3

Source: Calculated from Domingo G. Rodrigues (1984a), op. cit., pp.
150–3.

the 1964 reforms underscores the increase in financial vulnerability of
the Brazilian financial system and firms as the financial system grew
extensively. In the face of this fragility, the solvency of the system
was maintained by the interventions outlined in sections 6.2 to 6.4,
which usually involved a socialisation of the costs through monetisation of financial institution deficits. The necessity of encouraging the
growth of equities markets in order to allow firms to increase their
capital relative to financial obligations through equity issues as opposed to debt deflation still remains a major challenge in Brazil.

6.7   SUMMARY AND CONCLUSIONS

This chapter has reviewed the changes in the structure of commercial
and investment banks and investigated the process of concentration
and conglomeration of the banking system. The main conclusion
regarding the asset and liability structure of commercial and invest-

ment banks was the increased 'internationalization' of their balance sheets. As international interest rates were lower on average than domestic loan interest rates, these inflows of foreign financial capital should have put significant downward pressure on the cost of loans. Even though real rates of interest were high over the period, it seems that foreign loans rendered the cost of loans cheaper, because real interest rates increased dramatically after 1982, when new foreign loans to Brazil dried up. The process of conglomeration was less successful on this score. The existing evidence does not show significant returns to scale existing in the Brazilian financial system, and even if economies of scale were exploited they were not translated into lower borrowing costs. Further, the process of conglomeration combined with high and accelerating inflation rates allowed the banks to keep the existing, inefficient cost structure with high unit costs per deposit and an extraordinary number and growth of agencies. In fact, it was through the vast network of commercial bank agencies that newly formed conglomerates were able to sell their larger variety of products. The 'carta patente' charter system fuelled these developments, as it created a large barrier to entry and so diminished competition.

Conglomeration clearly increased the profitability of the Brazilian financial system and allowed financial institutions to charge extremely high interest rates in real terms. This explains the vacillation described in the introduction between free interest rate policy and interest rate controls. Ironically, interest rate controls failed to achieve the objective of regulating the price charged by the oligopolistic financial institutions, but instead fostered further concentration of financial market power. Efficiency gains in the financial sector will not be made through the use of usury laws.

The large growth in the Brazilian financial system increased the financial vulnerability of firms as debt-equity ratios and financial costs grew between 1969 and 1981. The international financial crisis and the restrictive monetary policies of 1981–3 caused a major debt deflation without a substantial decrease in the financial costs of firms. Financial crisis was averted by Central Bank interventions, which usually entailed monetisation and abetted the process of conglomeration.

The fact that Brazil's financial sector has been the fastest growing sector over the period, the financial deepening which occurred in spite of high inflation, and the successful process of conglomeration all imply that Brazil has been able to develop a strong financial system. The new financial system has not, however, been able to solve some of the basic problems faced in 1964. Financial intermediation is still extremely costly in spite of the size of the financial system. The cost of capital is still extremely high. There are also the problems associated with indexation, a tendency for excessive credit expansion, excessive market segmentation, and small equities markets studied in earlier chapters. Other problems which are frequently mentioned in financial market surveys in Brazil but fall outside the scope of this study are the fact that underdeveloped regions in Brazil do not receive the quantity or the quality of services that are extended in the more dynamic (industrialised) centres of Brazil such as São Paulo and Rio de Janeiro in spite of fiscal and regulatory incentives. Paradoxically, the underdeveloped regions are net creditors to the developed ones, a clear indication that financial intermediation has had detrimental distributional effects.[28]

Any type of financial reform will have to address all of these issues. The essential difference between any new reform and the reforms of 1964 will be that Brazil now has a strong and dynamic financial sector. The 1964–7 reforms had first to develop a financial system; new policies should be focused on improving the existing system.

7 Summary and Concluding Remarks: Towards a New Financial Reform in Brazil

The objective of this study has been to provide a systematic analysis of the post-war Brazilian experience with financial and capital market development. The introduction motivates the study and outlines a macroeconomic chronology which serves as a backdrop throughout. Chapter 1 reviews a number of different theories concerning the importance of financial development and different policy prescriptions to attain this goal. Chapter 2 looks at the pre-reform financial system during the heyday of import substitution industrialisation (ISI) from 1945 to 1964. The same chapter argues that the lack of functioning financial and capital markets contributed to the exhaustion of ISI policies. It also pinpoints the areas where market and institutional failures led to serious problems in the intermediation process. Chapter 3 analyses the original objectives to the reformers in 1964–7, the structure of financial markets which resulted from the reforms, and the structure of the decision process of financial policy. The remaining chapters of the study investigate the longer-term ramifications of the reforms. Chapter 4 shows that the objectives of creating vigorous markets for equities took much longer than expected and had limited success. Chapter 5 analyses the implications of creating inflation-indexed debt instruments. Finally, Chapter 6 examines the changing balance sheet structure of Brazilian firms and financial institutions in addition to gauging the efficiency of the intermediation process in Brazil.

The financial reforms of 1964–7 were successful in promoting the growth of the Brazilian financial system. The resulting strong and sophisticated system, however, is not cost efficient. Also, it has a propensity for excessive credit creation owing to its institutional structure, the government's borrowing necessities, and the political power of those who use and supply credit.

The basic problem with the Brazilian financial system, as with those in most developing countries, is the high cost of credit, which is due in part to market failures resulting from inflation and default uncertainty. The Brazilian government tried to resolve these market failures through direct intermediation by the creation of institutions and indexation. Because the accountability of these institutions was minimal, many of their activities were ultimately financed through money creation. Indexation had a major role in the growth of the financial system at the cost of enhanced inflation feedback mechanisms, which made inflation stabilisation increasingly difficult. The advantages of having a strong financial market, however, should not be ignored. The most important, from a macroeconomic standpoint, is the fact that it allowed Brazil to avoid the massive capital flight that occurred in Argentina, Mexico, and Venezuela.[1] Any attempts at dismantling the system of financial indexation (e.g. the heterodox stabilisation attempts of the 'Cruzado Plan' (1986–7), the 'Bresser Plan' (1987), and the 'Summer Plan' (1989)), will have to reduce inflation permanently or face significant capital flight. The fact that each attempt at dismantling indexation resulted in a large increase in capital flight should make policy makers wary of living without indexation.[2]

One of the main conclusions of this study is that the creation of a strong financial system allowed for a relatively smooth internal transfer of resources from the private sector to the public sector, especially when a large external resource transfer became necessary after 1982. Financial development based upon the financial necessities of the government, however, is certainly unsustainable. A reduction of the borrowing requirements of the public sector is necessary to allow for efficiency improvements in the financial and capital markets in general, not to mention the reduction in the use of the inflation tax. The growth in the internal debt service burden of the Brazilian governments has led to the argument that the government should repudiate its internal financial liabilities.[3] This study has sought to demonstrate that the reforms of 1964–7 created a strong and vital financial market through policies that honoured the government's liabilities with a high degree of credibility. This author feels that any type of debt moratorium would be disastrous in that it would lead ultimately to a reversal of the development of financial markets over the last quarter century.[4] Unfortunately, true fiscal reform still needs to be undertaken.

One of the main barriers to the reduction of the cost of financial capital has been the excessively high cost structure of the banking system. This cost structure was inherited from the previous period and was the direct result of inflation. It was seen as the main barrier to the reduction of interest rates in the late 1960s and early 1970s. In order to exploit (supposed) economies of scale, the Brazilian government promoted conglomeration in an already concentrated sector and the subsidisation of bank activities. The combination of increased market power, accelerating inflation, and heavy government borrowing, especially after 1982, led banks to avoid changing cost structures in a way that would be translated into lower borrowing costs.

At the microeconomic level, the Brazilian financial system must become more competitive. A minor banking reform in 1988–9 took two important steps toward increasing competition. The first provision followed the Canadian example of allowing conglomerates to become 'multiple banks' (or 'financial holding companies'). In other words movement has been promoted away from financial institution specialisation.[5] This would minimise 'self-dealing' and the possible conflicts of interest associated with such operations. For example, most housing credit societies, which experienced extraordinary growth over the period, have increasingly become associated with financial conglomerates. In order to transfer funds within the conglomerate, these institutions have been known to sell mortgage paper to the investment bank in the conglomerate which had obtained funds by selling a certificate of deposit.[6] Many of the recent conglomerate failures were due in part to the abuse of such operations.[7] Secondly, the creation of such a bank would allow for a decline in the cost of redundant legal and administrative procedures existing in the present conglomerate system.

Along with the creation of 'multiple banks', the 'carta patente' or charter system was eliminated in order to increase the number auctioned, allowing for increased competition among suppliers of financial services.[8] The profitability of bankruptcy would also be reduced as the value of existing 'cartas patentes' would fall. This essential part of the reforms, however, might prove politically unpalatable to financial conglomerates and would resist through their substantial lobbying power.

To date, a few financial institutions have taken advantage of the reform to become multiple banks. On the other hand, no new financial institutions have been created in spite of these measures, owing to the fact that the other entry restrictions are still prohibitive. The reform, therefore, has not produced significant increases in the productive efficiency of the financial system. The Brazilian government should in the near future implement a programme that gradually reduces the barriers to entry into the financial services sector by foreign institutions as well as by domestic ones. A gradual opening would allow the existing banks to reorganise their production processes without large-scale bankruptcies. The high level of profit and capitalisation of existing Brazilian banks should allow them to absorb such a shock without excessive trauma.

The reform also extinguished the National Housing Bank (BNH) and integrated the Housing Finance System (SFH) institutions with the rest of the financial system (especially commercial banks), allowing them to lend and borrow at market rates.[9] It is only to be hoped that this will improve the poor balance sheet condition of these institutions through diversification.

Clearly, high inflation rates are the main obstacle to an improvement in the efficiency of the Brazilian financial system. If inflation is not stabilised at lower levels then formal and informal indexation and the associated distortions will exist in one form or another. Any type of financial reform will be doomed to limited success at best if inflation remains at present levels or accelerates. Further, a reduction in inflation implies a large structural adjustment in financial institutions compatible with the lower level of inflation. Policy makers would have to smooth the subsequent adjustment distress felt by financial institutions during a drastic inflation stabilisation while resisting monetary expansion and the subsequent subversion of the stabilisation attempt.

Finally, for any reform to succeed, the structure of the Brazilian monetary authorities would necessarily have to be rearranged. The Central Bank would have to become completely independent of the other government financial institutions. The elimination of the Bank of Brazil's powers as monetary authority in early 1986 was a first step along these lines. The power of the National Monetary Council (CMN) would have to be limited to monetary and regulatory policy. The many powers it enjoyed would have to be returned to the fiscal arena under the supervision of Congress, which would allow more transparency and less automatic monetary expansion.

Notes

Introduction

1. See Carlos Diaz-Alejandro (1985): 'Good-bye Financial Repression, Hello Financial Crash,' in *Journal of Development Economics*, Vol. 19; and Diaz-Alejandro (1981): 'Southern Cone Stabilization Plans,' in William Cline and Sidney Weintraub, eds.: *Economic Stabilisation in Developing Countries* (Washington, D.C.: Brookings Institution).

2. For good reviews of these policies over the period, see: Décio Munhoz (1982); *Controle de Taxas de Juros—A Viablilidade de Compatibilização da Dívida Externa e da Dívida Interna*, Working Paper No. 91, University of Brasília; Donald Syvrud (1972): 'Estrutura e Política de Juros no Brasil-1960/70,' in *Revista Brasileira de Economia*, Vol. 26, No. 1, Jan.–March; João Sayad (1977): 'Controles de Juros e Saldos Médios,' in *Revista Brasileira de Economia*, Vol. 31, No. 1, Jan.–March; Leif Christoffersen (1969): 'Taxas de Juros e A Estrutura de Um Sistema de Bancos Comerciais em Condições Inflacionárias,' in *Revista Brasileira de Economia*, Vol. 23, No. 2, April–June; Mario H. Simonsen (1970): *Inflação: Gradualismo vs. Tratamento de Choque* (Rio de Janeiro: Apec).

3. As we shall see in Chapter 3, commercial banks and finance companies were able to get around this usury law through a number of different schemes. The costs of such arrangements were significant, however, and hindered the development of a large and flexible financial market.

4. For a review of Brazil's financial opening to external finance during this period, see Alkimar R. Moura (1981): 'A Abertura Financeira Externa: Um Breve Relato da Experiencia Brasileira.' in *Revista de Economia Política*, Vol. 1, No. 1, Jan.–March.

5. Ibid., p. 145.

6. Ibid., p. 145.

7. For reviews of policy during this period, see: Samuel A. Morley (1971): 'Inflation and Stagnation in Brazil,' in *Economic Development and Cultural Change*, Vol. 19, No. 2; Albert Fishlow (1973): 'Some Reflections on Post-1964 Brazilian Economic Policy,' in Alfred Stepan, ed.: *Authoritarian Brazil* (New Haven: Yale University Press); Werner Baer (1983): *The Brazilian Economy: Growth and Development* (New York: Praeger); and Mario H. Simonsen (1970), op. cit., among many others.

8. For evidence that this was the explicit objective of the government, see Octávio Gouvêa de Bulhões (1969): 'Financial Recuperation for Economic Expansion,' in H. S. Ellis, ed.: *The Economy of Brazil* (Berkeley: University of California Press).

9. See Syvrud (1972), op. cit., and Werner Baer and Paul Beckerman (1980): 'The Trouble with Index-Linking: Reflections on the Recent Brazilian Experience,' in *World Development*, Vol. 8, No. 9, September.

10. See Júlio S. G. de Almeida (1985): 'A Crise do Mercado Paralelo de Letras: Causas e Consequencias Sobre a Reforma Finançeira de

1964–1966,' in *Revista Brasileira de Mercado de Capitais*, Vol. 11, No. 33, Jan.–March.

11. For a good discussion of these early policies, see David M. Trubek (1971): 'Law, Planning, and the Development of the Brazilian Capital Market,' in *The Bulletin*, Nos. 72–3, April, New York University Graduate School of Business Administration Institute of Finance.

12. See Morley (1971), op. cit.; Fishlow (1973), op. cit.; Syvrud (1972), op. cit.; Baer (1983), op. cit.; Edmar Bacha (1977): 'Issues and Evidence on Recent Brazilian Growth,' in *World Development*, Vol. 5, Nos. 1–2; and Pedro Malan and Regis Bonelli (1977): The Brazilian Economy in the Seventies: Old and New Developments,' in *World Development*, Vol. 5, Nos. 1–2, among many.

13. See Syvrud (1972), op. cit., pp. 126–133; Munhoz (1982), op. cit., pp. 22–44; and Sayad (1977), op. cit., pp. 229–234.

14. See note 11.

15. See Peter Knight, Michael Growe, and Alan Gelb (1984): *Brazil: Financial Systems Review* (Washington, D.C.: World Bank).

16. See Werner Baer (1984): 'Brazil: Political Determinants of Development,' in Robert Wesson, ed.: *Politics, Policies, and Economic Development in Latin America.* (Stanford: Hoover Institution Press); Carlos F. Diaz-Alejandro (1983): 'Some Aspects of the 1982–83 Brazilian Payments Crisis,' in *Brookings Papers on Economic Activity*, No. 2; Bacha (1977), op. cit.; and Malan and Bonelli (1977), op. cit.

17. See Luiz A. Perdigão (1983): *Conglomerados Financeiros: Análise do Seu Desempenho no Brasil: 1978–1981* (Rio de Janeiro: IBMEC) and Marcus A. R. Tavares and Nelson Carvalheiro (1985): *O Sétor Bancário Brasileiro: Alguns Aspectos do Crescimento e Concentração* (São Paulo: IPE/University of São Paulo Press).

18. See Werner Baer and Paul Beckerman (1980), op. cit.; Adroaldo Moura da Silva (1979): *Intermediação Financeira no Brasil* monograph, University of São Paulo; and Walter L. Ness, Jr. (1977): *A Influência da Correção Monetária no Sistema Financeiro* (Rio de Janeiro: IBMEC).

19. See Moura da Silva (1979), op. cit.

20. See Luciano G. Coutinho (1981): 'Inflexões e Crise da Política Economica: 1974–1980,' in *Revista de Economia Política*, Vol. 1, No. 1, Jan.–March.

21. See Moura (1981), op. cit., p. 149.

22. For an analysis, see Rudiger Dornbusch and Adroaldo Moura da Silva (1984): 'Taxas de Juros e Depósitos em Moeda Estrangeira no Brasil,' in *Revista Brasileira de Economia*, Vol. 38, No. 1, Jan.–March.

23. Moura (1981), op. cit., pp. 149–150.

24. See for the Argentine case, Roque B. Fernandez (1985): 'The Expectations Management Approach to Stabilization in Argentina during 1976–82,' in *World Development*, Vol. 13, No. 8; Guillermo Calvo (1983): 'Trying to Stabilize: Some Theoretical Reflections Based on the Experience of Argentina,' in Pedro A. Armella, Rudiger Dornbusch, and Maurice Obstfeld, eds.: *Financial Policies and the World Capital Market: The Problem of Latin American Countries* (Chicago: University of Chicago Press); Edward C. Epstein (1987): 'Recent Stabilization

Programmes in Argentina: 1973–1985,' in *World Development*, Vol. 15, No. 8; and Diaz-Alejandro (1985), op. cit.
25. For a good review of the period 1980–3, see Edmar Bacha (1983): 'Vicissitudes of Recent Stabilization Attempts in Brazil and the IMF Alternative," in John Williamson, ed.: *IMF Conditionality* (Washington D.C.: Institute for International Economics) and Carlos F. Diaz-Alejandro (1983): 'Some Aspects of the 1982–83 Brazilian Payments Crisis,' in *Brookings Papers on Economic Activity*, No. 2.
26. See Simonsen (1970), op. cit.; Persio Arida (1982): 'Reajuste Salarial e Inflação,' in *Pesquisa e Planejamento Economico*, Vol. 12, No. 2, August; Francisco Lopes (1984): 'Inflação Inercial, Hiperinflação, e Desinflação: Notas e Conjecturas,' in *Revista da ANPEC*, Vol. 7, No. 8, Nov.; Francisco Lopes and Edmar Bacha (1983): 'Inflation, Growth, and Wage Policy: A Brazilian Perspective,' in *Journal of Development Economics*, September; and Robert M. B. Macedo (1983): 'Wage Indexation and Inflation: The Recent Brazilian Experience,' in Rudiger Dornbusch and Mario H. Simonsen, eds.: *Inflation, Debt, and Indexation* (Cambridge, Mass.: MIT Press).
27. See note 24.
28. Bacha (1983), op. cit., p. 329.
29. See John H. Welch, Carlos A. P. Braga, and Paulo T. A. André (1987): 'Brazilian Public Sector Disequilibrium,' in *World Development*, Vol. 15, No. 8, and Celso L. Martone (1985): 'A Inconsisténcia do Modelo Brasileiro de Ajustamento,' in *Estudos Economicos*, Vol. 15, No. 1.
30. See Peri Agostinho da Silva (1981): *Desenvolvimento Financeiro e Política Monetária*. (Rio de Janeiro: Interciência).
31. See Carlos A. P. Braga (1985): *A Economia Brasileira na Segunda Metade dos Anos 80*, Working Paper No. 18, University of São Paulo, among others.
32. See John H. Welch (1987): '*A Note on Indexation. 'Inertial Inflation'*, and Incomes Policies in Brazil,' Working Paper No. 87–12, Oakland University, June, and Werner Baer and Paul Beckerman (1987): '*The Decline and Fall of Brazil's Cruzado*,' Working Paper No. 1393, Bureau of Economic and Business Research, University of Illinois at Urbana-Champaign, September.

1 Financial Growth and Economic Development

1. The list is far too long to enumerate in this note. A good portion of these works, however, will be listed in this chapter. The most recent and perhaps most importan⊾ arguments along this line are developed in Ronald I. McKinnon (1973): *Money and Capital in Economic Development* (Washington D.C.: Brookings Institution) and Edward S. Shaw (1973): *Financial Deepening in Economic Development* (New York: Oxford University Press).
2. The authors refer mainly to the Keynesian theory of liquidity preference. I would venture that a more appropriate name would be the 'Hicksian' interpretation of liquidity preference. It might be argued that Keynes's analysis, especially in reference to his artiᵤle 'The General Theory of

Employment,' in *Quarterly Journal of Economics*, February 1937, corresponds in a general way to the Gurley and Shaw (1955) analysis. For discussions of the Hicksian interpretation and Keynes's view, see Hyman Minsky (1977): 'The Financial Instability Hypothesis: An Interpretation of Keynes and an Alternative to "Standard" Theory,' in *Nebraska Journal of Economics and Business*, Winter, Vol. 16, No. 1; G. L. S. Shackle (1961): 'Recent Theories Concerning the Nature and the Role of Interest,' in *Economic Journal*, Vol. 71; E. Roy Weintraub (1975): 'Uncertainty' and the Keynesian Revolution,' in *History of Political Economy*, Vol. 7, No. 4; J. A. Kregel (1976): 'Economic Methodology in the Face of Uncertainty: The Modeling of Keynes and the Post-Keynesians,' in *Economic Journal*, Vol. 86, June.

3. John G. Gurley and Edward S. Shaw (1955): 'Financial Aspects of Economic Development,' in *American Economic Review*, Vol. 45, No. 4, September, pp. 516–17.
4. Ibid., p. 517.
5. Goldsmith (1969) disaggregates these relationships to a large extent, although it should be mentioned that much of his work on this subject was performed prior to and coincidental with Gurley and Shaw (1955). See Raymond Goldsmith (1969): *Financial Structure and Development*. (New Haven: Yale University Press.)
6. Gurley and Shaw (1955), op. cit., pp. 517–18.
7. Ibid., p. 518.
8. Ibid., pp. 518–19.
9. Ibid., p. 524.
10. As Gurley and Shaw show, the share of commercial banks' assets in the total assets of the U.S. financial system has decreased to a large extent since 1900. Goldsmith (1969) provides international evidence of this same phenomenon. Further, it would be instructive to list these other types of financial intermediaries outside the banking system. Goldsmith (1969), op. cit., p. 69, categorizes them as follows: (a) the central bank, (b) thrift institutions, (c) insurance organizations, including private insurance companies and private and public pension funds, (d) financial institutions of the second degree (whose liabilities accrue to other financial intermediaries), and (e) all other financial intermediaries.
11. Gurley and Shaw (1955) op. cit., p. 521.
12. This argument anticipates one of the main ones in John G. Gurley and Edward S. Shaw (1960): *Money in a Theory of Finance* (Washington, D.C.: Brookings Institution). They argued there that one should consider 'outside' money (money created by financial intermediaries) instead of just 'inside' money (the monetary base) in financial macroeconomic theories.
13. Gurley and Shaw (1955) op. cit., p. 521.
14. This analysis is similar in focus to James Tobin (1955): 'A Dynamic Aggregative Model,' *Journal of Political Economy*, April, published in the same year. We shall see later that Shaw's 'Debt Intermediation View', introduced in both Gurley and Shaw (1955 and 1960) and developed in Shaw (1973), is incompatible with both Tobin (1955) and Tobin (1965): 'Money and Economic Growth,' *Econometrica*, Vol. 33, No. 4, October.

15. Gurley and Shaw (1955), op. cit., pp. 525–7.
16. Ibid., p. 529.
17. Ibid., pp. 530–1.
18. Ibid., p. 532.
19. Ibid., p. 537.
20. Goldsmith (1969), op. cit., pp. 44–8.
21. The more recent study by U Tan Wai and Hugh T. Patrick (1973) came to a more cautious conclusion based upon recent financial market reforms in LDCs:

> Our survey of the available evidence on existing capital markets in LDCs indicates that, overall, their development impact has been small. Except for contemporary Brazil, the countries in our sample that have a relatively high ratio of security issues also have small capital markets. Almost all new issues in those countries are placed privately—government bonds to financial institutions and corporate securities either through the formation of new, private companies or to the existing stockholders . . . Our study has drawn attention to the dangers of expecting capital markets (as we have defined them) to have a sizable and rapidly increasing effect on the process of development in LDCs in the foreseeable future. This does not imply that policies to develop capital markets should not be used, but it should be recognized that their effects are limited. We support a positive and comprehensive but gradualist approach to capital market development by the government authorities. (U Tan Wai and Hugh T. Patrick (1973): 'Stock and Bond Issues and Capital Markets in Less Developed Countries,' in *IMF Staff Papers*, Vol. 20, No. 2, pp. 299–301.)

22. See David Levhari and Don Patinkin (1968): The Role of Money in a Simple Growth Model, in *American Economic Review*, September, for a good discussion of the models McKinnon (1973) and Shaw (1973) dismiss. These models include James Tobin (1965), op. cit.; Robert A. Mundell (1971): *Monetary Theory: Inflation, Interest, and Growth in the World Economy* (Santa Monica: Goodyear).
23. This is a critique of what Shaw (1973) refers to as the wealth view and Keynesian wealth view. They both also find fault in the full liquidity policy prescription. See Levhari and Patinkin (1968), op. cit., and Shaw (1973), op. cit.
24. Shaw (1973), op. cit., p. 59.
25. Ibid., pp. 55–6.
26. Ibid., p. 70.
27. These sector balance sheets are motivated and developed in Gurley and Shaw (1955 and 1960).
28. Ibid., p. 70.
29. Much of the following analysis, in addition to Shaw (1973) and McKinnon (1973), borrows from Maxwell J. Fry (1978): 'Money and Capital or Financial Deepening in Economic Development,' in *Journal of Money, Credit and Banking*, Vol. 10, No. 4 and Maxwell J. Fry (1982): 'Models of Financially Repressed Developing Countries,' in *World Development*, Vol. 10, No. 9.

30. McKinnon (1973), op. cit., Chapter 2, pp. 5–21 and pp. 57–8.
31. Ibid., p. 59.
32. Fry (1978), op. cit., pp. 46–7 and Fry (1982), op. cit., pp. 733–4.
33. In effect, McKinnon (1973) and Shaw's (1973) arguments represent a strong criticism of import-substitution industrialisation. See especially Shaw (1973), op. cit., pp. 12–15, and McKinnon (1973) op. cit., pp. 22–4 and pp. 68–9.
34. Shaw (1973), op. cit., p. 68.
35. The following analysis is similar to Fry (1978), op. cit., pp. 465–6, and Fry (1982), op. cit., pp. 731–3.
36. The five countries are: Jamaica, Burma, India, Greece, and Turkey. The balance of the countries in the sample are: Argentina, Brazil, Colombia, Mexico, Indonesia, Korea, Malaysia, Philippines, Singapore, Taiwan, Thailand, Portugal, and Kenya. For more information see Alberto Giovannini (1985): 'Saving and the Real Interest Rate in LDCs,' in *Journal of Development Economics*, Vol. 18.
37. Joseph E. Stiglitz and Andrew Weiss (1981): 'Credit Rationing in Markets with Imperfect Information,' in *American Economic Review*, June, pp. 393–7. Their argument is as follows. Let θ be an index of projects and for each project there is a probability function of gross returns, R. Different firms have different probability functions but the only parameter the bank can perceive of the distribution is the mean return, i.e. it cannot ascertain the riskiness of the project. Let $f(R, \theta)$ and $F(R, \theta)$ be the density and distribution functions of returns, respectively. Let greater θ correspond to greater risk in a mean preserving spread sense defined as follows.

$\theta_1 > \theta_2$ if

$$\int_0^\infty Rf(R, \Theta_1)\, dR = \int_0^\infty Rf(R, \Theta_2)\, dR$$

(in other words, the mean returns for θ_1 and θ_2 are equal) and

$$\int_0^y F(R, \Theta_1)\, dR \geq \int_0^y F(R, \Theta_2)\, dR.$$

In other words, there is more probability in the tails for the θ_1 distribution than for the θ_2 distribution. Let B be the amount an individual borrows at interest rate r. Default on a loan by an individual is defined as the following

$$C + R \leq B(1 + r^*)$$

where C equals collateral. The net return (profit) to the borrower is

$$\pi = \max[R - (1 + r^*)B; - C].$$

The return to the bank is

$$\rho(R, r) = \min[R + C; B(1 + r^*)].$$

Under the conditions of risk neutrality on the parts of lenders and borrowers, we must show that there exists an r^* which maximises expected returns to the bank. Since profits are a convex function of R, for any given interest r, there is a critical value $\hat{\theta}$ such that the firm borrows from the bank if and only if $\theta > \theta^*$. θ^* will also increase with the interest rate. Since as r^* increases, θ^* increases, successive groups of borrowers (corresponding to projects) drop out of the market and there will be a discrete fall in the average return to the bank from the remaining borrowers at interest rate r^*. In other words, after a certain point, the return to the bank decreases as r^* increases because the risk of the loan portfolio increases. Hence, there is a value for r^* which maximises the banks' expected return. If there is an interior maximum for the average return to the banks' portfolio, $\bar{\rho}^*(r)$, then there exist supply of funds schedules for which competitive equilibrium entails credit rationing. Loan demand, L^D, is downward sloping in (L, r^*) space.

Assuming the banking system to be perfectly competitive, profits will equal zero and deposit rates will equal the average return to the portfolio, ρ^*. We can depict credit rationing in a perfectly competitive credit market in Figure 1.N37.

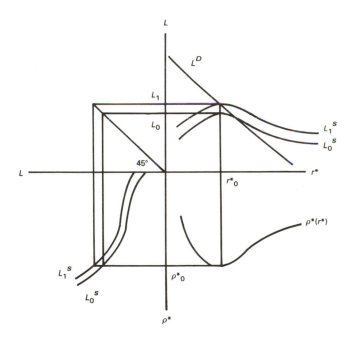

Figure 1.N37

Bank expected profits are maximised at ρ_0^*. Notice that the supply of loanable funds has been drawn as an increasing function of the deposit rate ρ. With an initial loan supply of L_0^s there is credit rationing of $(L_1 - L_0)$ at interest rate r_0^*. From the figure, there will be only one loanable funds schedule, L_1^s, which entails no credit rationing. Finally, if there was to be a shift out of the loan schedule from L_0^s to L_1^s, loanable funds would increase without any change in the loan interest rate, r_0^*.

38. For another example, see Stiglitz and Weiss (1981), op. cit., p. 408.
39. If real interest rates in curb markets are high compared with rates in the controlled section of the financial system, then this conclusion follows.
40. McKinnon (1973) refers to Samuel Morley (1971): 'Inflation and Stagnation in Brazil,' in *Economic Development and Cultural Change*, Vol. 19, No. 2, January in this passage. The importance of working capital in Brazil, paradoxically, provided the motivation of the models which show perverse output and price effects of interest rate liberalisation schemes analysed in the next section. It will figure importantly throughout this thesis.
41. McKinnon (1973), op. cit., p. 87.
42. Ibid., p. 88.
43. See Sweder Van Wijnbergen (1983a): 'Interest Rate Management in LDCs,' in *Journal of Monetary Economics*, Vol. 12, pp. 433–52.
44. McKinnon (1973), op. cit., p. 137.
45. Shaw (1973), op. cit., pp. 178–80.
46. Ibid., pp. 215–26, and McKinnon (1973), op. cit., pp. 155–61.
47. Ibid., pp. 166–9. If we ignore risk, the interest arbitrage condition is approximated by

$$i = i^* + \dot{e}^e$$

where i = domestic interest rate, i^* = foreign interest rate, and $\dot{e}^e$ = expected rate of exchange depreciation.
   If $i - \dot{e}^e > i^*$, then capital flows into the domestic energy until $i = i^* + \dot{e}^e$. If $\dot{e}^e$ moves appropriately, however, this capital inflow may be reduced. For a more thorough discussion of these conditions for LDCs which accounts for taxes, costs of intermediation, and systematic risk, see Vito Tanzi and Mario J. Blejer (1982): 'Inflation, Interest Rate Policy and Currency Substitution in Developing Countries: A Discussion of Some Major Issues,' in *World Development*, Vol. 10, No. 9.
48. McKinnon (1973), op. cit., pp. 166–7.
49. For a nice review of the formal modelling of the McKinnon–Shaw hypothesis, see Maxwell J. Fry (1982): 'Models of Financially Repressed Economies,' *World Development*, Vol. 10, No. 9 and Maxwell J. Fry (1988): *Money, Interest, and Banking in Economic Development* (Baltimore: Johns Hopkins University Press).
50. Basant K. Kapur (1976): 'Alternative Stabilization Policies in Less Developed Countries,' in *Journal of Political Economy*, Vol. 84, No. 4. The following analysis borrows much from Fry (1982), op. cit.
51. This fact is pointed out by Fry (1982), op. cit., p. 736.
52. Donald Mathieson (1980): 'Financial Reform and Stabilization Policy in

a Developing Economy,' in *Journal of Development Economics*, Vol. 7, p. 367.

53. It is assumed that the post-reform interest rate i will be everywhere higher than the pre-reform rate, i^*. This will hold in general during the initial stages of interest rate liberalisation. As saving is assumed to increase with the increase in the deposit rate, i^d, however, i may fall to make loans earning i^* desirable to hold on the part of banks. This case is ignored here.

54. Mathieson (1980), op. cit., pp. 390–5.

55. It is important to the results of this model that some capital inflows are induced. The capital inflows come from an assumed large degree of currency substitution, i.e. domestic residents hold a relatively large stock of foreign assets in a financially repressed economy. What should be avoided, however, is a large inflow of foreign saving, which crowds out domestic saving.

56. For a good discussion, see David Felix (1986): 'On Financial Blowups and Authoritarian Regimes in Latin American,' in Jonathan Hartlyn and Samuel A. Morley (1986): *Latin American Political Economy: Financial Crisis and Political Change* (Boulder: Westview).

57. Van Wijnbergen (1983a), op. cit., attempts to explain through supply side effect the stylised fact that in many LDCs orthodox deflationary policy leads to stagflation. He names this the 'Cavallo effect' after Domingo Cavallo, who qualifies it for Argentina in his 'Stagflationary Effects of Monetarist Stabilization Policies,' in M. June Flanders and Assaf Razin, eds.: *Development in an Inflationary World* (New York: Academic Press). This idea, however, is not new. For example, see Morley (1971), op. cit., and Ruben Almonacid and Alfonso Pastore (1975): 'Gradualismo ou Tratamento de Choque,' in *Pesquisa e Planejamento Economico*, Vol. 5. Van Wijnbergen essentially bases his model on that of Kapur, adding a full set of sectoral balance sheets, an explicit supply side equation, and long-term effects. Others that explicitly take working capital into account on the supply side are: Michael Bruno (1979): 'Stabilization and Stagflation in a Semi-Industrialized Economy,' in Rudiger Dornbusch and Jacob Frenkel, eds.: *International Economic Policy: Theory and Practice* (Baltimore: Johns Hopkins University Press); Lance Taylor (1981): 'IS/LM in the Tropics: Diagrammatics of the New Structuralist Macro Critique,' in William Cline and Sidney Weintraub, eds.: *Economic Stabilisation in Developing Countries* (Washington D.C.: Brookings Institution); and Lance Taylor (1983): *Structuralist Macroeconomics: Applicable Models for the Third World* (New York: Basic Books).

58. Van Wijnbergen (1983a), op. cit., pp. 445–51.

59. See Juan Carlos Lerda (1985): '"Marshall-Lerner" num Contexto de Disequilibrio Externo: O Caso do Brasil,' in *XIII Encontro Nacional de Economia* (ANPEC).

60. Edward Buffie (1984); 'Financial Repression, the New Structuralists, and Stabilization Policy in Semi-Industrialized Economies,' in *Journal of Development Economics*, Vol. 14.

61. See Felix (1986), op. cit.; Carlos Diaz-Alejandro (1985): 'Goodbye

Financial Repression, Hello Financial Crash,' in *Journal of Development Economics*, Vol. 19; Domingo F. Cavallo and A. Humberto Petrei (1983): 'Financing Private Business in an Inflationary Context: The Experience of Argentina,' in Pedro Aspe Armella, Rudiger Dornbusch, and Maurice Obstfeld, eds. (1983): *Financial Policies and the World Capital Market* (Chicago: The University of Chicago Press); Vittorio Corbo, Jaime de Melo, and James Tybout (1986): 'What Went Wrong in the Southern Cone?' in *Economic Development and Cultural Change*, Vol. 34, No. 3, April; Guillermo A. Calvo (1983): 'Fractured Liberalism under Martinez de Hoz,' in Aspe Armella, *et al.*, op. cit.; and James Tybout (1986): 'A Firm Level Chronicle of Financial Crisis in the Southern Cone,' in *Journal of Development Economics*, Vol. 24.

62. See Ronald I. McKinnon (1988): *Financial Liberalisation and Economic Development: A Reassessment of Interest Rate Policies in Asia and Latin America* (San Francisco: International Center for Economic Growth), and Vittorio Corbo and Jaime de Melo, eds. (1985): *Liberalisation with Stabilisation in the Southern Cone of Latin America*, a special edition of *World Development*, Vol. 13, No. 8.

63. Felix (1986), op. cit.; Diaz-Alejandro (1985), op. cit.; Cavallo and Petrei (1983), op. cit.; Corbo, de Melo, and Tybout (1986), op. cit.; Calvo (1983), op. cit.; and Tybout (1986), op. cit.

64. Sebastian Edwards and Sweder Van Wijnbergen (1986): 'The Welfare Effects of Trade and Capital Market Liberalization,' in *International Economic Review*, Vol. 27, No. 1, February, and (1987): 'On the Timing and Speed of Economic Liberalization in Developing Countries,' in Michael Connally and Claudio Gonzalez-Vega, eds. (1987): *Economic Reform and Stabilisation in Latin America* (New York: Praeger).

65. Ronald I. McKinnon (1985): 'How to Manage a Repressed Economy,' in Armin Gutowski, A. A. Arnaúdo, and Hans-Eckart Scharrer, eds. (1985): *Financing Problems of Developing Countries* (London: Macmillan).

66. See Roque B. Fernandez (1985): 'The Expectations Management Approach to Stabilization in Argentina during 1976–1982,' in *World Development*, Vol. 13, No. 8.

67. Bruce Greenwald, Joseph E. Stiglitz, and Andrew Weiss(1984): 'Informational Imperfections in the Capital Market and Macroeconomic Fluctuations,' in *American Economic Review*, May.

68. Joseph Stiglitz (1985): 'Credit Markets and the Control of Capital,' in *Journal of Money, Credit and Banking*, Vol. 17, No. 2, May.

69. See Stiglitz and Weiss (1981), op. cit..

70. Bruce Lloyd (1977): 'A Eficiência das Instituições e Mercados Financeiros,' *Mercado de Capitais e Desenvolvimento Economico* (Rio de Janeiro: IBMEC), p. 73.

71. For a good description, see Antonín Basch and Milic Kybal (1971): *Capital Markets in Latin America* (New York: Praeger), Chapter 3, and U Tan Wai and Hugh T. Patrick (1973), op. cit.

72. Hyman Minsky (1982): *Can 'It' Happen Again?: Essays on Instability and Finance* (New York: M. E. Sharpe).

73. In Minsky's terminology firms have changed from a hedged financed

position into a speculative finance position. A hedged finance unit is one whose receipts are expected to always exceed contractual payments on debt outstanding in every period in the foreseeable future. Speculative finance units are those whose total receipts over the foreseeable future exceed total cash payments on debt outstanding but short-term payments exceed short-term cash flows. Hedge financing units experience a continual decline in debt-asset ratios while speculative units experience a rise in debt-asset ratios in the short term decreasing in the long term.

74. Whether a particular firm is affected positively or negatively depends upon the correlation of the firm's profits with the variables undergoing the shock. For a good discussion see Julio Dreizzen (1985): 'Fragilidade Financeira, Inflação e Credito Indexado,' *Revista Brasileira de Economia*, Vol. 39, No. 3.

75. In Minsky's terminology, the unit becomes a Ponzi financed unit. The demand for credit becomes upward sloping in (i, y) space.

76. See David Felix (1986), op. cit.; Carlos Diaz-Alejandro (1981): 'Southern Cone Stabilization Plans,' in William Cline and Sidney Weintraub, eds.: *Economic Stabilisation in Developing Countries* (Washington D.C.: Brookings Institution); Diaz-Alejandro (1985), op. cit.; and Alejandro Foxly (1981): 'Stabilization Policies and Their Effects on Employment and Income Distribution,' in William Cline and Sidney Weintraub, op. cit.

77. The disdain for such development is reflected in the following quotation: 'The virtual neglect of securities markets in the literature of development economics reflects a general academic attitude that the subject is unimportant. Opinion in under developed countries and international agencies has been similar to that of academics, save for the institution building attitude sometimes found among politicians and officials.' Paul Drake (1977): 'Securities Markets in Less Developed Countries,' in *The Journal of Development Studies*, Vol. 13, No. 2, January, p. 73. Both Shaw (1973) and McKinnon (1973) reveal scepticism, if not discouragement, of such institution-creating policies.

78. The word development in this sense includes in its meaning economic growth but is not synonymous with it. For a discussion, see Werner Baer (1984): 'Semi-Industrialization and Semi-Development: The Legacy of Import-Substitution on Development Problems and on Development Economics,' in *METU Studies in Development*, Vol. 11, Nos. 1–2.

2 Development with Inflationary Finance: 1945–63

1. Under the law of similars (which dates back to 1911) domestic firms could apply for protection if their product was similar to one imported and if they could supply the market. For a discussion, see Werner Baer (1983): *The Brazilian Economy: Growth and Development* (New York: Praeger), pp. 74–5.

2. The most popular form this took, and which is still prevalent today, is the 'duplicata' system. Under this system, commercial banks would discount accounts receivable for firms seeking working capital. The bank would then collect the money owed on delivery of goods and services. This

system was fortified by the Letras de Cambio (bills of exchange) market which appeared in the late 1950s. As we shall see, the duplicata system played an important role in financial markets throughout the post-war period. For a discussion of the duplicata and Letra de Cambio see Mario H. Simonsen (1969): 'Inflation and the Money and Capital Markets of Brazil,' in H. S. Ellis, ed. (1969): *The Economy of Brazil* (Berkeley: University of California Press), pp. 140–5.

3. See Werner Baer (1983), op. cit., pp. 59–91; and Albert O. Hirschman (1969): 'The Political Economy of Import-Substitution Industrialization,' in *The Quarterly Journal of Economics*, Vol. 82, No. 1, February.

4. Walter J. Ness (1972): 'Some Effects of Inflation on Financing Investment in Argentina and Brazil' in Arnold W. Sametz, ed.: *Financial Development and Economic Growth: The Economic Consequences of Underdeveloped Capital Markets* (New York: New York University Press), pp. 247–8. Ness did not use the national accounts data presented in Table 2.4, but flow of funds accounts that he constructed in his statistical analysis.

5. For a discussion see Mario H. Simonsen (1969) op. cit., and Mario H. Simonsen (1966): *Situação Monetária, Creditícia, e do Mercado de Capitais* (Rio de Janeiro: EPEA).

6. Albert O. Hirschman (1968), op. cit., finds fault with simple exhaustion models of ISI. His discourse, however, does not concern itself with possible financial limitations to ISI.

7. Werner Baer (1965): *Industrialisation and Economic Development in Brazil* (Homewood: Irwin), p. 116.

8. The following example is based upon ones appearing in Douglas Gale (1982): *Money: In Equilibrium* (New York: Cambridge University Press), pp. 154–5, and Walter J. Ness, (1976): 'Inflação e o Mercado de Capitais,' in *Mercado de Capitais e Desenvolvimento Economico* (Rio de Janeiro: IBMEC), pp. 264–6.

9. See Douglas Gale (1982), op. cit., pp. 156–9, for this extension.

10. Ibid., pp. 157–8.

11. The economists at the Fundação Getulio Vargas had been predicting an inflationary recession for a few years before 1964.

> In the article on Corporation Results relating to 1962, published in our issue of February, 1964, page 115, when comparing the percentage increases in the working capital of corporations from 1959 to 1962, we stated that should that trend continue, there would be a reduction in the physical volume of business. (*Conjuntura Economica*, February, 1965, p. 129.)

12. See Joseph Stiglitz (1985): 'Credit Markets and the Control of Capital' in *Journal of Money, Credit and Banking*, Vol. 17, No. 2, May, for a discussion of how control may be better served by debt finance than equity finance, especially loans from commercial banks. Debt financing was effective in the Brazilian context, because all debt was tied to accounts receivable. The main creditors, e.g. the 'financeiras' and the commercial banks, were partly responsible for ensuring the payment of

the debt through monitoring the collection of accounts receivable. In this way, the financing arrangements accorded debt financing reduced uncertainty to the creditor and offered a service to firms which greatly increased their control of the firm's operations. Equity financing proved greatly inferior in terms of control as information about the firms' activities was all but non-existent to possible outside investors in the stock market. This argument differs from Stiglitz (1986) in that Brazilian firms looked to banks and other non-monetary financial intermediaries for a service which improved control for the few stockholders, while Stiglitz argues that banks become a dominant source of control owing to the existence of a large number of stockholders.

13. See Ness (1972), op. cit., pp. 234–5.
14. Octavio Gouvêa de Bulhões, the Minister of Finance under the Castelo Branco government which took over in 1964 and one of the architects of the reforms, summarised the motivation for the reforms in the following way.

> With inflation, the government's credit disappeared. Its re-establishment became imperative if government investments were to be freed from the exigencies of taxation. With inflation, the banking system had been swept clean of time deposits, an excellent source of cheap commercial credit. With inflation, the floatation of commercial bonds had been halted, though they are normally an excellent means of capturing resources to complement shareholder capital. . . . Between 1960 and 1963, entrepreneurs invested relatively little and resorted heavily to credit . . . The solution consists of reducing loans and increasing corporation's own working and shareholder capital. . . . As long as we insist on basing the expansion of firms on short-term credit, and persist in financing public works through surtaxes, we can be sure that inflation will always be a danger and promising economic development a dream.

Octavio Gouvêa de Bulhões (1969): 'Financial Recuperation for Economic Expansion,' in H. S. Ellis, ed. (1969): *The Economy of Brazil* (Berkeley: University of California Press).

15. A similar argument is developed in Maria de Conceição Tavares (1972): *Da Substuição de Importações ao Capitalismo Financeiro* (Rio de Janeiro: Zahar), pp. 125–153.
16. See Hirschman (1968), op. cit.
17. Ness (1972), op. cit., p. 244, estimated that less than 0.2 % of national saving was channelled through insurance companies.
18. See Antonio M. Silveira (1971): *Studies of Money and Interest Rates in Brazil*. Ph.D. Dissertation, Carnegie-Mellon University, republished in Portuguese by Edições Multiplic.
19. Antonio M. Silveira (1971), op. cit., estimated adaptive inflation expectations formation in terms of a Fisher equation framework based upon interest rates similar to those in Table 2.10 but which excluded compensating balances. His results show a lag in expectation formation of nearly three years. This clearly overestimates the true lag, because banks had

more flexibility in changing effective rates due to the use of compensating balances. It would not be worth while to reproduce his regressions using the data presented in Table 2.11 as the choice of compensating balance rate would be arbitrary with the true average one used unknown. It seems clear, however, that the *ex post* inflation premium implicit in the lending rates of commercial banks was formulated in an adaptive way because all real lending rates turned negative as inflation accelerated, e.g. 1961–3, and jumped sharply positive when inflation fell, e.g. 1954–5.

20. See Robert Barro (1972): 'A Theory of Monopolistic Price Adjustment,' in *Review of Economic Studies*, Vol. 39.

21. See Simonsen (1969), op. cit., pp. 145–6 and Simonsen (1966), op. cit., pp. 135–6.

22. It should be noted that the buyer of goods faces two prices, the spot or 'a vista' price of the good and the term or 'a prazo' price of the good. The price of working capital credit was thus passed on completely into the price of the good. Direct consumer credit did not exist at this time in Brazil. Although this system substituted for direct consumer credit, they should not be considered equivalent. Firms today, even after the institution of consumer credit, rely mainly on the discounting of duplicates for working capital loans.

23. See 'Bills of Exchange' in *Conjuntura Economica*, March, 1964, pp. 53–62; 'Sociedades Financeiras e Taxas de Juros' in *Conjuntura Economica*, June 1969; and Simonsen (1966), op. cit.

24. Simonsen (1966), op. cit., p. 139.

25. Ibid., pp. 142–5, and Júlio S. G. de Almeida (1985): 'A Crise do Mercado Paralelo de Letras: Causas e Consequencias sobre a Reforma Financeira de 1964–1966,' in *Revista Brasileira de Mercado de Capitais*, Vol. 11, No. 3.

26. Simonsen (1966), op. cit., p. 144.

27. Simonsen (1966), op. cit., estimated that the parallel bills of exchange market was from 8 to 10 times as large as the official market (p. 136). As Julio S. G. de Almeida (1985), op. cit., points out, however, it does not seem likely that the market for marginal borrowing serving mainly firms with a high credit risk would be so large (p. 69). The monthly journal from APEC editors, *A Economia Brasileira e Suas Perspectivas*, estimated the size of the market to be around 8.8 % of all credit extended to the private sector which would situate its size at about that of the official bills market. Another fact that supports the latter estimate is that this market attracted small sums of capital from a large amount of investors. This became evident when a major borrower on the parallel market, the Mannesman Group, went bankrupt in 1965 and refused to honor its obligations contracted in this 'illegal' manner.

28. See 'Bills of Exchange' in *Conjuntura Economica*, March 1964, pp. 61–2.

29. Simonsen (1966), op. cit., pp. 76–7.

30. The following analysis is based upon Affonso C. Pastore (1972): 'A Oferta de Moeda no Brasil—1961/72' in *Pesquisa e Planejamento Economico*, Vol. 3, No. 4, December; Affonso C. Pastore (1973): 'Aspectos da Política Monetária Recente no Brasil' in *Estudos Economicos*, Vol. 3,

No. 3; Affonso C. Pastore and Ruben D. Almonacid (1975): 'Gradua-lismo ou Tratamento de Choque' in *Pesquisa e Planejamento Econ-omico*, Vol. 5, No. 2, December; and Celso L. Martone (1976): 'Um Esquema para a Oferta de Moeda e Credito' in *Revista Brasileira de Economia*, Vol. 30, No. 4, Oct.–Dec.
31. From equation 2.2, we have

$$B = R^{v} + R^{c} + D^{bb} + C. \tag{i}$$

Multiplying and dividing the right-hand side of (i) by $D = D^{bc} + D^{bb}$, we get

$$B = \left[\frac{R^{v}}{D} + \frac{R^{c}}{D} + \frac{D^{bb}}{D} + \frac{C}{D} \right] D = [r^{v} + r^{c} + d^{bb} + c]D \tag{ii}$$

where r^{v} is the proportion of total deposits kept as voluntary (free) reserves, r^{c} is the proportion of total deposits kept as required reserves, d^{bb} is the proportion of total deposits held at the Bank of Brazil, and c is the ratio of currency to deposits. From equation 2.2 it is clear that

$$M = D + C = (1 + c)D. \tag{iii}$$

Solving for D in (iii) and substituting into (ii) yields

$$M = \left[\frac{1 + c}{r^{v} + r^{c} + d^{bb} + c} \right] B = mB. \tag{iv}$$

3 The Reforms of 1964–5

1. Donald Syvrud (1974): *Foundations of Brazilian Economic Growth* (Washington, D.C.: American Enterprise Institute), p. 232.
2. See Octávio Gouvêa de Bulhões (1969): 'Financial Recuperation for Economic Expansion,' in H. S. Ellis, ed.: *The Economy of Brazil* (Berkeley: University of California Press). Dr Bulhões was the Finance Minister for the Castello Branco government while the Minister of Planning was Roberto de Oliveira Campos. Together they designed the reforms of 1964–7. Many of their original intentions of the reforms are contained in Ellis (1969).
3. Syvrud (1974), op. cit., p. 107.
4. The acquisition of a 'casa propria' or 'own house' is now considered almost a right among the urban working class, much as landless peasants regard having their own piece of land.
5. A more detailed discussion of the CMN, the monetary budget, and the policy decision process in making financial policy follows later in this chapter.
6. This point was suggested to me by Juarez de Souza.
7. See Ernane Galveas (1982): 'Evolução do Sistema Financeiro e do Mercado de Capitais,' in *Revista de Economia do Nordeste*, Vol. 13, No. 1,

pp. 44–5, and Peter Knight, Michael Growe, and Alan Gelb (1984): *Brazil: Financial Systems Review* (Washington, D.C.: World Bank).

8. Galveas (1982), op. cit., p. 45.
9. Galveas, op. cit., pp. 42–3.
10. António Carlos F. Pinto (1985): *Os Investidores Institucionais no Brasil* (Rio de Janeiro: IBMEC), p. 6.
11. This is the main conclusion of Pinto (1985), op. cit. In order to come to it he calculated the efficient portfolio (based on the capital asset pricing model) for each institution and showed that it was significantly superior to the actual portfolio held by them.
12. David M. Trubek (1971): 'Law, Planning, and the Development of Brazilian Capital Markets,' in *The Bulletin* (New York: New York University Graduate School of Business Administration Institute of Finance), Nos. 72–3, April, p. 32.
13. Ibid., pp. 36–7.
14. Ibid., p. 37.
15. Ibid., pp. 37–8.
16. Mario H. Simonsen (1965): *O Mercado Brasileiro de Capitais* (Rio de Janeiro: EPEA), p. 82.
17. Trubek (1971), op. cit., p. 39.
18. Ibid., p. 40–1.
19. See Werner Baer (1983): *The Brazilian Economy: Growth and Development* (New York: Praeger).
20. Trubek (1971), op. cit., p. 36.
21. See Samuel Morley (1971): 'Inflation and Stagnation in Brazil,' in *Economic Development and Cultural Change*, Vol. 19, No. 2, January.
22. Trubek (1971), op. cit., pp. 46–7.
23. Ibid., p. 48.
24. See Walter L. Ness Jr. (1974): 'Financial Markets Innovation as a Development Strategy: Initial Results from the Brazilian Experience,' in *Economic Development and Cultural Change*, April, pp. 458–9.
25. This section is based upon José Leite Correa e Costa (1973): 'Fundos, Programas, e Linhas Especiais de Credito,' in *Conjuntura Economica*, Vol. 27, No. 11, November, and Annibal V. Villela and Werner Baer (1980): *O Setor Privado Nacional: Problemas e Políticas para Seu Fortalecimento* (Rio de Janeiro: IPEA).
26. See the introductory chapter for a description of the PND-II.
27. Martus A. R. Tavares and Nelson Carvalheiro (1985): *O Setor Bancário Brasileiro: Alguns Aspectos do Crescimento e da Concentração* (São Paulo: FIPE/USP), Table 25, p. 43.
28. Ibid., p. 43.
29. See Mario H. Simonsen (1974): 'A Imaginação Reformista,' in Roberto Campos and Mario H. Simonsen, eds.: *A Nova Economia Brasileira* (Rio de Janeiro: Livraria José Silva).
30. For a more detailed discussion see Chapter 2.
31. Simonsen (1974), op. cit., p. 125.
32. The BB's role as monetary authority was not extinguished until February 1986. Now that the BB is now only a (publicly owned) commercial bank, monetary authorities can conduct monetary policy with more control.

The BB's deficits, which previously had been financed by the 'conta de movimento' (described below), however, have become fiscal deficits. Hence, the BB still contributes to money creation to the extent that these deficits are monetised.

33. See Knight, *et al.* (1984), op. cit., and Paulo França (1986): 'A Conta de Movimento entre o Banco Central e o Banco do Brasil,' in *Conjuntura Economica*, Vol. 40, No. 3, March, pp. 47–8.

34. The workings of the 'saque especial' were described to me in a discussion with Luiz Bresser Pereira, ex-Minister of Finance in Brazil and ex-President of BANESPA.

35. See Syvrud (1972), op. cit., pp. 63–4.

36. See Mario H. Simonsen and Rubens P. Cysne (1986): 'O Sistema Monetário,' in *Macroeconomia* (Rio de Janeiro: Simposium Consultoria e Serviços, LTDA), pp. 9–10.

37. Jorge Vianna Monteiro (1983): 'Mecanismos Decisórios da Política Economica no Brasil,' in *Revista IBM*, No. 16, June, p. 21.

38. Ibid., p. 11; Also see Celso L. Martone (1983): 'Mudanças Estruturais no Mercado Monetário e Suas Implicações,' Working Paper No. 24, University of São Paulo, for a good discussion of the balance sheet framework of the monetary authorities and the financial system.

39. See Jorge Vianna Monteiro (1983), op. cit.; Jorge Vianna Monteiro (1982): *Fundamentos de Política Pública* (Rio de Janeiro: IPEA); and Jorge Vianna Monteiro (1983): 'Uma Análise do Processo Decisório do Sétor Público: O Caso do Conselho de Desenvolvimento Economico,' in *Pesquisa e Planejamento Economico*, April. For a discussion of the macroeconomic backdrop to these events, see the introductory chapter.

40. Mario H. Simonsen (1984): 'Inflation and Anti-Inflationary Policies in Brazil,' in *Brazilian Economic Studies*.

4 The Development of Equities Markets in Brazil: 1964–85

1. Werner Baer (1989): *The Brazilian Economy: Growth and Development* (New York: Praeger).

2. For a description of the closed family ownership structure of firms, see Mario Henrique Simonsen (1972): *Brasil 2002* (Rio de Janeiro: APEC), pp. 111–130.

3. Comissão de Valores Mobiliários (1979): *Sistema de Intemediação de Valores Mobiliários: II. Evolução Histórica* (Rio de Janeiro: CVM), pp. 94–101 and Roberto Teixeira da Costa (1982): 'Capital Markets in Brazil: Analysis of Performance and Outlook,' in Nicholas Bruck, ed. (1982): *Capital Markets Under Inflation* (Buenos Aires: Stock Exchange of Buenos Aires and the Inter-American Development Bank), p. 46.

4. Marcelo Fernandes Machado (1982): 'Um Balanço dos Incentivos Fiscais do DL 157: Evolução, Situação Atual e Aspectos Críticos,' in *Revista Brasileira de Mercado de Capitais*, Vol. 8, No. 22, p. 7. These maturities were changed again in 1974, allowing withdrawal of 50% in the fifth year and 50% in the sixth year.

5. Note that the data in Table 4.6 are not perfectly comparable with those in Table 4.7, owing to a change in national income accounting methods

in 1980. This fact, however, does not affect any of the conclusions drawn in this chapter.

6. Ney O. de Brito and Hélio Touriel (1980): 'A Estrutura Empresarial e a Atuação do BNDE no Mercado de Capitais,' in *Revista de Administração*, Universidade de São Paulo, Vol. 15, No. 2, June, as reprinted in Ney O. de Brito (1981): *O Mercado de Capitais e a Estrutura Empresarial Brasileira* (Rio de Janeiro: Guanabara Dois), pp. 39–40.

7. Walter L. Ness, Jr. (1978): 'A Empresa Estatal no Mercado de Capitais,' *Revista Brasileira de Mercado de Capitais*, Vol. 4, No. 12, p. 366.

8. Thomas J. Trebat (1983): *Brazil's State-Owned Enterprises: A Case Study of the State as Entrepreneur* (New York: Cambridge University Press), p. 212.

9. See for example Raymundo Magliano Filho (1986): 'O Estado e O Mercado de Capitais,' in *Conjuntura Economica*, Vol. 40, No. 3, March.

10. Ness (1978), op. cit.

11. Ness (1978) estimates the real annual return to a holder of Banco do Brasil stock to be around 30 % for the period 1955 to 1977. Ness (1978), op. cit., p. 367.

12. Ness (1978) estimates the average price–earnings ratio for state enterprises to be around 4 for 1978. Ness (1978), op. cit., p. 369.

13. Ness (1978), op. cit., pp. 370–1.

14. Ness (1978), op. cit., p. 365.

15. Data are based upon a sample of 199 firms holding 84 % of the 570 firms traded on the stock exchange collected by the CVM, as reported in Magliano Filho, op. cit., p. 105.

16. Trebat (1983). op. cit., pp. 78–9 and 84–93.

17. Simonsen (1972), op. cit., pp. 123–6.

18. Simonsen (1972), op. cit., p. 125. One should note that in a perfect capital market with high liquidity according to all stocks, the performance of a stock should not depend upon the distribution of dividends because the value of the firm should reflect the higher level of investment.

19. Ney O. Brito and Haroldo S. Portela (1976): 'Mercados Acionários: Sua Conceitação e a Nova Lei das Sociedades Anônimas,' *Revista de Administração de Empresas*, Vol. 16, No. 5, Sept.–Oct.

20. Not surprisingly, Mario Henrique Simonsen, the Minister of Finance in the Geisel administration, was the main author of the legislation. See Comissão de Valores Mobiliários (1987): *Brazilian Capital Markets Legislation* (Brasilia: Republica Federativa do Brasil).

21. Brito and Portela (1976), op. cit.

22. Abram Szajman (1988): 'A Lei das S. A. Está Vencida, ' in *Exame*, 2 November 1988.

23. Withholding taxes on interest income are deductible in the year-end tax statement.

24. With the writing of a new constitution in late 1988 came new tax provisions. One of these was to increase the taxation of short-term debt instruments *vis-à-vis* long-term ones. See Celso L. Martone (1989): 'The Structure of Taxes on Financial Instruments in Brazil,' manuscript, University of São Paulo.

25. See Chapter 5.
26. This is now referred to in economic circles as the 'Olivera–Tanzi effect.'
27. Martone (1989), op. cit., pp. 3–4.
28. Coopers and Lybrand (1986): *Profile of Banking and Finance in Brazil* (São Paulo: Coopers and Lybrand), p. 35, and Banco Central do Brasil (1985): *Boletim*, Jan.–Feb 1986.
29. Machado (1982), op. cit., p. 7.
30. Ibid., p. 7.
31. Ibid.
32. Ibid., p. 8.
33. Ibid., p. 8.
34. Ney R. O. de Brito and Antonio R. M. Neves (1984): 'O Desempenho Recente de Fundos de Investimento,' in *Revista Brasileira de Mercado de Capitais*, Vol. 10, No. 31, July–September, pp. 234–9.
35. Ibid, pp. 239–42.
36. The difference in all periods, however, is not statistically different from zero. Ibid., pp. 247–8.
37. Machado (1982), op. cit., pp. 20–2, and Comissão de Valores Mobiliários (1979), op. cit., pp. 135–6.
38. Comissão de Valores Mobiliários (1979), op. cit., pp. 136–8. See also Machado (1982), op. cit., pp. 22–3.
39. Roberto M. Montezano (1983): *Capital de Risco: Uma Alternativa de Financiamento* (Rio de Janeiro: IBMEC).
40. Ibid., pp. 45–6.
41. These include purchasing equities with repurchase clauses, convertible debentures, and preferred shares with a call option. Ibid., pp. 55–60.
42. With the possible exception of BRASILPAR Comércio e Participações S. A. Ibid., pp. 48–50.
43. Ibid., pp. 48–50.
44. Annibal V. Villela and Werner Baer (1980): *O Setor Privado Nacional: Problemas e Políticas para Seu Fortalecimento* (Rio de Janeiro: IPEA), pp. 95–107.
45. Montezano, op. cit., p. 63.
46. Ibid., p. 95.
47. Ibid., p. 64.
48. Ibid., p. 63.
49. BNDES (1982): *Relatório*, pp. 30–3.
50. Ibid., p. 65.
51. Villela and Baer (1980), op. cit., p. 67.
52. Ney O. de Brito and Hélio Touriel (1980): 'Estrutura Empresarial e a Atuação do BNDE no Mercado de Capitais,' in *Revista de Administração*, Universidade de São Paulo, Vol. 15, No. 2, June, as reprinted in Ney O. de Brito (1981): *O Mercado de Capitais e a Estrutura Empresarial Brasileira* (Rio de Janeiro: Guanabara Dois), p. 40.
53. Ibid., pp. 32–5.
54. Ibid., pp. 36–7.

5   The Indexation of Financial Assets in Brazil

1. See Mario H. Simonsen (1970): *Inflação: Gradualismo vs. Tratamento de Choque* (Rio de Janeiro: Apec), pp. 9–12.
2. See Chapter 1 for a discussion of these distortions and Chapter 3 for a discussion of the choice of indexation over eliminating the usury law.
3. See Ephraim Kleiman (1985): *The Indexation of Debt in Israel*, Working Paper No. 85.04, The Maurice Falk Institute of Economic Research in Israel, among many.
4. Werner Baer and Paul Beckerman (1980): 'The Trouble with Index-Linking: Reflections on the Recent Brazilian Experience,' in *World Development*, Vol. 8, No. 9, September.
5. Much of their work is based in part on work done by Adroaldo Moura da Silva, e.g. Adroaldo Moura da Silva (1979): *Intermediação Financeira no Brasil*. Manuscript, University of São Paulo.
6. See Basant Kapur (1982): 'Problems of Indexation in Financially Liberalized Less Developed Economies,' in *World Development*, Vol. 10, No. 3, among others.
7. See Thomas Sargent (1986): *Rational Expectations and Inflation* (New York: Harper Row).
8. For good discussions of the recent Latin American experience with inflations and specifically inflation feedback mechanisms, see Werner Baer and John H. Welch, eds. (1987): 'The Resurgence of Inflation in Latin America,' special edition of *World Development*, Vol. 15, No. 8 August.
9. Milton Friedman (1974): 'Monetary Correction,' in *Essays on Inflation and Indexation* (Washington D.C.: American Enterprise Institute) and James Tobin (1971): 'An Essay on the Principals of Debt Management,' in James Tobin: *Essays in Economics*. Vol. 1 (Chicago: Markham).
10. Stanley Fischer (1975): 'The Demand for Indexed Bonds.' in *Journal of Political Economy*, June.
11. Nominal bonds are bonds not indexed on an *ex post* basis. In other words, nominal bonds carry nominal interest rates known at the time they are purchased, which is not true of indexed bonds.
12. This is because the firm which issues the equity may either be helped, hurt, or unaffected by inflation in terms of earnings.
13. See Walter L. Ness, Jr. (1974): 'Financial Markets Innovation as a Development Strategy: Initial Results from the Brazilian Experience,' in *Economic Development and Cultural Change*, April, p. 458; Donald Syvrud (1972): 'Estrutura e Política de Juros no Brasil—1960/70,' in *Revista Brasileira de Economia*, Vol. 26, No. 1, Jan.–March, p. 136; and Júlio S. G. de Almeida (1985): 'A Crise do Mercado Paralelo de Letras: Causas e Consequencias sobre a Reforma Financeira de 1964–1966,' in *Revista Brasileira de Mercado de Capitais*, Vol. 11, No. 33, Jan.–March, pp. 73–5.
14. Claudio R. Contador (1976): 'Financial Development and Monetary Policy,' in *Brazilian Economic Studies*, No. 2, among his many other studies.
15. Kleiman (1985), op. cit., pp. 4–7.

16. David Levhari and Nissan Liviatan (1977): 'Risk and the Theory of Indexed Bonds,' in *American Economic Review*, June.
17. Paul Beckerman (1979): *Essays on the Theory of Indexed-Linking and Its Implementation in Brazil*, Ph.D. Dissertation, Princeton University.
18. Stanley Fischer (1983): 'On the Non-existence of Privately Issued Indexed Bonds,' in R. Dornbusch and M. H. Simonsen, eds.: *Inflation, Debt, and Indexation* (Cambridge: MIT Press).
19. This statement is derived from conversations with Howard A. Welch, Jr. and Gilberto A. Guizzelini, both of the tax department of Arthur Andersen and Co. Dividends are subject to non-deductible withholding taxes of 23% for individual investors and 25% for institutional investors according to the Corporation Law of 1976. For a more detailed discussion of the dividend taxes for the period 1964–76, see Chapter 3.
20. Milton Friedman (1974): 'Monetary Correction,' in *Essays on Inflation and Indexation* (Washington, D.C.: American Enterprise Institute).
21. The proof is as follows. $da^*/d\Pi$ will be negative when

$$\ln(1 + \Pi) < \Pi \tag{i}$$

Using the Taylor series expansion of $\ln(1 + \Pi)$ around $(1 + \Pi) = 1$ (i.e., $\Pi = 0$) with a remainder, equation (i) becomes:

$$\ln(1 + \Pi) = \Pi - \int_1^{(1+\Pi)} \frac{1 + \Pi - t}{(1 + \Pi)^2} \, dt < \Pi \tag{ii}$$

This will be true when the integral term is positive. Solving the integral, we obtain

$$\frac{1}{2} - \frac{1}{1 + \Pi} + \frac{1}{2(1 + \Pi)^2} > 0 \tag{iii}$$

Solving, condition (iii) reduces to $\Pi^2 > 0$, which is always true for Π not equal to zero. Hence, a sufficient condition for $da^*/d\Pi < 0$ is $\Pi > 0$ or $\Pi < 0$.
22. A detailed description of day trading in Brazil's so-called overnight market was given to the author by one of the most important traders in that market, Eliseu Tadao Hirata, in April 1986, who was then affiliated with Unibanco.
23. Clearly, this would have to be compared, in present value terms, to any cost incurred when selling bonds at a discount.
24. Some of this reasoning developed from discussions with Joaquim E. C. de Toledo of the University of São Paulo.
25. This section is based in part on John H. Welch, Carlos Alberto Primo Braga, and Paulo de Tarso Afonso de André (1987): 'Brazilian Public Sector Disequilibrium,' in *World Development*, Vol. 15, No. 8.
26. For a discussion of continuous as compared with discrete models, see Welch, Braga, and André (1987), op. cit.
27. Integrating equation 5.9 from $t - 1$ to t yields

$$\int_{t-1}^{t} [\dot{m}(s) + \dot{b}(s)] \, ds = \Delta m(t) + \Delta b(t)$$

$$= \int_{t-1}^{t} [g(s) + \tau(s)] \, ds + \rho \int_{t-1}^{t} b(0)e^{(B^* - \pi)s} \, ds - \pi \int_{t-1}^{t} e^{(M^* - \pi)s} \, ds \quad \text{(i)}$$

where B^* and M^* are the instantaneous growth rates of the nominal monetary base and the nominal stock of indexed bonds. Integrating (i), and assuming that the cumulative government deficit over the period is some positive constant δ, yields:

$$\Delta m(t) + \Delta b(t) = \delta + \rho \frac{b(0)}{(B^* - \pi)} e^{(B^* - \pi)(t-1)} [e^{(B^* - \pi)} - 1]$$

$$- \pi \frac{m(0)}{(M^* - \pi)} e^{(M^* - \pi)(t-1)} [e^{(M^* - \pi)} - 1] \quad \text{(ii)}$$

Since an exponential function expanded around $x = 0$ yields

$$e^x = 1 + x + \frac{x^2}{2!} + \frac{x^3}{3!} + \frac{x^4}{4!} + \ldots$$

then, if x is small, e.g. $|x| < 1$, $\exp[x]$ is approximately equal to $1 + x$. We assume that M^* and B^* are roughly equal to the inflation rate. This is not a strong assumption, because the period of adjustment is sufficiently small, i.e. one month. Also, recent estimates of the semi-elasticity (in years) of real money demand to inflation are between -0.6 and -0.9 which on a monthly basis is between -7.2 and -10.8. Hence, the *change* in the annual inflation rate would have to be on the order of 100 % and the change in the monthly inflation rate would have to be on the order of 9.3 to 14 percentage points to render the $M^* - \pi$ larger than one in magnitude, in which case this approximation is inappropriate. Hence, equation (ii) collapses to equation 5.10 in the text. Estimates of the semi-elasticity of real money demand to inflation can be found in Rubens P. Cysne (1985): 'Moeda Indexada,' in *Revista Brasileira de Economia*, Vol. 39, No. 1, and Claudio R. Contador (1986): 'O Espaço para o Déficit Público em 1986,' in *Conjuntura Economica*, April.

28. See Phillip Cagan (1956): 'The Monetary Dynamics of Hyperinflation,' in Milton Friedman, ed.: *Studies in the Quantity Theory of Money* (Chicago: University of Chicago Press), p. 7.

29. In order to see this, merely substitute r for II in note 21.

30. Cagan (1956), op. cit., p. 80.

31. See Baer and Welch (1987), op. cit.

32. The price level was measured by the average General Price Index (IGP-DI) from *Conjuntura Economica*; all other variables were taken from *Conjuntura Economica* and the Banco Central do Brazil *Boletim*.

33. Indexation clauses were used prior to the introduction of ORTNs on some loans extended by the National Economic Development Bank

(BNDE). BNDE loans, however, did not become significant until after the 1964 reforms.

34. Law 4357 of 17 July 1964. For descriptions, see Werner Baer and Paul Beckerman (1974): 'Indexing in Brazil,' in *World Development*, Vol. 2, Nos. 10–12; Albert Fishlow (1974): 'Indexing Brazilian Style: Inflation without Tears?,' *Brookings Papers on Economic Activity*, No. 1; Walter L. Ness, Jr. (1974): 'Financial Markets Innovation as a Development Strategy: Initial Results from the Brazilian Experience,' in *Economic Development and Cultural Change*, April; Werner Baer and Paul Beckerman (1980): 'The Trouble with Index-Linking: Reflections on the Recent Brazilian Experience,' *World Development*, Vol. 8, No. 9; and Walter L. Ness, Jr. (1977): *A Influência da Correção Monetária no Sistema Financeiro* (Rio de Janeiro: IBMEC).

35. See Chapter 3.

36. It should be noted that the term 'indexed' refers to *ex post* or post-fixed indexed assets, while the terms 'non-indexed' or 'nominal' assets refer to *ex ante* or pre-fixed indexed assets. Also, see note 10.

37. Ness (1977), op. cit., p. 454.

38. Ness (1977), op. cit, p. 467 and Baer and Beckerman (1980), op. cit., p. 679.

39. Alberto Giovannini (1985): 'Saving and the Real Interest Rate in LDCs,' in *Journal of Development Economics*, Vol. 18.

40. See the introductory chapter for a more detailed discussion of this policy.

41. See Baer and Beckerman (1980), op. cit., and Ness (1977), op. cit., for similar conclusions.

42. See Ness (1977), op. cit., and Ness (1974), op. cit.

43. The Mannesman default is described in more detail in the Introduction and in Chapter 2.

44. See Welch, Braga, and André (1987), op. cit., for a discussion of this process.

45. Baer and Beckerman (1980), op. cit., pp. 685–6.

46. The following quote from the then Minister of Finance, Octávio Bulhões, describes the nature of private sector resistance to indexing liabilities.

> Borrowers and lenders in the private market refuse to follow the system of monetary correction used in Treasury obligations. Their objection lies in the difficulty the borrower has in making an additional payment at the end of the loan, to compensate the creditor for capital depreciation due to inflation over the period.

> In other words, *ex post* indexation would make the use of compensating balances difficult to justify and would make charging interest at the time the loan is made impossible. Hence, indexation would make the collection of monopoly rents disguised as 'risk premia' increasingly difficult. Octávio Gouvêa de Bulhões (1969): 'Financial Recuperation for Economic Expansion,' in H. S. Ellis, ed.: *The Economy of Brazil* (Berkeley: University of California Press).

47. Leif E. Christoffersen (1969): 'Taxas de Juros e a Estrutura de Um

Sistema de Bancos Comerciais em Condições Inflacionárias: O Caso do Brasil,' in *Revista Brasileira de Economia*, Vol. 23, No. 2.

48. Christoffersen (1969) calculated these average interest rates by dividing the year's interest earnings by the average stock of loans. Since these stocks of loans are overstated owing to the use of compensating balances, the interest rate will be understated.

49. The correlation coefficient between the spread and the inflation rate is 0.74, which is significantly positive at the 0.5 % level.

50. It should be noted that 'pre-fixed' indexed assets fall into the 'non-indexed' asset category used above.

51. Baer and Beckerman (1980), op. cit., p. 698.

52. See note 45.

53. Bulhões (1969), op. cit., p. 170. For similar discussions, see Kenneth King (1972): *Recent Brazilian Monetary Policy*, monograph, CEDE-PLAR—Federal University of Minas Gerais, Belo Horizonte, pp. 24–6.

54. For discussions of the Brazilian open market , see Roberto Fendt, Jr. (1977): *Mercado Aberto e Política Monetária* (Rio de Janeiro: IBMEC); Peri Agostinho da Silva (1981): *Desenvolvimento Financeiro e Política Monetária* (Rio de Janeiro: Editora Interciência); Peri Agostinho da Silva (1983): *Técnicas de Mercado Aberto* (Rio de Janeiro: IBMEC); and Fernando T. R. do Val (1983): 'Efeitos das Operações de Mercado Aberto sobre as Reservas dos Bancos Comerciais Brasileiros,' in *Revista Brasileira de Mercado de Capitais*, Vol. 9, No. 28, Oct.–Dec.

55. See the Introduction for a full description of the policies used to reduce real interest rates which included direct subsidies to commercial banks. King (1972), op. cit., pp. 28–9, argues that these policies were only partially effective if at all in decreasing real interest rates faced by borrowers.

56. See Fendt (1977), op. cit., pp. 6–10; Moura da Silva (1979), op. cit., pp. 83–4; Baer and Beckerman (1980), op. cit., pp. 687–92; and Ness (1977), op. cit., pp. 82–90.

57. Ness (1977), op. cit., p. 99.

58. See Moura da Silva (1979), op. cit., pp. 82–93, and Ness (1977), op. cit., pp. 96–102.

59. Moura da Silva (1979), op. cit., p. 85.

60. See Baer and Beckerman (1980), op. cit., p. 689.

61. The last part of 1979 and the year 1980 do not fall in this category, as interest rates were controlled during this period on both pre-fixed in-dexed and post-fixed indexed assets because of the policy of prean-nounced monetary correction rates. This period should be viewed an attempt to escape the ills of indexation described here by partially de-indexing the economy. Unfortunately, the attempt was a failure.

62. Welch, Braga, and André (1987), op. cit.

63. Agostinho da Silva (1983), op, cit., pp. 54–5.

64. Carlos Brandão (1989): 'A Dívida Pública Interna: Seus Problemas e Soluções,' in *Conjuntura Economica*, October, pp. 55–6.

65. See José Júlio Senna (1985): 'Correção Monetária em Discussão,' in *Carta Andima*, No. 52, May, and José Júlio Senna (1985): 'Correção Vai se Estabilizar em 3 ou 4 Meses,' in *Arthur Andersen Sinopse Empresar-*

ial, Vol. 2, No. 8. Dr Senna was one of the creators and main apologists of this indexation scheme as Central Bank director of the public debt under Minister of Finance Dornelles.

66. This analysis owes very much to many discussions with Celso L. Martone of the University of São Paulo during the period in which this took place.

67. Décio Kadota and Adroaldo Moura da Silva (1982): 'Inflação e Preços Relativos: O Caso Brasileiro 1970/79,' *Estudos Economicos*, Vol. 12, No. 1.

68. John H. Welch (1989): 'The Variability of Inflation in Brazil: 1974–1982,' *Journal of Economic Development*, Vol. 14, No. 1.

69. See Werner Baer (1987): 'The Resurgence of Inflation in Brazil,' in *World Development*, Vol. 15, No. 8, and Luiz Bresser Perreira (1987): 'Inertial Inflation and the Cruzado Plan,' in *World Development*, Vol. 15, No. 8.

70. See Werner Baer and Paul Beckerman (1987): 'The Decline and Fall of Brazil's Cruzado Plan,' Faculty Working Paper No. 1393, BEBR, University of Illinois at Urbana-Champaign.

6 Commercial Banks, Investment Banks, Conglomeration, and the Financial Structure of Firms

1. Ailton C. Filho (1980): 'A Controvérsia dos Conglomerados Financeiros: O Caso do Brasil,' in *Revista Brasileira de Mercado de Capitais*, Vol. 6, No. 18, Sept.–Dec., p. 289.

2. The term 'total liabilities' includes the capital account, or in other words one can look at these as the proportion of each liability item to total assets. It should be noted that in all the tables in this chapter, figures for the years before 1967 are not strictly comparable with those after and including 1967, owing to a change in accounting standards.

3. This remittance maturity was decreased early in 1986 to fifteen days.

4. Calculated from Table 6.2.

5. For a description of '432 accounts', see the Introduction and Chapter 3.

6. For a description of the role of investment banks in the Brazilian financial system, see Chapter 3.

7. For a nice review of government policy concerning commercial bank expansion, see Martus A. R. Tavares and Nelson Carvalheiro (1985): *O Setor Bancário Brasileiro: Alguns Aspectos do Crescimento e da Concentração* (São Paulo: FIPE/University of São Paulo Press), pp. 147–86.

8. See the Introduction and Chapter 1.

9. Some such studies include Sebastião M. Vital (1973): 'Economias de Escala em Bancos Comerciais Brasileiros,' in *Revista Brasileira de Economia*, Vol. 27, No. 1; José Brito Alves (1974): *Fatores Determinantes da Eficiência dos Bancos Comerciais* (Rio de Janeiro: Sindicato dos Bancos do Estados de Guanabara); Antonio C. Meirelles (1974): *Economias de Escala e a Estrutura do Sistema Financeiro: O Caso Brasileiro* (Rio de Janeiro: Sindicato dos Bancos do Estado de Guanabara); and Oseas Maurer (1980): *Eficiência e Economias de Escala no Banco do Brasil* (Rio de Janeiro: EPGE).

10. Diana Hancock (1985a): 'The Financial Firm: Production with Monetary

and Non-Monetary Goods,' in *Journal of Political Economy*, Vol. 93, No. 5; Diana Hancock (1985b): 'Bank Profitability, Interest Rates, and Monetary Policy,' in *Journal of Money, Credit, and Banking*, Vol. 17, No. 2, May; and Diana Hancock (1986): 'A Model of the Financial Firm with Imperfect Asset and Deposit Elasticities,' in *Journal of Banking and Finance*, Vol. 10, No. 1, March.

11. Filho (1980), op. cit., pp. 294–6, develops a simple theoretical model of multi-market conglomeration and the conditions necessary to generate results similar to those obtained under perfect competition. These conditions generally include the independence of a conglomerates actions across the different goods produced, which seem rather restrictive when one is looking at financial products.

12. See Ney O. Brito and Ricardo F. Franco (1981): 'Retornos de Escala em Bancos Comerciais: A Experiencia Brasileira,' in *Revista Brasileira de Mercado de Cepitais*, Vol. 7, No. 21.

13. Filho (1980), op. cit., pp. 298–9.

14. See Tavares and Carvalheiro (1985), op. cit., pp. 53–4.

15. Ibid., p. 54.

16. For an account of the 'extra-judicial' or 'out-of-court' liquidations, see *Gazeta Mercantil International Weekly Edition*, 23 December 1985, p. 12. In December 1985 President Sarney changed the existing legislation such that the liabilities of banks would also be subject to inflation indexation which was precipitated by the failure of the banks Auxiliar, Comind, and Maisonnave in November, 1985. For an account see Carlos Drummond (1985): 'O Negocio é Credibilidade,' in *Senhor*, 4 December 1985, pp. 61–2.

17. For a journalistic account of such cases, see J. Carlos de Assis (1984a): *A Chave do Tesouro: Anatomia dos Escândalos Financeiros no Brasil* (Rio de Janeiro: Paz e Terra) and J. Carlos de Assis (1984b): *A Dupla Face da Corrupção* (Rio de Janeiro: Paz e Terra).

18. Modesto Carvalhosa (1979): *Oferta Pública de Aquisição de Ações* (Rio de Janeiro: IBMEC), pp. 112–14.

19. These subsidies took the form of allowing those banks in compliance to hold an increasing proportion of required reserves in the form of indexed government bonds. For a more detailed explanation, see the Introduction.

20. Tavares and Carvalheiro (1985), op. cit., p. 54.

21. Ibid., p. 55, pp. 179–81.

22. Ibid., p. 144.

23. Ibid., pp. 144–5.

24. See the Introduction and Chapter 5 for description of why 1980 is an outlier year. Effectively, interest rates were controlled by the government well below the inflation rate.

25. These data may understate the true effective rate, according to my own calculations, based upon the same compensating balance rate and payment techniques reported in *Análise Financeira*, nominal interest rate between 1982 and 1983 reached almost 1200 % per year on 'duplicata discounts' or a real rate of interest between 300 % and 650 % per year!

26. Luiz A. Perdigão (1983): *Conglomerados Financeiros: Análise do Seu*

Desempenho no Brasil. (Rio de Janeiro: IBMEC).
27. The data for the following analysis were taken from Alvaro A. Zini, Jr. (1984): 'Evolução da Estrutura Financeira das Empresas no Brasil 1969–1977,' in *Estudos Economicos*, Vol. 14, No. 1, January–April; Domingo G. Rodrigues (1984a): 'A Evolução das Empresas Não-Financeiras no Brasil no Periódo 1975–82,' in *Revista Brasileira de Mercado de Capitais*, Vol. 10, No. 30, April–June; and 'Balanço de Mil Sociedades por Ações,' in *Conjuntura Economica*, December 1988, pp. 55–117.
28. Celso L. Martone (1986): 'Reforma Bancária: Quais Os Objetivos?' in *O Plano Cruzado: Na Visão dos Economistas da USP* (São Paulo: Livraria Pioneira), p. 212.

7 Summary and Concluding Remarks: Towards a New Financial Reform in Brazil

1. Cuddington (1987) estimates that Brazil's cumulative capital flight over the 1975 to 1982 period amounted to 1.35 % of that of Argentina, 0.63 % of that of Mexico, and 1.9 % of that of Venezuela. Brazil's capital flight was insignificant in relative terms. See John T. Cuddington (1987): 'Capital Flight,' in *European Economic Review*, Vol. 31, p. 383.
2. See John H. Welch (1990): 'Monetary Policy, Hyperinflation, and Internal Debt Repudiation: Reflections on Brazil and Argentina,' Working Paper,University of North Texas.
3. Alvaro Zini, Jr. (1989): 'Fundar a Dívida,' *Informações FIPE*, January.
4. At time of writing, the newly elected Collor administration has effected what amounts to internal debt repudiation by freezing 80% of the liabilities of the financial system in March 1990. The main reason was to diminish the borrowing requirements of the public sector. For a critical analysis of this policy, see Welch (1990), op. cit.
5. See Carlos Drummond (1986): 'A Segunda Geração das Reformas,' in *Senhor*, 4 August 1986, pp. 26–30. For an examination of the Canadian case, see Garry J. Schinasi (1985): 'Canadian Financial Markets: The Government's Proposal for Reform,' *International Finance Discussion Papers*, No. 269.
6. Jorge R. Wahl (1984): 'Todo Poder aos Bancos,' in *Senhor*, 6 June 1984, p. 42.
7. See José Carlos de Assis (1984): *A Chave do Tesouro: Anatomia dos Escândalos Financeiros no Brasil* (Rio de Janeiro: Paz e Terra), especially the chapters on the TAA case, the Delfin group case, and the Vitória-Minas case, pp. 181–230.
8. See Celso L. Martone (1986): 'Reforma Bancária: Quais os Objectivos?,' in *O Plano Cruzado: Na Visão de Economistas da USP* (São Paulo: Livraria Pioneira), p. 213.
9. Celso L. Martone (1986): 'Indexação, Inflação Subjacente, e Políticas de Controle de Demand,' in *Indexação, Juros, e Inflação* (São Paulo: ANDIMA), pp. 42–3 and Celso L. Martone, Carlos A. Luque, and Luiz M. Lopes (1986): *Mercado Financeiro e Ajustamento Macroeconomico Brasileiro: 1978–1985* (São Paulo: IPE/USP), pp. 63–4.

Bibliography

A Economia Brasileira e Suas Perspectivas (Rio de Janiero: APEC Editora).

Agostino da Silva, Peri (1981): *Desenvolvimento Financeiro e Política Monetária* (Rio de Janeiro: Interciência).

—— (1983): *Técnicas de Mercado Aberto* (Rio de Janeiro: IBMEC).

Almeida, Júlio S. G. de (1985): 'A Crise do Mercado Paralelo de Letras: Causas e Consequencias sobre a Reforma Finançeira de 1964–1966,' in *Revista Brasileira de Mercado de Capitais*, Vol. 11, No. 33, Jan.–March.

Almonacid, Ruben and Alfonso Pastore (1975): 'Gradualismo ou Tratamento de Choque,' in *Pesquisa e Planejamento Economico*, Vol. 5.

Análise Financeira. (São Paulo: Análise Editora, S. A.), various issues

Arida, Persio (1982): 'Reajuste Salarial e Inflação,' in *Pesquisa e Planejamento Economico*, Vol. 12, No. 2.

Arida, Persio and André Lara Resende (1985): *Inertial Inflation and Monetary Reform in Brazil*, Working Paper No. 85, Catholic University of Rio de Janeiro (PUC).

Assis, José Carlos de (1984): *A Chave do Tesouro: Anatomia dos Escândalos Financeiros no Brasil* (Rio de Janeiro: Paz e Terra).

—— (1984): *A Dupla Face da Corrupção* (Rio de Janeiro: Paz e Terra).

Bacha, Edmar (1977): 'Issues and Evidence on Recent Brazilian Growth,' in *World Development*, Vol. 5, Nos. 1–2.

—— (1983): 'Vicissitudes of Recent Stabilization Attempts in Brazil and the IMF Alternative,' in John Williamson, ed.: *IMF Conditionality* (Washington, D.C.: Institute for International Economics).

Bacha, Edmar and Francisco Lopes (1984): 'Inflation, Growth, and Wage Policy: A Brazilian Perspective,' in *Journal of Development Economics*, September.

Baer, Werner (1965): *Industrialisation and Economic Development in Brazil* (Homewood: Irwin).

—— (1983): *The Brazilian Economy: Growth and Development* (New York: Praeger).

—— (1984): 'Semi-Industrialization and Semi-Development: The Legacy of Import-Substitution Industrialization on Development Problems and on Development Economics,' in *METU Studies in Development*, Vol. 11, Nos. 1–2.

—— (1984): 'Brazil: Political Determinants of Development,' in Robert Wesson, ed.: *Politics, Policies, and Economic Development in Latin America* (Stanford: Hoover Institution Press).

—— (1987): 'The Resurgence of Inflation in Brazil,' in *World Development*, Vol. 15, No. 8.

Baer, Werner and Paul Beckerman (1974): 'Indexing in Brazil,' in *World Development*, Vol. 2, Nos. 10–12.

—— (1980): 'The Trouble with Index-Linking: Reflections on the Recent Brazilian Experience,' in *World Development*, Vol. 8, No. 9, September.

—— (1987): '*The Decline and Fall of Brazil's Cruzado Plan*,' Working Paper

212

No. 1393, BEBR, University of Illinois at Urbana-Champaign.

Baer, Werner and Annibal Villela (1980): *O Setor Privado Nacional: Problemas e Políticas para Seu Fortalecimento* (Rio de Janeiro: IPEA).

Baer, Werner and John H. Welch (1987): 'The Resurgence of Inflation in Latin America,' special edition of *World Development*, Vol. 15, No. 8.

Barro, Robert (1972): 'A Theory of Monopolistic Price Adjustment,' in *Review of Economic Studies*, Vol. 39.

Basch, Antonín and Milis Kybal (1971): *Capital Markets in Latin America* (New York: Praeger).

Baumol, William (1965): *The Stock Market and Economic Efficiency* (New York: Fordham University Press).

Beckerman, Paul (1979): *Essays on the Theory of Index-Linking and Its Implementation in Brazil*. Ph.D. Dissertation, Princeton University.

Bonelli, Regis and Pedro Malan (1977): 'The Brazilian Economy in the 1970s: Old and New Developments.' in *World Development*, Vol. 5, Nos. 1–2.

Bresser Perreira, Luiz (1987): 'Inertial Inflation and the Cruzado Plan,' in *World Development*, Vol. 15, No. 8.

Brito, Ney O. and Ricardo F. Franco (1981): 'Retornos de Escala em Bancos Comerciais: A Experiencia Brasileira,' in *Revista Brasileira de Mercado de Capitais*, Vol. 7, No. 21.

Brito, Ney R. O. and Antonio R. M. Neves (1984): 'O Desempenho Recente de Fundos de Investimento,' in *Revista Brasileira de Mercado de Capitais*, Vol. 10, No. 31, July–September.

Brito, Ney R. O. and Fernando A. Paiva (1987): 'Bancos de Investimento: Evolução e Estrutura Financeira,' in *Revista Brasileira de Mercado de Capitais*, Vol. 13, No. 38.

Brito, Ney O. and Haroldo S. Portela (1976): 'Mercados Acionários: Sua Conceitação e a Nova Lei das Sociedades Anônimas,' *Revista de Administração de Empresas*, Vol. 16, No. 5, Sept.–Oct.

Brito, Ney O. de and Hélio Touriel (1980): 'Estrutura Empresarial e a Atuação do BNDE no Mercado de Capitais,' in *Revista de Administração*, Universidade de São Paulo, Vol. 15, No. 2, June, as reprinted in Ney O. de Brito (1981): *O Mercado de Capitais e a Estrutura Empresarial Brasileira* (Rio de Janeiro: Guanabara Dois).

Brito Alves, José (1974): *Fatores Determinantes da Eficiência dos Bancos Comerciais* (Rio de Janeiro: Sindicato dos Bancos do Estado de Guanabara).

Bruno, Michael (1979): 'Stabilization and Stagflation in a Semi-Industrialized Economy,' in Rudiger Dornbusch and Jacob Frenkel, eds.: *International Economic Policy: Theory and Evidence* (Baltimore: Johns Hopkins University Press).

Buffie, Edward (1984): 'Financial Repression, the New Structuralists, and Stabilization Policy in Semi-Industrialized Economies,' in *Journal of Development Economics*, Vol. 14.

Bulhões, Octávio Gouvêa (1969): 'Financial Recuperation for Economic Expansion,' in H. S. Ellis, ed.: *The Economy of Brazil* (Berkeley: University of California Press).

Cagan, Phillip (1956): 'The Monetary Dynamics of Hyperinflation,' in Milton

Friedman, ed.: *Studies in the Quantity Theory of Money* (Chicago: University of Chicago Press).

Calvo, Guillermo (1983): 'Trying to Stabilize: Some Theoretical Reflections Based on the Experience of Argentina,' in Pedro A. Armella, Rudiger Dornbusch, and Maurice Obstfeld, eds.: *Financial Policies and the World Capital Market: The Problem of Latin American Countries* (Chicago: University of Chicago Press).

—— (1983): 'Fractured Liberalism under Matinez de Hoz,' in Pedro Aspe Armella, Rudiger Dornbusch, and Maurice Obstfeld, eds.: *Financial Policies and the World Capital Market*. (Chicago: University of Chicago Press).

Cardoso, Eliana (1977): 'Moeda, Renda, e Inflação: Algumas Evidencias da Economia Brasileira,' in *Pesquisa e Planejamento Economico*, Vol. 7, No. 2.

Carneiro Netto, Dionísio D. and Arminio Fraga Neto (1984): 'Variaveis de Credito e Endogeneidade da Oferta de Moeda no Brasil,' in *Pesquisa e Planejamento Economico*, Vol. 14, No. 1.

Cavallo, Domingo F. (1981): 'Stagflationary Effects of Monetarist Stabilization Policies in Economies with Persistent Inflation,' in M. June Flanders and Assaf Razin, eds.: *Development in an Inflationary World* (New York: Academic).

Christofferson, Leif (1969): 'Taxas de Juros e A Estrutura de Um Sistema de Bancos Comerciais em Condições Inflacionárias,' in *Revista Brasileira de Economia*, Vol. 23, No. 2, April–June.

Comissão de Valores Mobiliários (1987): *Brazilian Capital Markets Legislation* (Brasilia: Republica Federativa do Brasil).

Conceição Tavares, Maria (1972): *Da Substituição de Importações ao Capitalismo Financeiro* (Rio de Janeiro: Zahar).

Conjuntura Economica. (Rio de Janeiro: Fundação Getúlio Vargas), various issues.

Contador, Claudio (1976): 'Financial Market Development and Monetary Policy,' in *Brazilian Economic Studies*, No. 2.

—— (1978): 'A Exogeneidade da Oferta de Moeda no Brasil,' in *Pesquisa e Planejamento Economico*, Vol. 8, No. 2.

—— (1986): 'O Espaço para o Déficit Público em 1986,' in *Conjuntura Economica*, April.

Coopers and Lybrand (1986): *Profile of Banking and Finance in Brazil* (São Paulo: Coopers and Lybrand).

Corbo, Vittorio and Jaime de Melo, eds. (1985): *Liberalization with Stabilization in the Southern Cone of Latin America*, a special edition of *World Development*, Vol. 13, No. 8.

Corbo, Vittorio, Jaime de Melo, and James Tybout (1986): 'What Went Wrong in the Southern Cone?' in *Economic Development and Cultural Change*, Vol. 34, No. 3. April.

Correa e Costa, José L. (1973): *Fundos, Programas, e Linhas Especiais de Credito,'* in *Conjuntura Economica*, Vol. 27, No. 11.

Costa, Roberto Teixeira da (1982): 'Capital Markets in Brazil: Analysis of Performance and Outlook,' in Nicholas Bruck, ed.: *Capital Markets Under Inflation* (Buenos Aires: Stock Exchange of Buenos Aires and Inter-American Development Bank).

Coutinho, Luciano (1981): 'Inflexões e Crise da Política Economica: 1974–1980,' in *Revista de Economia Política*, Vol. 1. No. 1, Jan.–March.

Cuddington, John T. (1987): 'Capital Flight,' in *European Economic Review*, Vol. 31.

Cysne, Rubens P. (1985): 'Moeda Indexada,' in *Revista Brasileira de Economia*, Vol. 39, No. 1.

Diaz-Alejandro, Carlos (1981): 'Southern Cone Stabilization Plans,' in William Cline and Sidney Weintraub, eds.: *Economic Stabilization in Developing Countries* (Washington D.C.: Brookings Institution).

—— (1983): 'Some Aspects of the 1982–83 Payments Crisis,' *Brookings Papers on Economic Activity*, No. 2.

—— (1985): 'Goodbye Financial Repression, Hello Financial Crash,' in *Journal of Development Economics*, Vol. 19.

Dornbusch, Rudiger and Adroaldo Moura da Silva (1984): 'Taxas de Juros e Depósitos em Moeda Estrangeira no Brasil,' in *Revista Brasileira de Economia*, Vol. 38, No. 1, Jan.–March.

Drake, Paul (1977): 'Securities Markets in Less Developed Countries,' in *The Journal of Development Studies*, Vol. 13, No. 2, January.

Dreizzen, Julio (1985): 'Fragilidade Financeira, Inflação e Credito Indexado,' in *Revista Brasileira de Economia*, Vol. 39, No. 3.

Drummond, Carlos (1985): 'O Negocio é Credibilidade,' in *Senhor*, 4 December 1985.

—— (1986): 'A Segunda Geração das Reformas,' in *Senhor*, August 1986.

Edwards, Sebastian and Sweder Van Wijnbergen (1986): 'The Welfare Effects of Trade and Capital Market Liberalization,' in *International Economic Review*, Vol. 27, No. 1, February.

—— (1987): 'On the Timing and Speed of Economic Liberalization in Developing Countries,' in Michael Connally and Claudio Gonzalez-Vega, eds.: *Economic Reform and Stabilization in Latin America* (New York: Praeger).

Engle, Robert F. (1982): 'Autoregressive Conditional Heterskedasticity with Estimates of U.K. Inflation,' *Econometrica*, Vol. 50.

Epstein, Edward C. (1987): 'Recent Stabilization Attempts in Argentina: 1973–1985', in *World Development*, Vol. 15, No. 8.

Felix, David (1986): 'On Financial Blowups and Authoritarian Regimes in Latin America', in Jonathan Harleyn and Samuel A. Marley (eds), *Latin America Political Economy: Financial Crisis and Political Change* (Brussels: Westview Press).

Fendt, Roberto Jr. (1977): *Mercado Aberto e Política Monetária* (Rio de Janeiro: IBMEC).

Fernandez, Roque B. (1985): 'The Expectations Management Approach to Stabilization in Argentina during 1976–1982,' in *World Development*, Vol. 13, No. 8.

Filho, Ailton C. (1980): 'A Controvérsia dos Conglomerados Financeiros: O Caso do Brasil,' in *Revista Brasileira de Mercado de Capitais*, Vol. 6, No. 18, Sept.–Dec.

Fischer, Stanley (1975): 'The Demand for Indexed Bonds,' in *Journal of Political Economy*, June.

—— (1983): 'On the Non-existence of Privately Issued Indexed Bonds,' in

Rudiger Dornbusch and Mario H. Simonsen, eds.: *Inflation, Debt, and Indexation* (Cambridge, Mass.: MIT Press).

Fishlow, Albert (1973): 'Some Reflections on Post-1964 Brazilian Economic Policy,' in Alfred Stepan, ed.: *Authoritarian Brazil* (New Haven: Yale University Press).

—— (1974): 'Indexing Brazilian Style: Inflation without Tears?' in *Brookings Papers on Economic Activity*, No. 1.

Foxley, Alejandro (1981): 'Stabilization Policies and Their Effects on Employment and Income Distribution,' in William Cline and Sidney Weintraub, eds.: *Economic Stabilization in Developing Countries* (Washington, D.C.: Brookings Institution).

França, Paulo (1986): 'A Conta de Movimento' entre o Banco Central e o Banco do Brasil,' in *Conjuntura Economica*, Vol. 40, No. 3, March.

Friedman, Milton (1974): 'Monetary Correction,' in *Essays on Inflation and Indexation* (Washington, D.C.: American Entrprise Institute).

Fry, Maxwell J. (1978): 'Money and Capital or Financial Deepening in Economic Development?' in *Journal of Money, Credit, and Banking*, Vol. 10, No. 4, November.

—— (1980): 'Saving, Investment, Growth and the Cost of Financial Repression,' in *World Development*, Vol. 8.

—— (1982): 'Models of Financially Repressed Developing Economies,' in *World Development*, Vol. 10, No. 9.

—— (1988): *Money, Interest, and Banking in Economic Development* (Baltimore: Johns Hopkins University Press).

Gale, Douglas (1982): *Money: In Equilibrium* (New York: Cambridge University Press).

Galveas, Ernane (1982): 'Evolução do Sistema Financeiro e do Mercado de Capitais,' in *Revista de Economia do Nordeste*, Vol. 13, No. 1.

Gazeta Mercantil International Edition. (São Paulo: Gazeta Mercantil Journal S. A.), various issues.

Giovannini, Alberto (1985): 'Saving and the Real Interest Rate in LDCs,' *Journal of Development Economics*, Vol. 18.

Goldsmith, Raymond (1969): *Financial Structure and Development* (New Haven: Yale University Press).

Greenwald, Bruce, Joseph E. Stiglitz, and Andrew Weiss (1984): 'Information Imperfections in the Capital Market and Macroeconomic Fluctuations,' in *American Economic Review*, May.

Gurley, John G. and Edward S. Shaw (1955): 'Financial Aspects of Economic Development,' in *American Economic Review*, Vol. 45, No. 4, September.

—— (1960): *Money in a Theory of Finance* (Washington, D.C.: Brookings Institution).

Hancock, Diana (1985): 'The Financial Firm: Production with Monetary and Non-Monetary Goods,' in *Journal of Political Economy*, Vol. 93, No. 5.

— (1985): 'Bank Profitability, Interest Rates, and Monetary Policy,' in *Journal of Money, Credit, and Banking*, Vol. 17, No. 2, May.

—— (1986): 'A Model of the Financial Firm with Imperfect Asset and Deposit Elasticities,' in *Journal of Banking and Finance*, Vol. 10, No. 1, March.

Hirschman, Albert O. (1968): 'The Political Economy of Import-Substitution Industrialization,' in *Quarterly Journal of Economics*, Vol. 82, No. 1, February.

Kadota, Décio and Adroaldo Moura da Silva (1982): 'Inflação e Preços Relativos: O Caso Brasileiro 1970/79,' *Estudos Economicos*, Vol. 12, No. 1.

Kapur, Basant K. (1976): 'Alternative Stabilization Policies for Less Developed Economies,' in *Journal of Political Economy*, Vol. 84, No. 4.

—— (1976): 'Two Approaches to Ending Inflation,' in Ronald I. McKinnon, ed.: *Money and Finance in Economic Growth and Development* (New York: Marcel Dekker).

—— (1982): 'Problems of Indexation in Financially Liberalized Less Developed Countries,' in *World Development*, Vol. 10, No. 3.

—— (1983): 'Optimal Financial and Foreign-Exchange Liberalization of Less Developed Economies,' *The Quarterly Journal of Economics*, February.

Keynes, John M. (1937): 'The General Theory of Employment,' in *Quarterly Journal of Economics*, February.

King, Kenneth (1972): *Recent Brazilian Monetary Policy*, monograph, CEDPLAR—Federal University of Minas Gerais, Belo Horizonte.

Kleiman, Ephraim (1985): *The Indexation of Debt in Israel*. Working Paper No. 85.04, The Maurice Falk Institute of Economic Research in Israel, Jerusalem.

Knight, Peter, Michael Growe, and Alan Gelb (1984): *Brazil: Financial Systems Review* (Washington, D.C.: World Bank).

Kregel, J. A. (1976): 'Economic Methodology in the Face of Uncertainty: The Modeling Methods of Keynes and the Post-Keynesians,' in *Economic Journal*, Vol. 86, June.

Krugman, Paul and Lance Taylor (1978): 'Contractionary Effects of Devaluation,' in *Journal of International Economics*, Vol. 8.

Lerda, Juan Carlos (1985): '"Marshall-Lerner" num Contexto de Disequilibrio Externo: O Caso do Brasil,' in *XIII Encontro Nacional de Economia* (ANPEC.)

Levhari, David and Nissan Liviatan (1977): 'Risk and the Theory of Indexed Bonds,' in *American Economic Review*, June.

Levhari, David and Don Patinkin (1968): 'The Role of Money in a Simple Growth Model,' in *American Economic Review*, September.

Lloyd, Bruce (1977): 'A Eficiência das Instituições e Mercados Financeiros, in *Mercado de Capitais e Desenvolvimento Economico* (Rio de Janeiro: IBMEC).

Lopes, Francisco L. (1976): 'Inflação, Correção Monetária, e Controles de Preços,' in *Revista Brasileira de Economia*, Vol. 30, No. 4.

—— (1984): 'Inflação Inercial, Hiperinflação, e Desinflação: Notas e Conjecturas,' in *Revista da ANPEC*, Vol. 7, No. 7.

Macedo, Roberto B. M. (1983): 'Wage Indexation and Inflation: The Recent Brazilian Experience,' in Rudiger Dornbusch and Mario H. Simonsen, eds.: *Inflation, Debt, and Indexation* (Cambridge, Mass.: MIT Press).

Machado, Marcelo Fernandes (1982): 'Um Balanço dos Incentivos Fiscais do DL 157: Evolução, Situação Atual e Aspectos Críticos,' in *Revista Brasileira de Mercado de Capitais*, Vol. 8, No. 22.

Magliano Filho, Raymundo (1986): 'O Estado e O Mercado de Capitais,' in *Conjuntura Economica*, Vol. 40, No. 3, March.

Marques, Maria S. B. (1983): 'Moeda e Inflação: A Questão de Causalidade,' in *Revista Brasileira de Economia*,Vol. 37, No. 1.

Martone, Celso L. (1976): 'Um Esquema para a Oferta de Moeda e Credito,' in *Revista Brasileira de Economia*, Vol. 30, No. 4, Oct.–Dec.

—— (1983): *Mudanças Estruturais no Mercado Monetário e Suas Implicações*. Working Paper No. 24, University of São Paulo.

—— (1985): 'A Inconsisténcia do Modelo Brasileiro de Ajustamento,' in *Estudos Economicos*, Vol. 15, No. 1.

—— (1986): 'Reforma Bancária: Quais os Objetivos?' in *O Plano Cruzado: Na Visão dos Economistas da USP* (São Paulo: Livraria Pioneira).

—— (1986): 'Indexação, Inflação Subjacente, e Políticas de Controle de Demanda,' in *Indexação, Juros, e Inflação* (São Paulo: ANDIMA).

—— (1989): 'The Structure of Taxes on Financial Instruments in Brazil,' manuscript, University of São Paulo.

Martone, Celso, Carlos A. Luque, and Luiz M. Lopes (1986): *Mercado Financeiro e Ajustmento Macroeconomico Brasileiro: 1978–1985* (São Paulo: IPE/USP).

Mathieson, Donald (1979): 'Financial Reforms and Capital Flows in a Developing Country, in *IMF Staff Papers*, Vol. 26, No. 3.

—— (1980): 'Financial Reform and Stabilization Policy in a Developing Economy,' in *Journal of Development Economics*, Vol. 7.

Maurer, Oseas (1980): *Eficiência e Economias de Escala no Banco do Brasil* (Rio de Janeiro: EPGE).

McKinnon, Ronald I. (1973): *Money and Capital in Economic Development* (Washington D.C.: Brookings Institution).

—— (1976): *Money and Finance in Economic Growth and Development* (New York: Dekker).

—— (1985): 'How to Manage a Repressed Economy,' in Armin Gutowski, A. A. Arnaúdo, and Hans-Eckart Scharrer, eds. (1985): *Financing Problems of Developing Countries* (London: Macmillan).

—— (1988): *Financial Liberalization and Economic Development: A Reassessment of Interest Rate Policies in Asia and Latin America* (San Francisco: International Center for Economic Growth).

Meirelles, Antonio C. (1974): *Economias de Escala e a Estrutura do Sistema Financeira: O Caso Brasileiro* (Rio de Janeiro: Sindicato dos Bancos do Estado de Guanabara).

Minsky, Hyman (1977): 'The Financial Instability Hypothesis: An Interpretation of Keynes and An Alternative to Standard Theory,' in *Nebraska Journal of Economics and Business*, Vol. 16, No. 1, Winter.

—— (1980): 'The Federal Reserve: Between a Rock and a Hard Place,' in *Challenge*, May/June.

—— (1982): *Can 'It' Happen Again?: Essays on Instability and Finance* (New York: M. E. Sharpe).

Modigliani, Franco and Marcus Miller (1958): 'The Cost of Capital, Corporation Finance, and the Theory of Investment,' in *American Economic Review*, June.

Monteiro, Jorge Vianna (1982): *Fundamentos de Política Pública* (Rio de Janeiro: IPEA).
—— (1983): 'Mecanismos Decisórios da Política Economica no Brasil,' in *Revista IBM*, No. 16, June.
—— (1983): 'Uma Análise do Processo Decisório do Setor Público: O Caso do Conselho de Desenvolvimento Economico,' in *Pesquisa e Planejamento Economico*, April.
Montezano, Roberto M. (1983): *Capital de Risco: Uma Alternativa de Financiamento* (Rio de Janeiro: IBMEC).
Morley, Samuel (1971): 'Inflation and Stagnation in Brazil,' in *Economic Development and Cultural Change*, Vol. 19, No. 2, January.
Moura, Alkimar R. (1981): 'A Abertura Financeira Externa: Um Breve Relato Sobre da Experíencia Brasileira,' in *Revista de Economia Política*, Vol. 1, No. 1, Jan.–March.
Moura da Silva, Adroaldo (1979): *Intermediação Financeira no Brasil*, monograph, University of São Paulo.
Mundell, Robert (1971): *Monetary Theory: Inflation, Interest, and Growth in the World Economy* (Santa Monica: Goodyear).
Munhoz, Décio (1982): *Controle de Taxas de Juros—A Viabilidade de Compatibilização da Dívida Externa e da Dívida Interna*, Working Paper No. 91, University of Brasília.
Ness, Walter L. J. (1972): 'Some Effects of Inflation on Financing Investment in Argentina and Brazil,' in Arnold W. Sametz, ed.: *Financial Development and Economic Growth: The Economic Consequences of Underdeveloped Capital Markets* (New York: New York University Press).
—— (1974): 'Financial Markets Innovation as a Development Strategy: Initial Results from the Brazilian Experience,' in *Economic Development and Cultural Change*, April, Vol. 22, No. 3.
—— (1976): 'Inflação e o Mercado de Capitais,' in *Mercado de Capitais e Desenvolvimento Economico* (Rio de Janeiro: IBMEC).
—— (1977): *A Influência da Correção Monetária no Sistema Financeiro* (Rio de Janeiro: IBMEC).
—— (1978): 'A Empresa Estatal no Mercado de Capitais,' *Revista Brasileira de Mercado de Capitais*, Vol. 4, No. 12.
Pastore, Affonso C. (1972): 'A Oferta de Moeda no Brasil—1961/72,' in *Pesquisa e Planejamento Economico*, Vol. 3, No. 4, December.
—— (1973): 'Aspectos da Política Monetária Recente no Brasil,' in *Estudos Economicos*, Vol. 3, No. 2, December.
Perdigão, Luiz A. (1983): *Conglomerados Financeiros: Análise do Seu Desempenho no Brasil* (Rio de Janeiro: IBMEC).
Pinto, Antonio C. F. (1985): *Os Investidores Institucionais no Brasil* (Rio de Janeiro: IBMEC).
Primo Braga, Carlos A. (1985): *A Economia Brasileira na Segunda Metade dos Anos 80.* Working Paper No. 18, University of São Paulo.
Rodrigues, Domingo G. (1984): 'A Evolução das Empresas Não-Financeiras no Brasil no Periódo 1975–82,' in *Revista Brasileira de Mercado de Capitais*, Vol. 10, No. 30, April–June.
Sargent, Thomas (1976): 'The Observational Equivalence of Natural and

Unnatural Rate Theories of Macroeconomics,' in *Journal of Political Economy*, Vol. 84, No. 3.

—— (1986): *Rational Expectations and Inflation* (New York: Harper & Row).

Sargent, Thomas and Neil Wallace (1976): 'Rational Expectations and the Theory of Economic Policy,' in *Journal of Monetary Economics*, No. 2.

Sayad, João (1977): 'Controles de Juros e Saldos Médios,' in *Revista Brasileira de Economia*, Vol. 31, No. 1, Jan.–March.

Senna, José Júlio (1985): 'Correção Monetária em Discussão,' in *Carta Andima*, No. 52.

—— (1985): 'Correção Vai se Estabilizar em 3 ou 4 Meses,' in *Arthur Andersen Sinopse Empresarial*, Vol. 2, No. 8.

Shackle, G. L. S. (1961): 'Recent Theories Concerning the Nature and Role of Interest,' in *The Economic Journal*, Vol. 71, June.

—— (1967): *Time in Economics* (Amsterdam: North-Holland).

Shaw, Edward S. (1973): *Financial Deepening in Economic Development* (New York: Oxford University Press).

Sheshinski, Etan and Yoram Weiss (1977): 'Inflation and the Costs of Price Adjustment,' in *Review of Economic Studies*, Vol. 7, No. 8.

Shinasi, Garry J. (1985): 'Canadian Financial Markets: The Government's Proposal for Reform,' in *International Finance Discussion Papers*, No. 269.

Silveira, Antonio M. (1971): *Studies of Money and Interest Rates in Brazil*. Ph.D. Dissertation, Carnegie-Mellon University, republished in Portuguese by Edições Multiplic.

Simonsen, Mario H. (1966): *Situação Monetária, Creditícia, e do Mercado de Capitais* (Rio de Janeiro: EPEA).

—— (1965): *O Mercado Brasileiro de Capitais* (Rio de Janeiro: EPEA).

—— (1969): 'Inflation and the Money and Capital Markets of Brazil,' H. S. Ellis, ed.: *The Economy of Brazil* (Berkeley: University of California Press).

—— (1970): *Inflação: Gradualismo vs. Tratamento de Choque* (Rio de Janeiro: Apec).

—— (1972): *Brasil 2002* (Rio de Janeiro: APEC).

—— (1974): 'A Imaginação Reformista,' in Roberto Campos and Mario H. Simonsen, eds.: *A Nova Economia Brasileira* (Rio de Janeiro: Livraria José Silva).

—— (1984): 'Inflation and Anti-Inflationary Policies in Brazil,' in *Brazilian Economic Studies*.

Simonsen, Mario H. and Rubens P. Cysne (1986): 'O Sistema Monetário,' in *Macroeconomia* (Rio de Janeiro: Simposium Consultoria e Serviços, LTDA).

Stiglitz, Joseph E. (1985): 'Credit Markets and the Control of Capital,' in *Journal of Money Credit and Banking*, Vol. 17, No. 2, May.

Stiglitz, Joseph and Andrew Weiss (1981): 'Credit Rationing in Markets with Imperfect Information,' in *American Economic Review*, June.

Syvrud, Donald (1972): 'Estrutura e Política de Juros no Brasil—1960–70,' in *Revista Brasileira de Economia*, Vol. 26, No. 1, Jan.–March.

—— (1974): *Foundations of Brazilian Economic Growth* (Washington, D.C.: American Enterprise Institute).

Szajman, Abram (1988): 'A Lei das S.A. Está Vencida,' in *Exame*, 2 November 1988.

Tanzi, Vito and Mario I. Blejer (1982): 'Inflation, Interest Rate Policy, and Currency Substitution in Developing Countries: A Discussion of Some Major Issues,' in *World Development*, Vol. 10, No. 9.

Tavares, Martus A. R. and Nelson Carvalheiro (1985): *O Setor Bancário Brasileiro: Alguns Aspectos do Crescimento e da Concentração* (São Paulo: IPE/ University of São Paulo Press).

Taylor, Lance (1981): 'IS/LM in the Tropics: Diagrammatics of the New Structuralist Macro Critique,' in William Cline and Sidney Weintraub, eds.: *Economic Stabilization in Developing Countries* (Washington D.C.: Brookings Institution).

—— (1983): *Structuralist Macroeconomics: Applicable Models For The Third World* (New York: Basic Books).

Tobin, James (1955): 'A Dynamic Aggregative Model,' in *Journal of Political Economy*, April.

—— (1971): 'An Essay on the Principals of Debt Management,' in James Tobin: *Essays in Economics*. Vol. 1 (Chicago: Markhan).

Trebat, Thomas J. (1983): *Brazil's State-Owned Enterprises: A Case Study of the State as Entrepreneur* (New York: Cambridge University Press).

Trubek, David M. (1971): 'Law, Planning, and the Development of the Development of the Brazilian Capital Market,' in *The Bulletin*, Nos. 72–73, April, New York University School of Business Administration Institute of Finance.

Turnovsky, Stephen J. (1977): *Macroeconomic Analysis and Stabilization Policy* (London: Cambridge University Press).

Tybout, James (1986): 'A Firm Level Chronicle of Financial Crisis in the Southern Cone,' in *Journal of Development Economics*, Vol. 24.

Val, Fernando T. R. do (1983): 'Efeitos das Operações de Mercado Aberto sobre as Reservas dos Bancos Comerciais Brasileiros,' in *Revista Brasileira de Mercado de Capitais*, Vol. 9, No. 28, Oct.–Dec.

Van Wijnbergen, Sweder (1983a): 'Interest Rate Management in LDCs,' in *Journal of Monetary Economics*, Vol. 12.

—— (1983b): 'Credit Policy, Inflation, and Growth in a Financially Repressed Economy,' in *Journal of Development Economics*, Vol. 13.

Vital, Sebastião M. (1973): 'Economias de Escala em Bancos Comerciais Brasileiros,' in *Revista Brasileira de Economia*, Vol. 27, No. 1.

Wahl, Jorge R. (1984): 'Todo Poder aos Bancos,' in *Senhor*, 6 June 1984.

Wai, U Tan (1977): 'Estrategias e Politicas de Estimulo e Desenvolvimento do Mercado de Capitais,' in *Mercado de Capitais e Desenvolvimento Economico* (Rio de Janeiro: IBMEC.)

—— and Hugh T. Patrick (1973): 'Stock and Bond Issues and Capital Markets in Less Developed Countries,' in *IMF Staff Papers*, Vol. 20, No. 2.

Weintraub, E. Roy (1975): '"Uncertainty" and the Keynesian Revolution,' in *History of Political Economy*, Vol. 7, No. 4.

Welch, John H. (1989): 'The Variability of Inflation in Brazil: 1974–1982,' *Journal of Economic Development*, Vol. 14, No. 1.
—— (1990): 'Monetary Policy, Hyperinflation, and Internal Debt Repudiation: Reflections on Brazil and Argentina,' Working Paper, University of North Texas.
Welch, John H., Carlos A. Primo Braga, and Paulo T. A. André (1987): 'Brazilian Public Sector Equilibrium,' in *World Development*, Vol. 15, No. 8.
Zini, Jr., Alvaro A. (1984): 'Evolução da Estrutura Financeira das Empresas no Brasil 1969–1977,' in *Estudos Economicos*, Vol. 14, No. 1, January–April.
—— (1989): 'Fundar a Dívida,' *Informações FIPE*, January.

Index

Adjustable Obligations of the National
    Treasury (ORTNs)   7, 69, 124,
    136–7, 138
  change in indexation rule (1985)   149
  'go round' auction   148
  'purged' index   146
  repurchase agreements   147
  see also indexation
adjustment   9, 13–14
administrative costs of loans   171–2
agriculture
  commercial bank loans to   158, 159
  growth   5
  subsidised credit   67
  'superharvest' policy   12
amortisation window   62, 64
arbitrage mechanism   11
Argentina   12
  capital flight   182, 211
  financial system   169–72 passim
  neo-liberal reform   37, 38, 40
asset structures
  commercial banks   156–8
  firms   174–5
  investment banks   160, 161
Auxiliar bank   210

Baer, W.   48
  indexation   124, 128; inflation   147,
    149; private sector   139, 142–3
Banco do Estado de Minas Gerais   55,
    56
Bank of Amazônia (BASA)   72, 73
Bank of Brazil (BB)   184
  agencies   164
  'Bank Reform Act'   6, 69
  bills of exchange   61–2
  'conta de movimento'   85, 86
  credit to private sector   54, 78, 79
  funds and programmes managed
    by   76
  loan windows   76
  monetary base   64
  money creation   6, 62, 85, 201
  rediscount window   62, 64
  role   6, 62, 85, 86, 200–1
bank charters   162–3, 179, 183
Bank of the Northeast (BNB)   72, 73
'Bank Reform Act' (1964)   6, 69

bankruptcies   32–3, 160, 163, 210
bearer bonds   109
Beckerman, P.   127
  indexation   124; inflation   147, 149;
    private sector   128, 139, 142–3
bills of exchange market   140, 196
  and indexed bonds   127, 138
  inflationary finance   59–62
  parallel market   61, 198
black credit markets   35–6, 61, 198
BNCC (National Cooperative Credit
    Bank)   54, 72
BNDE see National Economic (and
    Social) Development Bank
BNDESPAR (BNDES Participações)
    77, 117, 118, 119
  financing   118, 121
  holdings   118, 120
  performance   120, 121
BNH see National Housing Bank
Bolivia   169–71 passim
Bresser Plan   182
Brito, N. O. de   102, 112, 113, 120
Bruno, M.   36
Buffie, E.   37
Bulhões, O. Gouvéia de   124, 199, 207

cadernatas de poupança (passbook
    savings accounts)   70, 137, 138
Cagan, P.   132, 136
Caixas Economicas Estaduais (state
    savings banks)   70, 78, 80
Caixas Economicas Federais (federal
    savings banks)   70, 71 78, 80
Campos, R. de Oliveira   124, 199
Canadian Wheat   77
capital flight   182, 211
capital flows, liberalisation of   38–9
'Capital Markets Law' (1965)   6–7, 69,
    93, 158, 206
  democratic capitalism   91
  equities markets   73
  extension of indexation rules   137
capitalism, democratic   91, 110
'cartas patentes' (bank charters)   162–
    3, 179, 183
Carvalheiro, N.   79, 80, 166
Castello Branco administration   6–8,
    68, 124

CCAs (Equity Purchase
Certificates) 110–11
CDI (Economic/Industrial Development
Council) 87
Central Bank (BCB)
'Bank Reform Act' 6, 69
BB's 'conta de movimento' 85
conglomeration 179
'extra-judicial' liquidations 163
foreign capital inflows 7, 9
432 accounts 11
funds and programmes managed
by 77
'go round' auctions 15, 148–9
independence 184
institutional investors 73
open capital companies 74–5
re-lending policy 146
Resolution 16 74
Resolution 21 75
Resolution 63 7
Resolution 106 74–5
certificates of deposit 141, 143
charter system 162–3, 179, 183
Chile 37, 38, 40, 169–72 *passim*
Christoffersen, L. 140
CIP (Industrial Price Council) 87
CMN *see* National Monetary Council
Collor administration 211
Colombia 169–71 *passim*
Comind bank 210
Comissão de Valores Mobiliários
(CVM) 106, 112
commerce, loans to 158, 159
commercial banks 152
administrative costs 171–2
agencies 59, 164, 165
concentration 152–3, 165–7
conglomeration 112, 152–3, 163–7
duplicata discount system 53
financial layering 19–20
inflation tax 15
interest rates 140–2; and
inflation 55–7
'internationalization' 178–9
loans to private sector 57, 58, 78,
79, 82, 84
LTNs 144
political power 15, 68
private 78, 79, 163–4, 165
short-term credit 71–2
state 78, 79, 164
structure 153–8, 159; assets 156–8;
liabilities 153–6; profile of loans
158, 159

U.S. 188
usury law 68
compensatory refinancing 146
competition 183
conglomeration 10, 152–3, 160–9, 179,
209–10
see also multiple banks
constant-purchasing-power units of
account 125–6
see also dollar; Adjustable
Obligations of the National
Treasury
consumption boom 71
'conta de movimento' (movement
account) 85
Contador, C. 127
control, stock market and 99–107
'Corporations Law' (1976) 106, 205
corporate ownership structure 49–50,
122–3
see also equities markets
costs, financial 176, 177, 178, 182–3
see also interest rates
Costa e Silva administration 8
credit
black markets 35–6, 61, 198
commercial banks 158, 159, 165–6,
167; operations 156–8
costs 51–2, 182–3;
administrative 171–2; *see also*
interest rates
efficiency index 170–1
-to-GDP ratios 169, 170
investment banks 160, 161
long-term 45, 53, 54, 72–3
medium-term 72–3
policy 64–5
private sector 53, 54; growth 82–3;
percentage of GDP 81–2;
structure of loans 78–81
rationing 27–8, 40, 191–2; interest
rates 55–7, 58
short-term 45, 53, 54, 71–2; *see also*
bills of exchange; duplicata
discount
Cruzado Plan 15, 71, 151, 182
curb market loans 35–6
Customs Policy Council 87
CVM (Comissão de Valores
Mobiliários) 106, 112

day trading 130, 205
debt *see* credit; foreign debt;
government debt

debt–asset ratios 18, 51, 52
    interest rate liberalisation 41–2
debt deflation 173–6, 179
debt–equity ratios 41, 51–2, 66, 173,
    176, 177
debt financing 39–40, 41, 128, 196–7
debt–income ratios 17, 21
debt-intermediation model 22–4, 25
Decree Law 157 funds *see* 157 funds
Delfim-Netto, A. 8, 12
demand deposits 57, 58, 140, 153,
    154–5, 156
democratic capitalism ·91, 110
deposit rates 24–5, 26–31, 32
    see also interest rates
deposits, commercial banks' 164–6,
    167
devaluation
    interest rate liberalisation 31, 33–4,
    36–7
    maxi- 12, 14
development, economic *see* financial
    growth
development banks 72–3
    state 72, 80, 81
    see also National Economic (and
    Social) Development Bank
Diaz-Alejandro, C. 39
direct finance 18
dollar, U.S. 11, 86, 125–6, 134
    see also 432 accounts
Dornelles, F. 149
DUNEBE (Cattle Development
    Fund) 77
duplicata discount system 45, 195–6
    inflationary finance 53–62
    interest rates 141, 143, 167–8

economic development *see* financial
    growth
Economic Development Council
    (CDI) 87
Ecuador 169–71 *passim*
Edwards, S. 38
efficiency 169–72, 182
EMBRAMEC (Brazilian
    Mechanics) 77, 115–16, 117, 119,
    146
Engle, R. F. 150
entry restrictions 183–4
equities markets 73–5, 91–123, 126,
    181, 195
    capital market liberalisation and 40
    historical experience 92–9
    interpretation 99–107

mutual funds 113
    performance of 157 funds 110–12
    role of BNDE 115–21
    tax structure of financial
    instruments 107–10
    venture capital companies 113–15
equity financing 39–40, 41, 50, 197
Equity Purchase Certificates
    (CCAs) 110–11
exchange rate policy 31, 34–5
EXIMBANK 76
'extra-judicial' liquidations 163, 210

FAD (German Development Fund) 76
FDI (Industrial Development
    Fund) 76
FDU (Urban Development Fund) 76
federal savings banks (Caixas
    Economicas Federais) 70, 71, 78,
    80
Felix, D. 39
FGTS (Job Tenure Guarantee
    Fund) 6, 70, 137, 139
FIBASE (Insumos Básicos S. A.) 77,
    116, 117, 119, 146
FIBEP (Productive Goods Import
    Financing) 77
Filho, M. 105
FIMEO (Equipment and Machinery
    Financing) 76
FINAME (Special Agency of Industrial
    Financing) 54, 71, 72, 76, 77
'financeiras' (finance companies) 59,
    71
    bills of exchange market 59–60
    growth of credit 60, 62, 79, 80
financial costs 176, 177, 178, 182–3
    see also interest rates
financial growth and economic
    development 16–44, 181
    neo-liberal approach 22–35
    neo-structuralist approach 35–7
    reconsideration of theory 40–2
    relationship 16–22
    Southern Cone 37–40
financial holding companies 183
financial repression 25–6, 41
financial sector
    asset–GNP ratios 1, 2–3
    bankruptcies and interest rate
    liberalisation 32–3
    efficiency 169–72, 182
    financial development 19–20, 21
    growth 179–80, 181
    institutions: development 40–1, 42,

financial sector, institutions, *cont.*
195; in existence 152–3
participation in national income 83–4, 169, 170
U.S. 188
see also under names of institutions
FINEX (Export Finance Fund) 77
FINSOCIAL (Social Investment Fund) 77
FIPEME (Small and Medium Size Enterprise Finance Programme) 76
FIRAE (Foreign Branch Financing) 76
FIREX (Industrial Financing with Foreign Loans) 76
firms' financial structure 172–8
FIRUN (Capital Goods and Services Import Financing) 76
fiscal mutual funds 73
fiscal policy 10, 30–1, 38–9
see also taxation
Fischer, S. 126, 127–8
'float' funds 72, 154–5, 156
FMRC (Commercial Modernisation and Reorganisation Fund) 77
FMRI (Industrial Modernisation and Reorganisation Fund) 76, 119
FNRR (National Rural Refinancing Fund) 77
forced-savings funds 9, 45, 69, 137, 139
see also 157 funds; Job Tenure Guarantee Fund
foreign debt/loans 4
contraction 8–9
and cost of loans 179
432 accounts 11
investment banks 158, 159, 160, 161
Law 4131 7
public sector debt and 13, 148
quantitative restrictions 11
resolution 63 7, 69
foreign exchange operations 154–5, 156, 157, 158
foreign firms 173–8 *passim*
432 (dollar) accounts 11, 86, 87, 157, 158
FRE (Economic Retooling Fund) 76
Friedman, M. 126, 128, 150
Fry, M. J. 26–7
FUMCAP (Capital Market Development Fund) 75, 77
FUNAGRE (Agricultural Export Fund) 77

FUNDAG (Special Agricultural Development Fund) 77
FUNDECE (Fund for the Democratization of Corporate Capital) 75, 77
FUNDRIA (Industrialisation of Agriculture, Livestock and Fisheries Fund) 76
FUNGIRO (Special Working Capital Fund) 77
FUNTEC (Technology and Scientific Research and Development Fund) 76

Gale, D. 49
Geisel administration 9–10
Giovannini, A. 27
'go round' auctions 15, 148–9
gold exchange clause 46
Goldsmith, R. 21–2, 188
government bonds 15, 46
indexed and inflation tax 128–36
see also indexation
government debt, indexation of 7, 42, 128, 130–6
gross domestic product (GDP)
assets–GDP ratios 1, 3
financial sector share 83–4, 169, 170
inflation tax as percentage of 133, 134
loans to private sector as percentage of 81–2
savings as percentage of 137, 141
gross national product (GNP)
assets–GNP ratios 1, 2
stock issues as percentage of 99–101
growth rates, real 5, 47
Gurley, J. G. 17–21 *passim*, 43

Halles group 146
hedge financing units 194–5
housing bonds 70, 137, 138
housing credit societies 70, 183
Housing Finance System (SFH) 6, 69, 69–71, 184
growth in participation 78–9, 80

IBRASA (Investimento Brasileiros) 77, 115–18, 119, 146
illusory profits 91
import substitution industrialisation (ISI) 45–52, 53, 65–6, 181
imported inputs 33–4
indexation 7, 69, 124–51
Brazilian experience with 136–49

capital flight and dismantling 182
desirability of indexed bonds 126–8
inflation and *see* inflation; inflation
tax
prefixed rates 12, 13
shift from pre- to post- 10, 144–6
and usury law 68, 140
see also Adjustable Obligations of the
National Treasury
indirect finance 18–19
Industrial Development Council
(CDI) 87
industrialisation, import substitution
(ISI) 45–52, 53, 65–6, 181
industry
commercial bank loans to 158, 159
real growth 5
inflation 4
chronology: 1945–64 5–6; 1964–7
7, 8; 1967–73 8; 1974–6 9,
10; 1980 12; 1981–2 14; 1983–6
14, 15
commercial banks and usury law 68
economic growth and 20–1, 33, 35;
neo-structuralist approach 35–6
future reforms 184
indexation and 14–15, 124–6, 137,
144, 150–1, 182; feedback
mechanisms strengthened 147–9;
inflation rate, inflation variance and
uncertainty 149–50; *see also*
inflation tax
industrialisation and 45–66, 197;
duplicata discount and bills of
exchange 53–62; monetary
authorities' structure 62–5
loan interest rates and 55–7, 197–8
real rates 5, 47
inflation tax 15
government indexed bonds and 128–
36, 205–6
institution building 68–9
institutional investors 73, 111–12, 114,
115
institutions' role in development
process 40–1, 42, 195
interest rates 1
bills of exchange 60, 61
Castello Branco administration 7, 68
conglomeration 162, 163, 167–9,
179, 210
credit expansion 8
domestic linked to foreign 11
duplicata discount system 55–7, 197–8

financial growth and 41–2, 43, 192;
credit rationing 27–8, 190–2; neo-
liberalism 26–33; neo-structuralism
35, 37
Geisel administration 9–10
indexation and 7, 124, 140–8 *passim*
negative 12
regimes 4
usury law 4
Interministerial Price Council (CIP) 87
internal debt repudiation 182, 211
International Monetary Fund
(IMF) 13, 14
investment banks 73, 91
157 funds 110, 112
participation 79–80
structure 158–60, 161, 178–9
investment capital, stock markets and
99–107, 122

Job Tenure Guarantee Fund
(FGTS) 6, 70, 137, 139

Kadota, D. 150
Kapur, B. K. 32, 33, 36, 37
Kleiman, E. 127
Krugman, P. 36

labour costs 171–2
Latin America 169–72
see also Southern Cone; *and under
individual countries*
lending *see* credit
less-developed countries (LDCs) 21–2,
189
financial repression 25–6
letras de cambio *see* bills of exchange
market
letters of intent 14
Levhari, D. 127, 128
liability structures 209
commercial banks 153–6
firms 174–5
investment banks 158–60
liberalisation 16
neo-liberal approach to financial
growth 22–35, 39–40
Southern Cone 37–40
liquidations, 'extra-judicial' 163, 210
liquidity 17
liquidity preference 20, 187
Liviaton, N. 127, 128
Lloyd, B. 41

loans *see* credit
long-term credit   53, 54, 72–3

M_2 169, 170, 171
Maisonnave bank   210
managers   105–6
Mannesman group   127, 138, 198
Mathieson, D.   32–3, 34–5
maxidevaluation   12, 14
McKinnon, R. I.   27, 28, 32, 41, 52, 190
  economic growth theory   22, 31, 43;
    anti-inflationary monetary
    policy   29–30; capital inflows   38;
    financial repression   25; inside
    money   24–5
medium-term credit   53, 72–3
Mexico
  capital flight   182, 211
  debt moratorium   13, 14
  financial sector   170, 171
minority shareholders' rights   105–6
Minsky, H.   42
monetary authorities' structure
  future reforms   184
  1945–64   62–5, 66
  1964 reforms   84–8
  see also under individual names
monetary base   86–7
  expansion   62–4
  indexed bonds and inflation tax
    130–6 *passim*
  relationship with money supply   64–5, 199
monetary budget   86, 87, 88–9
monetary policy   144
  financial growth   21; anti-
    inflationary   29–30
  indexation and   145–9
  restrictive   10, 35
money
  creation   5–6, 46–7, 85; *see also*
    inflation
  financial growth   22–5, 32
  supply and monetary base   64–5, 199
money multiplier   65, 85
monopoly rents   143–4
Montezano, R. M.   113
Morley, S.   35
Moura da Silva, A.   150
movement account ('conta de
  movimento')   85
multiple banks   183
multiplier, money   65, 85

mutual funds   91, 113–15
  see also   157 funds

National Cooperative Credit Bank
  (BNCC)   54, 72
National Economic (and Social)
  Development Bank (BNDE)   67, 71
  'Bank Reform Act'   6
  forced-savings funds   9, 72
  funds and programmes managed
    by   76–7
  growth in participation   80, 81
  long-term credit   53, 54, 72
  re-lending scheme   146
  role   115–21
National Housing Bank (BNH)   6, 69, 69–70, 184
  growth in participation   78, 80
  long-term credit   54
National Monetary Council (CMN)   6, 69, 85–6
  BNDE   72
  composition   88, 89, 90
  role   86; economic policy   87–8;
    future   184
  SFH   70
National Treasury   6, 62, 63–4, 85
National Treasury Bills (LTNs)   9, 144, 148, 149
neo-liberalism   22–35, 39–40
neo-structuralism   35–7
Ness, W. L. J.   45, 102–4, 105
Neves, A. R. M.   112, 113
nominal bonds   126, 127, 128, 204

oil price shocks   4
157 funds   8, 75
  absorbed into mutual funds
    system   113
  creation   8, 75, 93
  modification of rules   94–7
  performance   110–12, 114, 115, 116, 117, 118
open capital companies (SCAs)   69, 74–5
  'Corporations Law'   106
  157 funds   110, 111
  taxation   107–9
open-market operations   9, 148–9
ORTNs *see* Adjustable Obligations of
  the National Treasury
overnight market (SELIC)   14, 92
ownership structure   49–50, 106–7, 122–3
  see also equities markets

parallel credit markets 35–6, 61, 198
participation companies 113–15
participation funds 59
PASEP (Public Employees Financial
    Reserve Fund) 9, 72, 77, 137, 139
passbook savings accounts
    (cadernetas) 70, 137, 138
Patrick, H. T. 189
PCAS (Warehouse and Silo
    Construction Programme) 76
PEB (Development Bank Loan
    Programme) 77
Perdigão, L. A. 168–9
Peru 169–71 *passim*
PIB-NE (Northeastern Industry
    Financial Support Programme) 77
PIS (Programme of Social
    Integration) 9, 72, 77, 137, 139
POC (Joint Operations
    Programme) 76
post-fixed indexation 10, 144–6
    see also indexation
preferred stock 106
pre-fixed indexation 142–4, 208
    see also indexation
prices 5, 198
    see also inflation
primary equities market 100, 101
    composition 101–2
    157 funds 111, 112, 116
    percentage of savings 98–9
    private sector and 104–5
private commercial banks 78, 79,
    163–4, 165
private investment banks 73
private sector
    equities markets 104–5, 106–7, 122–3
    firms' financial structure 173–8
        passim
    indexation 125, 126, 128, 139–49,
        151, 207
    loans to 78–83; Bank of Brazil 54,
        78, 79; commercial banks 57, 58,
        78, 79, 82, 84; growth 82–3;
        percentage of GDP 81–2;
        structure 78–81
PRODESAR (Storage Infrastructure
    Development Programme) 76
PRODOESTE (Centre-West
    Development Programme) 77
profits
    financial costs as percentage of 176,
        177, 178
    illusory 91

Programme for Social Integration
    (PIS) 9, 72, 77, 137, 139
PROTERRA (North and Northeast
    Land Redistribution and
    Agroindustry Fund) 77
PROVALE (Special Vale do São
    Francisco Programme) 77
public commercial banks 78, 79, 164
public development banks 72, 80, 81
Public Employees Financial Reserve
    Fund (PASEP) 9, 72, 77, 137, 139
public sector
    borrowing requirement 183, 211
    debt and foreign debt 13, 148
    equities markets 102–5, 122
    financial structure of firms 173–8
        passim

rational expectations 33
recession 49, 137, 196
rediscount window 62–4
reforms 1964–5 6–7, 67–90, 181
    credit institutions 71–3
    equities markets 73–5
    financial market 68–9; structural
        changes 77–84
    housing finance system 69–71
    institutional investors 73
    monetary authorities 84–8
Regional Development Bank of the
    Extreme South (BRDE) 72
re-lending 10, 146, 159, 160, 161
repression, financial 25–6, 41
repurchase agreements 13–14, 147
required reserves 63, 156, 157
    see also voluntary reserves
'Resolution 63' loans 167–8
Rio de Janeiro stock exchange 100,
    104
    index 92, 93
    volume of stock traded 95, 97
risk
    conglomeration and
        diversification 162
    credit rationing 27–8, 190–2
    indexation 127–8; inflation 130–3

sales, financial costs as percentage
    of 176, 178
sales promoters 71
São Paulo stock exchange 100
    index 92, 94
    volume of stock traded 96, 97

'saque especial' (special withdrawal
   right) 85
savings
   decline 12
   indexation and 137–8
   neo-liberal approach to growth 35
   as percentage of GDP 45, 46, 137,
   141
   primary market issues as percentage
   of 98, 99
savings and loan associations 70
scale economies 160–2, 179
SCAs *see* open capital companies
secondary equities markets 97–8
   157 funds 111, 112, 117
   state enterprise stock 104–5
self-dealing 183
SELIC (overnight market) 14, 92
SFH *see* Housing Finance System
Shaw, E. S. 27, 52, 190
   economic growth 32, 41, 43; debt-
   intermediation 22, 23, 28, 32;
   financial growth and 17–21
short-term credit 45, 53, 54, 71–2
   see also bills of exchange market;
   duplicata discount system
similars, law of 45, 195
Simonsen, M. H. 11, 202
   equities markets 105–6
   minority shareholders 74
   resignation from Planning
   Ministry 12
   stabilisation 10, 88–9
social accounts 17
Sociedades de Credito, Financiamento e
   Investimento *see* financeiras
Southern Cone 37–40
   see also under individual countries
Special Agency of Industrial Financing
   (FINAME) 54, 71, 72, 76, 77
special withdrawal right ('saque
   especial') 85
speculative finance units 195
stabilisation 4, 10–11, 15, 43
stagflation 35–6
state banks 85
state commercial banks 78, 79, 164
state development banks 72, 80, 81
state enterprises *see* public sector
state savings banks (Caixas Economicas
   Estaduais) 70, 78, 80
structuralist approach to growth 35–7
Stiglitz, J. E. 27, 28, 43, 190–2

subsidies
   banks and interest rate controls 8,
   163, 210
   tax-cum-subsidy schemes 40–1
Summer Plan 182
Superintendency of Amazônia
   (SUDAM) 72, 73
Superintendency of Money and Credit
   (SUMOC) 6, 7, 62, 64, 69, 85
Superintendency of Northeastern
   Development (SUDENE) 72, 73
Syvrud, D. 68

Tavares, M. A. R. 78–9, 80, 166
tax-cum-subsidy schemes 40–1
tax float 72, 154–5, 156
taxation
   indexed bonds 127–8, 205
   structure of financial
   instruments 107–10, 202
   see also inflation tax
Taylor, L. 36
time deposits 140
   commercial banks 153, 154–5, 156
   investment banks 158–60
   interest rates 60
   shift away from 57, 58
Time for Service Guarantee Fund
   (FGTS) 6, 70, 137, 139
timing of policy measures 31, 33, 34–
   5, 38
Tobin, J. 126
Touriel, H. 102, 120
trade liberalisation 30–1, 38–9
Treasury, National 6, 62, 63–4, 85
treasury bills 62
   see also National Treasury Bills
   (LTNs)
Trubek, D. M. 74

underdeveloped regions 180
United States (U.S.) 171–2
   commercial banks 188
   inflation 150
   interest rates 173
Uruguay 37, 38, 39, 169–71 *passim*
US Wheat 77
usury law (1933) 4, 5, 66
   circumvention 54, 68, 185
   indexation and 68, 140
   inflation 46
   subversion 61–2, 68
usury laws, financial repression and 25

Van Wijnbergen, S.   35–6, 36–7, 38
Venezuela   169–71 *passim*, 182, 211
venture capital companies   113–15
voluntary reserves   156, 157
  see also required reserves

Wai, U. Tan   189
Weiss, A.   27, 28, 43, 190–2

Welch, J. H.   150
withholding taxes   107, 108–9, 202
working capital   75
  import substitution
    industrialisation   48–51, 52
  interest rates   141, 143, 167–8
  neo-structuralist growth model   35